THE REALITIES OF HUMAN RESOURCE MANAGEMENT
MANAGING THE EMPLOYMENT RELATIONSHIP

Keith Sisson and John Storey

Open University Press
Buckingham · Philadelphia

Open University Press
Celtic Court
22 Ballmoor
Buckingham
MK18 1XW

e-mail: enquiries@openup.co.uk
world wide web: http://www.openup.co.uk

and 325 Chestnut Street
Philadelphia, PA 19106, USA

First Published 2000

A catalogue record of this book is available from the British Library

ISBN   0 335 20620 4 (pb)   0 335 20621 2 (hb)

Library of Congress Cataloging-in-Publication Data
Sisson, Keith.
    The realities of human resource management : managing the
employment relationship / Keith Sisson and John Storey.
        p. cm – (Managing work and organizations series)
    Includes bibliographical references and index.
    ISBN 0-335-20620-4 – ISBN 0-335-20621-2
    1. Personnel management.   2. Strategic planning.
    3. Organizational change.   I. Storey, John, 1947–   II. Title.   III. Series.
HF5549.S654 2000
658.3–dc21

                                                                    99-088067

Typeset by Type Study, Scarborough
Printed in Great Britain by St Edmundsbury Press Ltd, Bury St Edmunds,
Suffolk

CONTENTS

Contents

PREFACE

This book builds upon our previous volume (Storey and Sisson, 1993) in this series and, like that book, it has been written with two main audiences in mind: practising managers, and students of business and management. The managers whom we seek to address are just as likely to be in line, general and project positions as they are to be specialist human resource or industrial relations (HR/IR) practitioners. A crucial feature of the new developments in the area has been the way in which vital new initiatives have been driven, as well as delivered, by managers from outside the specialist function. The adage that every manager needs to be his or her own people-manager has rarely been as relevant as it is now.

The issues discussed in this book are all of critical contemporary importance. Restructuring, continuous improvement, involvement and participation, pay and working time, training and development, recruitment and selection, and other themes associated with managing in a highly competitive environment constitute the heart of the analysis. We have tried to deal with them in both a practical and an academically rigorous fashion. Critically, the book eschews the approach of so many recent management books that purport to offer easy solutions. We do not believe there are any quick fixes of this kind: indeed, in our experience most are likely to end in tears.

In bringing the results of research to bear upon issues of the day, however, we are also conscious of the need to deal with the 'so what?' question. Here our experience is that most managers are looking for directions rather than specific recipes. Our treatment should therefore serve the large part of the needs of most practising managers who want to be briefed on the main themes. For this segment of our audience the book can be used either for private reading or as part of a short course programme.

The second audience whose needs we have tried to meet will be found among the student population. Here we have in mind MBA students and undergraduates typically taking a course in human resource management (HRM). The latter group of readers is likely to be from a wide range of courses – business, engineering and many more. The common element is the need for a relatively short, affordable, up-to-date analysis of themes and topics relevant to the management of human resources today. With the trend towards modularization there are increasing numbers of students who are exposed to just one main course (or 'module') on the management of the human resource. Conventional texts are not geared to the needs of these students. It is intended that this one will be. To meet their needs, the content is up to date and relevant to contemporary organizational management practice. The style is intended to be approachable, to the point and not literature-bound. The material is arranged into chapters each of which could appropriately constitute the required reading for a week-by-week programme extending over ten weeks (an increasingly standard module in higher education).

The book is distinctive in two other key regards. Most books are either 'about' HRM (as personnel management has increasingly come to be known) or 'about' industrial relations. This one is about both, which is why the term 'employment relations' or the acronym HR/IR is used in this book. In the real world, problems of motivation, communication, discipline and the wage/effort bargain are suffused with collective and individual aspects. Moreover, collective bargaining continues to affect nearly half the working population in the UK and recent and forthcoming legislation is likely to put a premium on information and consultation with collective forms of employee representation, be they union or non-union. In our view, managing the employment relationship will demand both an individual and a collective perspective and so this is how we approach the issues.

There is a further central rationale to this book. Not only is the great bulk of material, certainly on human resource management, which managers and students of management are likely to come across, highly prescriptive but it also gives the strong impression that there is a 'universal' solution. Typically, it consists of statements asserting how managers *should* devise training programmes, evaluate training, conduct appraisal and so on, regardless of the situation. Alternatively, it takes the form of the presentation of so-called leading edge thinking arising from the experience of one of the world's large multinational companies at one moment in time or a development in Silicon Valley or somewhere equally remote. The problem with this type of literature is not that advice is proffered or thought stimulated (on the contrary these are laudable objectives), rather it is that it takes no account of the context – and context is absolutely critical. The vast majority of workplaces in most developed countries belong to small and medium-sized enterprises and their managers have to grapple with a particular framework of legislation, corporate governance arrangements, trade union structure, historical legacy and so on.

The problem is compounded because much of this literature lacks any basis in empirical evidence. The result is that a totally misleading impression is often given about trends and developments. No wonder, as Chapter 1 argues, there is such an enormous gap between the rhetoric and the reality of managing employment relations.

This is increasingly unforgivable as more and more evidence becomes available from surveys and cases. Indeed, it is not too much of an exaggeration to say that the field in the UK has exploded since the publication of our *Managing Human Resources and Industrial Relations* in 1993. Outlets for serious research, such as the *Human Resource Management Journal* and the *International Journal of Human Resource Management*, have firmly established themselves, while the Institute of Personnel and Development has sponsored major investigations into such issues as performance management and the 'lean organization'. The first findings of the wide-ranging *1998 Workplace Employee Relations Survey* are also available, with the detailed results to come.

Reflecting these weaknesses in so much of the literature, we have set ourselves the objectives of analysing the complexities of process and context, taking close note of empirical research findings about actual practice, while at the same time identifying what it all means for the practitioner. The task has proved to be a demanding one in the wake of the election of a Labour government with a massive majority, the signing of the 'social chapter' of the EU Maastricht Treaty and the prospect of economic and monetary union, coupled with the substantial increase in research evidence.

LIST OF ABBREVIATIONS

ACAS	Advisory, Conciliation and Arbitration Service
BIFU	Bank, Insurance and Finance Union
BPR	business process reengineering
BT	British Telecom
CAC	Central Arbitration Committee
CCT	compulsory competitive tendering
CEC	Commission of the European Communities
CIR	Commission on Industrial Relations
CLIRS	Company Level Industrial Relations Survey
CNC	computer numerical control
DfEE	Department for Education and Employment
DPA	departmental purpose analysis
DTI	Department of Trade and Industry
EDAP	Employee Development and Assistance Programme
EIRO	European Industrial Relations Observatory
EMU	economic and monetary union
ERT	European Round Table of Industrialists
GMB	General, Municipal and Boilermakers Union
GNVQ	General National Vocational Qualifications
HR	human resources
HRM	human resource management
HRP	human resource planning

ICL	International Computers Ltd
IES	Institute of Employment Studies
IiP	Investors in People
IPA	Involvement and Participation Association
IPD	Institute of Personnel and Development
IPM	Institute of Personnel Management
IPRP	individual performance-related pay
IR	industrial relations
IRRR	Industrial Relations Review and Report
IRRU	Industrial Relations Research Unit
IRS	Industrial Relations Services
IT	information technology
ITB	industrial training board
MCR	management of change report
MNC	multinational company
NAAFI	Navy, Army and Air Force Institutes
NACAB	National Association of Citizens Advice Bureaux
NEDO	National Economic Development Office
NVQ	National Vocational Qualification
OD	organizational development
plc	public limited company
PMS	performance management system
PRP	performance-related pay
SBU	strategic business unit
SME	small and medium-sized enterprises
TEC	Training and Enterprise Council
TQM	total quality management
UCW	Union of Communication Workers
VET	vocational and educational training
WERS	The 1998 Workplace Employee Relations Survey

INTRODUCTION: THE STORY SO FAR

The starting point: from rhetoric to reality

This book is about managing employment relations. Approximately half the total population of the country is in some form of paid work or employment and is thus directly party to such a relationship. In consequence, the way in which this part of the life experience is handled carries a wide range of political, social and economic implications. Central to the concerns of most managers and students of management reading this book, however, is likely to be the link between the management of employment relations and competitiveness.

Just about every book on the subject and many a company chairman's statement, make the same point: it is people which make the difference. The workforce is the most vital asset. Technology and capital can be acquired on varying terms by a wide range of players around the world: the real, sustainable competitive advantage, or edge, has to come ultimately from the way that capable and motivated teams utilize these resources. In Ulrich's (quoted in MacLachan, 1998: 37) words,

> Sooner or later, traditional forms of competitiveness – cost, technology, distribution, manufacturing and product features

– can be copied. They have become table stakes. You must have them to be a player, but they do not guarantee you will be a winner . . .

Winning will spring from organizational capabilities such as speed, responsiveness, agility, learning capacity and employee competence. Successful organizations will be those that are able to quickly turn strategy into action; to manage processes intelligently and efficiently; to maximize employee contribution and commitment; and to create the conditions for seamless change.

Statements such as these constitute the conventional wisdom. The message has been repeated *ad nauseam* by ranks of chief executives, management 'gurus' and politicians. The real cause for surprise today is not the message but that so little has been done to put it into effect: the management of employment relations remains the Cinderella function of management.

Signs of significant change are certainly easy to find. Indeed, it is possible to talk in terms of a restructuring of UK employment relations (see, for example, Gallie *et al.*, 1998). The most fundamental change has been the decline in joint regulation by collective bargaining. According to the first findings of the 1998 Workplace Employee Relations Survey (WERS), the proportion of workplaces recognizing trade unions had fallen from 66 per cent in 1984 to 53 per cent in 1990; between 1990 and 1998 it fell a further eight points to 45 per cent (Cully *et al.*, 1998: 28). Meanwhile, the proportion of workplaces with no union member increased from 27 per cent in 1984 to 36 per cent in 1990, to 47 per cent in 1998. In the words of the authors of the first findings, 'This signals, clearly, a transformation in the landscape of British employment relations, particularly when contrasted with the relative stability and continuity that has characterised the system for much of the post-war period' (Cully *et al.*, 1998: 28).

A second major change is the growth in the different forms of so-called atypical or non-standard forms of employment. Figure 1.1, which also comes from the first findings of the 1998 WERS, gives a good overview. Most obvious is the growth in part-time work. Part-time employees account for around one-quarter of the workforce and they make up the *majority* of the workforce in a

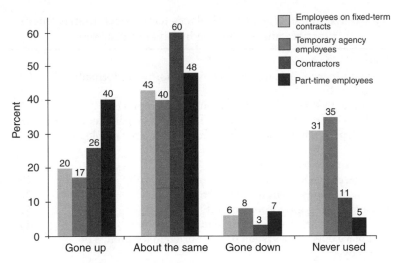

Figure 1.1 Change in the use of different forms of labour over the past five years
Source: Cully *et al.*, 1998

similar proportion of the workplaces. Significantly, this figure is up from 16 per cent in 1990 (Cully *et al.*, 1998: 6).

For the most part, however, these changes have largely reflected changes in the patterns of employment and are the unintended consequences of the business strategies and structures underpinning them. They have less commonly been the result of conscious management decisions about managing employment relations, let alone their redesign.

The yawning gap between the rhetoric and the reality of employment relations can be most graphically illustrated by studying the diffusion of the 'new' management practices which have been grouped according to four main areas of activity in Table 1.1. Although many of these practices are by no means new, they have nonetheless come to be associated with change and offer the most robust set of data with which to make our points.

In the case of *appraisal and reward* it will be seen that just over one-half of non-managerial employees are subject to some form of appraisal. Only one in ten of these employees has individual performance pay, however, raising questions about the amount

Table 1.1 Percentage of workplaces using 'new' management
practices and employee involvement schemes

Appraisal and reward	
Most non-managerial employees have performance formally appraised	56
Individual PRP scheme for non-managerial employees	11
Employee share ownership scheme for non-managerial employees	15
Profit-sharing scheme operated for non-managerial employees	30
Involvement and participation	
Workplace level joint consultative committee	28
Regular meetings of entire workforce	37
Problem-solving groups (e.g. quality circles)	42
Staff attitude survey conducted in last five years	45
Workplace operates a system of team briefing for groups of employees	61
Most employees work in formally designated teams	65
Training and development	
Most employees receive minimum of five days training a year	12
Most supervisors trained in employee relations skills	27
Status and security	
Guaranteed job security or no compulsory redundancy policy	14
'Single status' between managers and non-managerial employees	41
Workplace operates a just-in-time system of inventory control	29
Attitudinal test before making appointments	22

Base: all workplaces with 25 or more employees
Figures are weighted and based on response from 1,926 managers

Source: Cully *et al.* (1998)

of attention such arrangements have received in the prescriptive literature. More enjoy the benefits of share ownership (one in seven) and profit sharing (one in three), but they remain very much a minority.

In the case of *involvement and participation*, the signs of activity are greater but again for most types of activity less than half of workplaces were affected. Thus, 37 per cent of workplaces reported regular meetings, 42 per cent said they had some kind of problem-solving group such as quality circles and 45 per cent that they had used staff attitude surveys. Only teamworking and team briefing were reported as practised in a majority of workplaces.

The latter data need to be treated with some caution, however. Around two-thirds of workplaces (65 per cent) reported that employees worked in formally designated teams. Yet only a handful (5 per cent of those with teams) had something resembling the semi-autonomous teamworking which has come to be regarded as the leitmotif of new forms of work organization, i.e. respondents said team members had to work together, had responsibility for specific products or services, jointly decided how work was to be done, and appointed their own team leaders. If, in Peters's (1987: 302–3) uncompromising words, 'the only possible implementers' of a strategy of quality production are 'committed, flexible, multi-skilled, constantly retrained people, joined together in self-managed teams', the UK clearly has a very long way to go.

The next dimension is *training and development*. Here too the evidence is hardly supportive of a paradigm shift. Despite the widespread importance attached to training by the Government, only 12 per cent, or one in eight, said that most employees received a minimum of five days training per year. Perhaps even more surprising is that only 27 per cent, or one in four, said they trained most supervisors in employee relations skills. Such skills have been found to be strongly correlated with both the more advanced forms of involvement and participation and with their estimated success of these schemes more generally (see, for example, European Foundation for the Improvement of Living and Working Conditions, 1997: ch. 9).

The final cluster to be considered involves *status* and *security*. Here it will be seen from Table 1.1 that less than half of workplaces (41 per cent) had single-status arrangements between managerial and non-managerial employees, and only 14 per cent, or one in seven, guaranteed job security or had a no-compulsory redundancy policy.

Details of the combinations of practices are also illuminating (Cully *et al.*, 1998: 11). There is some evidence of practices operating together, possibly suggesting the development of a more strategic approach in the sense of the integration or 'bundling' of practices. Training, teamworking and supervisor training appear to go together, as do individual performance pay, profit sharing and share ownership. Single status is associated with the first cluster but not the second, however, suggesting that direct participation and financial participation are seen as alternatives rather than complementary as might have been expected.

Perhaps most telling, though, are the figures for the total number of practices. The practices listed, it hardly needs emphasizing, are far from being revolutionary. Indeed, most personnel texts seem to assume them to be standard in today's workplace. Moreover, the figures also measure workplace *incidence* only and not *scope* of the practice (as in the case of teamworking discussed above). In the circumstances, the finding that only one in five (20 per cent) had half or more of the 16 practices and only one in fifty (2 per cent) had 10 or more is little short of staggering.

The significance of this is that it looks as if the 1998 WERS findings will also provide further evidence, to add to that increasingly available for the USA (see, for example, Becker and Huselid, 1998) and EU member countries (see European Foundation for the Improvement of Living and Working Conditions, 1997) establishing a positive link between the adoption of these 'new' practices and performance. In the words of the team responsible for the 1998 WERS first findings (Cully *et al.*, 1998: 25), 'workplaces with a high number of "new" management practices were substantially more likely to report high productivity growth'.

Critically, too, the UK continues to lag behind the international competition as the Government's 1998 White Paper on competitiveness argues (DTI, 1998). Not everything can be laid at the door of the management of employment relations – lack of investment in R&D and plant and equipment is perhaps the major issue – yet it is a significant contributory factor. The UK remains in essence a low paid, low skill, low productivity economy.

Our task in this opening chapter is to put managing employment relations into context so that there can be a better understanding of the problem. The chapter goes back to basics in reminding us of some of the complexities of the employment relationship. It outlines the main developments in employment patterns and business strategies and structures which have been so important in recent years. It considers the main recipes put forward and their limitations. It evaluates the new agenda that is emerging.

The overall conclusion is that the significance of managing employment relations in competitive success will certainly grow. Most critically, however, the key to realizing the potential that improved performance in this area can bring does not lie in the pursuit of the latest techniques. Indeed, this is likely to be counter-productive, diverting attention from what really needs to be done and encouraging cynicism on the part of employees. Rather it will depend not only on doing more of the 'basic' things, such as training and development, and information and consultation, and but also on making sure that they are properly integrated in the sense that policies and practices are both complementary and compatible with business strategy. It is in showing how this might be done, despite all the obstacles, that the book tries to make its significant contribution.

The nature of the employment relationship

In discussing the employment relationship, it has become fashionable to emphasize the importance of the 'psychological contract'. The term is rarely spelt out but is generally understood to mean the expectations, aspirations and understandings which employers and employees have of each other (see Herriot *et al.*, 1998). It is highlighted because the rupture in the traditional contract, above all of managerial employees, is seen as a major issue in managing employment relations. In a nutshell, the worry is that intensifying competitive pressures, largely generated in a global marketplace, are encouraging continuous change and cost-cutting, meaning the employer can no longer deliver the job security, promotion opportunities and pay increases which have been the quid pro quo for employees' loyalty, commitment and skills.

Important though the debate is in highlighting the fundamental problem – the need to balance flexibility with security – it needs to be kept in perspective. It is not just that talk of a psychological contract has a hollow ring for many non-managerial employees: more worrying is the danger that it blinds people to the fact that the employment relationship has several key facets which have to be taken into account if it is to be effectively managed. Most obviously, it embraces an economic exchange or relationship. Employees make their contribution to achieving the organization's objective and, in return, they receive a level of remuneration. Putting a price on this contribution is no easy matter, however; the market rarely determines a unique price in the way that many economists lead us to believe. Especially difficult is ensuring that employees deliver what they are supposed to, which gets us into very difficult waters: there needs to be a variety of control mechanisms in place. This is not automatic. In effect, management is buying the right to exploit the individual's contribution and nothing more.

There are difficulties, too, in treating employees as a form of human capital as many pundits urge. One, the so-called information barrier, is that investment in human capital, being intangible, is difficult to measure and therefore difficult to justify. The other, the so-called externality problem, is that organizations cannot guarantee that they will capture the returns made on intangible investments. For example, performance-enhancing organizational innovations require up-front training investments of both a general and company-specific nature, which enterprises risk losing if employees leave before the returns can be captured.

The second distinguishing feature of the employment relationship is that it involves a social relationship. Typically, employees attend a workplace, be it fixed or transitory, where they interact with other employees and with managers. According to the WERS first findings quoted above, around two-thirds work in formally designated teams in which their colleagues affect their contribution. Inevitably, concepts such as a fair day's work come to be socially determined, as does what is acceptable and unacceptable behaviour on the part of employees and managers alike. In grouping people together in occupations and workplaces, work organization also creates the basis for collective action on the part of employees, which underpins trade unions and collective bargaining.

The employment relationship is also complicated because it involves a legal relationship. Employers are required by law to give employees a contract of employment. Although this contract of employment itself rarely spells out the mutual obligations of employers and employees, it provides the underpinning of specific obligations, rights and standards emanating from statutes and court judgements regulating the relationship.

This brings us to our final point. The fact that the employment relationship is a social and legal as well as an economic relationship means that it is deeply embedded in both particular national and organizational contexts. As Bach and Sisson (2000) emphasize, it has long been recognized that key features of the UK's business system are especially inhospitable to treating people as the key to success. The most important of these features can be summarized as follows:

1 An overwhelming emphasis on shareholder value as the key business driver as opposed to the interests of other stakeholders.
2 Institutional share ownership by investment trusts and pensions funds rather than banks which encourages a focus on short-term profitability as the key index of business performance rather than long-term market share or added value.
3 Relative ease of takeover, which not only reinforces the pressure on short-term profitability to maintain share price but also encourages expansion by acquisition and merger rather than by internal growth.
4 A premium on 'financial engineering' as the core organizational competence and the domination of financial management, both in terms of personnel, activities and control systems, over other functions.

Furthermore, two key features of the UK's overall industrial relations system mean there have been few, if any, of the countervailing pressures found in most other developed economies to encourage investment in human capital:

1 A tradition of 'voluntarism' in virtually every area of UK employment relations (including vocational education and training), which means that the framework of legal rights and obligations (individual and collective) is much less than in other EU countries.
2 A highly decentralized and diverse structure of collective bargaining, deeply embedded in procedural rather than substantive

rules, which means that the UK does not possess the detailed multi-employer agreements which supplement and extend the legislative framework in most other EU countries.

It is important to remember, too, that the 1980s and early 1990s saw the few countervailing pressures even further reduced. Individual employment rights were whittled away and the role of trade unions curtailed. Perhaps even more importantly, the Wages Councils, which had provided a statutory floor of pay and conditions, were abolished and there was further reduction in the coverage of the multi-employer agreements which had fulfilled a similar function elsewhere. Indeed, such agreements all but disappeared in key sectors such as metalworking. The decline of sector regulation means that there are few acknowledged standards or benchmarks for organizations to follow.

The changing patterns of employment

Our attention now turns to the changing patterns of employment which are one of the two sets of considerations which help to put both the changes in and diversity of employment relations practice into relief. These patterns are many and varied, but four stand out: the ongoing shift from manufacturing to services; the shrinking size of workplaces; the polarization of the occupational structure; and the feminization of the workforce.

A service economy

As the first column in Table 1.2 confirms, the UK is very much a service economy; less than one in five workplaces are in manufacturing. The changing balance between public and private services is also evident: for example, a significant proportion of employees in health services are now to be found in the private sector. The composition of the workforce, column 3 suggests, is also critically affected. Part-time working is much less prevalent in manufacturing, whereas it is the predominant pattern in sectors such as hotels and restaurants. Levels of pay and productivity are also closely correlated with sector, as columns 5 and 6 show clearly. Not only do

Table 1.2 The significance of sector

	Distribution of workplaces by sector (%)	Workplaces with no part-time employees (%)	Workplaces with most employees part-time (%)	Low paying workplaces (%)	High productivity growth workplaces (%)
Manufacturing	18	36	1	5	34
Electricity, gas, water	0	51	0	0	55
Construction	4	39	0	1	49
Wholesale and retail	18	14	43	8	51
Hotels and restaurants	6	3	55	48	29
Transport and communications	5	23	4	0	60
Financial services	3	20	5	0	62
Other business services	9	23	7	10	34
Public administration	6	9	1	0	42
Education	14	0	40	2	42
Health	13	1	50	17	34
Other community services	4	8	51	19	23
All workplaces	100	16	26	9	41

Base: all workplaces with 25 or more employees, except column 5, where it is all workplaces five or more years old with 25 employees

Figures are weighted and based on responses from 1,929 managers for column 1, 1,914 for columns 2 and 3, 1,890 for column 4 and 1,668 for column 5.

Source: Cully *et al.* (1998)

sectors such as hotels and restaurants have the largest proportions of employees earning less than £3.50 per hour, but they are also characterized by some of the lowest levels of productivity.

The first findings of the 1998 WERS do not give us a breakdown of union membership by sector. Fortunately a recent analysis of the Labour Force Survey data does (Cully and Woodland, 1998). It shows that the decline of manufacturing and the shift to the service sector have been associated with the decline of union recognition and collective bargaining.

The shrinking workplace

One of the developments that the shift from manufacturing to services has contributed to is shrinkage in the size of workplace. A strong impression of the significance of the size of workplaces comes from Table 1.3. Column 1 confirms the long-standing association between union membership and the size of workplace. Other things being equal, the larger the workplace, the more likely collective bargaining and vice versa. In addition, more than twice as many smaller workplaces had 25 per cent of employees earning less than £3.50 an hour as opposed to 9 per cent in the case of larger ones. Productivity growth was also less (33 per cent against 42 per cent, 50 per cent and 56 per cent for workplaces with 100–199 employees, 200–499 employees and 500 or more employees, respectively).

Smaller workplaces, it also emerges, are less likely to have the 'new' employment practices discussed in the previous section. The proportion with no practices (8 per cent) was four times that of larger workplaces, while the number with five or more (28 per cent) was only about half as many (Cully *et al.*, 1998: 26).

The polarization of the occupational structure

The occupational structure of the UK workforce has also altered markedly. Data from the Labour Force Survey in Table 1.4 show that the blue-collar workers in manufacturing represent a dwindling minority as manufacturing shrinks. The largest single groups are 'managers and administrators' (4,306,000) followed by 'clerical' (4,096,000). The two groups of 'professional' and 'professional and

Table 1.3 The significance of workforce size

Workplace size	Union density: % of employees who are members	Any union members: % of workplaces	Union recognition: % of workplaces	Low paying workplaces (%)	High productivity growth workplaces (%)
25–49	23	46	39	12	40
50–99	27	52	41	8	38
100–199	32	66	57	6	42
200–499	38	77	67	4	50
500 or more	48	86	78	2	56
All workplaces	36	53	45	9	41

Base for columns 1–4: all workplaces with 25 or more employees; for column 5 all workplaces five or more years old with 25 employees

Figures are weighted and based on responses from 1,889 managers for columns 1–3; 1,890 for column 4 and 1,668 for column 5.
Source: Cully *et al.* (1998)

Table 1.4 The significance of occupation

	Employment (%)	Union membership (%)
Managers and administrators	16	20
Professional	10	50
Associated professional and technical	10	46
Clerical	15	25
Craft and related	12	34
Personal and protective services	11	28
Sales	8	9
Plant and machine operators	9	38
Others	8	26

Source: column 1 *Labour Market Trends*, 1998b; column 2 *Labour Market Trends*, 1998a

technical' amount to 5,517,000, whereas 'craft and related' accounts for 3,370,000. More people are employed in 'personal and protective services' (2,986,000) than are 'plant and machine operators' (2,589,000).

Arguably, the main divide is no longer between blue-collar and white-collar but between managerial and professional groups, on the one hand, and the rest, on the other. Much of the interest and target of the human resource management (HRM) discussed later, it can be argued, is the managerial and professional group. Significantly, for example, the focus of many of the WERS questions is implicit recognition of this. Managers are expected to be subject to individual performance pay, appraisal, a special status and security whereas for other employees it is an open question. Occupation is not so relevant where membership of trade unions is concerned (see column 2 of Table 1.4). Important, however, is the pattern of regulation: even if members of trade unions and/or professional organizations, managers and professional employees are typically covered by individual contracts rather than by collective agreements.

Feminization

The fourth and final dimension to be considered is sex. The growth in the proportion of women in the labour force reflects the

14

Table 1.5 Workplaces by gender

	Workplaces largely male: > 75% male	Workplaces largely female: > 75% female	Workplaces mixed (%)
Private sector	32	22	46
Public sector	14	49	37

Base: all workplaces with 25 or more employees
Figures are weighted and based on responses from 1,914 managers
Source: Cully *et al.* (1998)

shifts in sector and occupation discussed above. As is clear from Table 1.5, the distribution remains skewed. Manufacturing and construction have relatively few women, whereas women predominate in sectors such as retail or hotels.

In terms of its implications for managing employment relations, the most important variable is working time. Nearly half the women in work are part-time. Other studies (see, for example, the review in Gallie *et al.*, 1998) tend to confirm that training and development opportunities are less for part-time employees as are pay levels and other benefits.

An interim conclusion

There have been fundamental and interrelated changes in the patterns of employment which help to explain much of both the restructuring and the diversity of employment relations to be observed in the UK. The decline of joint regulation, for example, can be associated with the reduction in the manufacturing workforce, along with highly unionized sectors such as coal, and a shrinking in the size of workplaces more generally. The growth in part-time work and the feminization of the workforce reflects the expansion in the service sector. The growing interest in HRM can be related, above all, to the increasing proportion of managers and professional workers in the workforce.

It would be wrong, however, to imply that it is possible to read off employment relations practice from a single set of structural variables. There is a number of crosscutting dimensions contributing to the enormous diversity of practice. Take training, development and security, for example. A part-time female employee of one of the large retail chains might be expected to enjoy greater *de facto* security, training and development opportunities than her counterpart in a small family-owned store. Less expectedly, the same is likely to be true of the comparison with male full-time employees in some sectors of manufacturing or protection services; it may even be true of managers in these sectors. Much depends on the business systems, strategy and structure of employing organizations, and so it to these that the analysis now turns.

Changing business strategies and structures

The 1980s and 1990s saw major changes in business strategies and structures underpinning the changes in both employment relations management and the patterns of employment. In the case of what might be termed the 'external face' of organizations there were considerable changes in the portfolio of many companies. For example, the second Company Level Industrial Relations Survey (CLIRS) found that, over the five years until 1992, more than two-thirds of companies with more than 1000 employees in the UK reported cases of merger and acquisition and a similar number investment in new locations. Almost the same number, however, reported the closure of existing sites, nearly half divestment and 40 per cent the rundown of existing sites. Many of these changes were associated with each other. Thus, the authors found that nearly three-quarters of the companies reported both growth and closure or rundown, with 20 per cent citing growth only and 8 per cent neither (Marginson *et al.*, 1995: 20).

A second significant change is the growing internationalization of the UK economy. In the preparatory work for CLIRS in 1992, 975 companies were identified as having more than 1000 employees in the UK. Of these, 759 were UK-owned and 216 foreign-owned. Of the UK-owned companies, almost half (360) were themselves multinational including about one-third of the companies, discussed below, that had been privatized since 1979 (Marginson *et al.*,

1995: 4, 20). Overall, then, almost seven out of ten large companies in the UK were multinational.

A third major change, externalization, involves the subcontracting of activities previously performed inside the organization. This is closely associated in many people's minds with privatization and programmes of compulsory competitive tendering. As Figure 1.1 has already confirmed, however, such developments are widespread and reflect the conventional wisdom that management should focus on its 'core' activities, allowing much greater play for the 'market' in areas of so-called ancillary services such as catering, cleaning and distribution.

There have also been significant changes on the inside of organizations, reflecting the revolution in information processing facilities. One, *divisionalization*, involves the break-up of the large-scale hierarchical organization into a number of semi-autonomous or 'quasi' businesses responsible for most, if not all, activities within their jurisdiction. Examples include teamworking under cellular manufacturing, 'executive agencies' and 'trusts' in the public services, the break-up of companies such as Courtaulds and ICI into separate and independent organizations and, in the case of multinational companies (MNCs), the coming of international product or service divisions with responsibility for individual products or related products either on a European or worldwide basis. The second, *budgetary devolution*, involves the allocation to the lowest possible unit within the organization of responsibility for managing activities within financial resources or targets. A third development is a variant of the externalization discussed in the previous section. It involves seeing the organization as an *internal market* in which 'services' are traded between 'purchasers' and 'providers' to ensure that different groups are more responsive to the needs of each other and that activities are cost effective. The NHS, where the district health authorities formerly responsible for total health care provision within a given area, have been split into purchaser authorities and provider trusts, is the extreme example.

Both these external and internal changes are profoundly important in understanding why there has been restructuring, but little redesign, of employment relations in the UK. For example, at the same time as the changing portfolios have reinforced many of the implications of the business system, they have also led to shifts out of manufacturing and reductions in the size of many organizations as the result of divestment and externalization. Many more workplaces in the UK find themselves competing for investment within the MNCs' internal market at the same time as they have to justify retaining activities in-house through market testing. Meanwhile, divisionalization, devolved budgeting and internal markets have involved a fundamental shift from management by task to management by financial performance. In the words of management consultants McKinsey & Co. discussing developments in the electronics sector:

> Decentralisation to small units has limited the scale of ambition to that of the units rather than the company as a whole. 'Numbers driven' rather than 'issue driven' planning has reinforced a focus on short term results rather than long term investment to create major new businesses. The limited role of the centre in many UK companies has meant that the potential synergies and scale benefits of a large company – in creating a customer franchise, in product development and in attracting and developing highly talented management – have not been achieved.
>
> (McKinsey & Co./NEDO, 1988: 49)

Coupled with the changing patterns of employment described in the previous section, these developments have also made a significant contribution to the diversity of employment relations practice. For example, developments such as the externalization of activities, divisionalization and budgetary devolution have combined to encourage the fragmentation of employment systems, leaving managers to cope in a contingent fashion in the best way they can. Critically, too, developments in the public sector mean that it no longer has the function of the model 'good employer'.

Most fundamentally, the sheer pace and extent of the change in business portfolios has been a consideration in its own right. Not only has it produced considerable insecurity on the part of managers and employees alike, which is inimical to developing long-term relationships, but it has also made it difficult to develop a consistency in approach of almost any kind. Indeed, organizations are littered with half-finished initiatives, which have had to be interrupted because of takeover or merger or change of business direction or divestment, leading to considerable cynicism not only on the part of employees but also on the part of senior managers who are supposed to be implementing them.

Changing recipes

The era of collective bargaining

For much of the period following the ending of the Second World War in 1945, personnel management played second fiddle to industrial relations. Personnel management, rightly or wrongly, was regarded as an administrative function concerned with operational matters relating to recruitment and selection, appraisal, reward and training policies and practices directed towards the *individual* employee. Industrial relations, which focused on trade unions, collective bargaining and the handling of grievances and disputes and so could be suitably regarded as concerned with *collective* labour issues, was seen as the area for strategic initiative.

Unusually for the UK, theory and practice were closely intertwined. Writers such as Flanders (1970) argued impressively the case for collective bargaining. Collective bargaining, he suggested, should be seen primarily not as a bargaining but as a rule-making process. Collective bargaining, for which he suggested a better description would be joint regulation, made it possible to agree the key procedural and substantive rules governing the employment relationship. An added advantage was that it enabled workers themselves to shape the decisions affecting them through democratic activity within the trade union. More to the point, others argued (see, for example, Clegg, 1960), collective bargaining was to be preferred to other vehicles for promoting participation and involvement such as works councils and worker directors.

Collective bargaining recognized that the enterprise involved a number of stakeholders with plural and, sometimes, conflicting interests. Trade unions did not compromise their independence in collective bargaining: they were the permanent opposition. In principle, other analysts (see, for example, McCarthy and Ellis, 1973) argued, collective bargaining could be extended to almost every aspect of the working environment. They saw collective bargaining shifting from simply dealing with claims, disputes and grievances, i.e. a largely reactive role, to a more proactive or 'predictive' function.

The practice seemed to bear out the theory. Collective bargaining was by far and away the most important process in UK industrial relations. Even the incoming Conservative government of Edward Heath in 1970 recognized this. Many saw the Industrial Relations Act 1971 as a legal attack on the power of trade unions, but it did not question the primacy of collective bargaining. This was explicitly accepted as the most important method of determining pay and conditions of employment. The number already covered by collective bargaining was extensive and there was optimism that it would grow as non-manual workers achieved recognition for their trade unions. The breadth and depth of collective bargaining was also impressive. Like other European countries, a framework of multi-employer agreements, most negotiated at national level, provided the foundations. To this, however, had been added throughout the 1950s and 1960s something that seemed to be lacking in the European practice, which was the deep involvement of shop stewards and other local trade union representatives at workplace level in the application and extension of the agreements reached at higher levels.

The conventional wisdom was that good practice equated with formalized procedures. Government led the way. A feature of all of the nationalization acts in the late 1940s was the inbuilt statutory requirement for managers of the new public corporations to negotiate and consult with recognized trade unions. Private sector companies were left in no doubt that they were to follow this example. Continuation of, and indeed elaboration of this formula could be seen clearly in the report of the Royal Commission on Trade Unions and Employers' Associations published in 1968: the prevailing levels of industrial conflict were too high and the source could be traced to inadequacies in the national or industry-level negotiating bodies such as the National Joint Industrial Councils which were supposed to regulate these things. For a host of reasons, much of the activity in industrial relations had shifted to the level of the workplace, where it was typically more difficult to control and regulate. The nature of the relations between, for example, plant managers and individual shop stewards was highly informal and fragmented, with agreements typically ad hoc, makeshift and unwritten. The Commission's classic recommendation was that the divide between the 'two systems' (the formal national-level arrangements and the informal local arrangements) should be closed by moving towards the formalizing of the latter.

Clearly reflecting this same recipe was the elaboration of procedures within individual companies for all manner of problems relating to discipline and grievance-handling. Indeed, the centrality of installing and following procedures became the leitmotif of acceptable practice. Sophisticated companies were, it was maintained, already pursuing these steps anyway. The need for the official spelling-out of these formal procedures was mainly to disseminate this modern good practice to the less enlightened. Illustrations include the codes of practice on discipline and grievance-handling as promulgated by the Advisory, Conciliation and Arbitration Service (ACAS). Notably, these 'codes' were not in themselves legally mandatory in any direct sense. However, observance or breach of these formulations of recommended practice could be used in tribunals and courts as evidence of behaviour should a case be brought to law.

It has become clearer since that this was very much the era of the large manufacturing workplace employing men in full-time jobs. Even at the time, it represented only a partial characterization. Large swathes of the economy, notably in services and among small and medium-sized enterprises (SMEs) more generally, remained untouched by trade unions and collective bargaining. Significantly, too, in the light of later developments, even where it was well ingrained, including the car industry, the famed workplace bargaining was relatively narrow in its scope, focusing largely on the 'wage/effort' relationship and rarely extending to wider issues.

A number of non-union companies such as IBM and Marks & Spencer were already pursuing what was to become known as the HRM approach. As early as 1974, for example, Fox had drawn attention to the variety of identifiable approaches with his codification of four styles – traditionalist; sophisticated paternalist;

sophisticated modern; and standard modern – which were to become the building-blocks of later modelling (see, for example, Purcell and Sisson, 1983). These, together with the dominant pragmatic approach, are set out below:

1 The *traditionalist* style was based on a firm belief in management's right to manage without interference. It was characterized by adamant hostility to trade unions and is associated therefore with a refusal to recognize unions, still less to negotiate with them.
2 The *sophisticated paternalistic* style was also marked by opposition to trade unionism but it differed from the former in the way in which the management of companies practising this style introduced an array of benefits and positive personnel devices to substitute for collective bargaining. These included above-average arrangements relating to pay, welfare and consultation.
3 *Sophisticated moderns* were sophisticated in a rather different way. They recognized that, at least in certain industries, it would be unrealistic to seek to defend absolute managerial prerogative. Workforce expectations of trade union representation were met with a set of measures which legitimate these expectations but which nonetheless sought to contain and channel the consequences. Thus joint procedures which contained and institutionalized conflict were honed.
4 *Standard moderns* represented the pragmatic stance. This was perhaps the predominant style in Britain. It was reactive and opportunistic rather then principled, the approach adopted at any one time depending primarily on the nature of the pressures experienced.

The coming of HRM

The term 'human resource management' (HRM) emerged in Britain in the mid to late 1980s and continues to be surrounded by controversy (Storey, 1995). A critical issue is the meaning to be attached to it. One way in which HRM has come to be used is a simple relabelling of personnel management and industrial relations, arguably designed to capture the benefits of the other meanings. For others, however, HRM denotes above all a more strategic approach. Four aspects are involved. One is the link between managing human resources and business strategy; it is the state of competition, which, in effect, is requiring management to make changes. A second is the key role which senior line managers are expected to play – managing human resources becomes their major activity. A third is the emphasis on the integration of policies and practices with each other as well as with business strategy. Fourthly, and finally, HRM has come to be associated with a very specific approach, which is discussed in detail in Chapter 2.

For the present, it is enough to appreciate the main contrast between the thinking associated with HRM and the era of collective bargaining. A number of common themes continually appear and reappear in the debate. The first emphasizes the model of management as a *strategic actor*. Management's approach to employment relations has to be business-focused, if not business-led. Senior line managers in particular can no longer afford to allow specialist HR/IR managers to maintain a 'system' for its own sake. The key decisions in employment relations must have regard to the business strategy and be taken by line managers. A second theme is an emphasis on flexibility: management, it is argued, needs to develop the capacity to respond more quickly to business conditions. This is reflected in developments as diverse as: the introduction of devolved organizational structures; the growth of outsourcing; and a range of flexibility in working time, task and functional flexibility. The third theme relates to arrangements for managing the employment relationship. Management is no longer supposed to see collective bargaining as the primary mechanism. Rather, more emphasis on the direct relationship with individual employees is regarded as the bedrock of the system. The implication is that unions are at best unnecessary and at worst to be avoided. Similarly, although it is a moot point whether the model can do without a firm basis in procedures to ensure consistency of behaviour, the impression given is that 'flexibility' is everything and the desired state is that management 'can do' and should be able to do anything it likes. This is hardly compatible with the notions of rights and obligations set out in legislation or collective agreements. Figure 1.2 summarizes the main contrasts.

A critical point to note is that there is a Jekyll and Hyde quality about HRM. Not only are there, as Chapter 2 outlines, a variety of

The realities of human resource management

	Dimension	Personnel and IR	HRM
	Beliefs and assumptions		
1	Contract	Careful delineation of written contracts	Aim to go 'beyond contract'
2	Rules	Importance of devising clear rules/mutuality	'Can do' outlook: impatience with 'rule'
3	Guide to management action	Procedures/consistency control	'Business need'/flexibility/commitment
4	Behaviour referent	Norms/custom and practice	Values/mission
5	Managerial task *vis-à-vis* labour	Monitoring	Nurturing
6	Nature of relations	Pluralist	Unitarist
7	Conflict	Institutionalized	De-emphasized
8	Standardization	High (e.g. 'parity' an issue)	Low (e.g. 'parity' not seen as relevant)
	Strategic aspects		
9	Key relations	Labour-management	Business-customer
10	Initiatives	Piecemeal	Integrated
11	Corporate plan	Marginal to	Central to
12	Speed of decision	Slow	Fast
	Line management		
13	Management role	Transactional	Transformational leadership
14	Key managers	Personnel/IR specialists	General/business/line managers
15	Prized management skills	Negotiation	Facilitation
	Key levers		
16	Foci of attention for interventions	Personnel procedures	Wide-ranging cultural, structural and personnel strategies
17	Selection	Separate, marginal task	Integrated, key task
18	Pay	Job evaluation: multiple, fixed grades	Performance-related: few if any grades
19	Conditions	Separately negotiated	Harmonization
20	Labour-management	Collective bargaining contracts	Towards individual contracts
21	Thrust of relations with stewards	Regularized through facilities and training	Marginalized (with exception of some bargaining for change models)
22	Communication	Restricted flow/indirect	Increased flow/direct
23	Job design	Division of labour	Teamwork
24	Conflict handling	Reach temporary truces	Manage climate and culture
25	Training and development	Controlled access to courses	Learning companies

Figure 1.2 IR and HRM: the differences
Source: Storey (1992: 35)

24

approaches including 'universal' and 'contingency' models, but it is conveniently forgotten in most formulations that there are so-called hard and soft versions too. In Storey's words,

> The one emphasises the quantitative, calculative and busi-ness-strategic aspects of managing the headcounts resource in as 'rational' a way as for any other economic factor. By con-trast, the 'soft' version traces its roots to the human-relations school: it emphasises communication, motivation and leader-ship.
>
> (Storey, 1989: 8)

Both versions share key elements of the analysis and the pre-scription of the HRM approach: that organizations are under pres-sure to rethink their approach to managing people; that they are and should be seeking a better fit between their human resource strategies and business strategies; and that they are and should be transforming their practice. The two versions differ fundamen-tally, however, in their views on the direction that this transform-ation should take. The 'soft' version entails a range of specific policies and practices, which are people-centred and designed to win commitment. On the other hand, the 'hard' version admits any practice that advances the business strategy. In certain cir-cumstances, the response might entail very low pay or substantial employment insecurity.

With the benefit of hindsight, it is not difficult to understand why the new paradigm received so much attention. Not only did it seem to offer a guide to best practice, which was far better grounded and integrated than ever before, but it was also extremely optimistic. Here was a model that appeared to be able to satisfy everyone (apart from unions): it met the demand for economic efficiency and yet could also seemingly make a signifi-cant contribution to improving the quality of working life. No less important, the stress on the significance of the management of human resources to the competitive advantage of the organization appeared to give the HR/IR function, if not necessarily specialist HR/IR managers, the status which so many commentators, in particular in the UK and USA, had been seeking. Important, too, was that HRM became institutionalized in business schools where it has provided an opportunity to develop new courses and to occupy a central place on MBA programmes. Personnel management, rightly or wrongly, had been seen largely as low-level administrative routine and so has been ignored in the curricula of key management programmes such as the MBA. Human resource management, with its emphasis on strategy, strategic choice and competitive advantage, has proved to be much more acceptable. Most importantly, HRM was ambiguous: it is not stretching the point too far to suggest that it admitted of any number of possibilities.

These sentiments chimed well with the political climate. Anxious to avoid what they saw as the failures of the past, the four Conservative governments in power between 1979 and 1997 sought to introduce an 'enterprise culture' in which individuals and organizations, rather than governments, were to be held responsible for economic performance. Thus, as well as rejecting the maintenance of full employment as a major policy objective, they in effect abandoned the commitment of their predecessors to voluntary collective bargaining as the most effective method of determining pay and conditions. Trade unions and collective bargaining were seen as major factors in the stickiness of the response of wages to changes in demand and supply; and the government has introduced a series of Employment Acts to limit the powers of trade unions. The following quotation from the 1992 White Paper dealing with industrial relations, *People, Jobs and Opportunity*, gives a very strong flavour of its ideal state, even if its descriptive accuracy is open to question:

There is new recognition of the role and importance of the individual employee. Traditional patterns of industrial relations, based on collective bargaining and collective agreements, seem increasingly inappropriate and are in decline. . .

Many employers are replacing outdated personnel practice with new policies for human resource management, which put the emphasis on developing the talents and capacities of each individual employee. Many are also looking to communicate directly with their employees rather than through the medium of a trade union or a formal works council. There is a growing trend to individually negotiated reward packages which reflects the individual's personal skills, experience, efforts and performance. Employees in turn have higher expectations of their employer. They are increasingly aware of the contribution they are making – as individuals – to the business for which they work. They want to know how it is performing and to contribute to its development. They increasingly expect to influence their own development and to be rewarded for their achievement and initiative . . .

They also want the opportunity to influence, in some cases to negotiate, their own terms and conditions of employment, rather than leaving them to the outcome of some distant negotiations between employers and trade unions . . .

(Employment Department, 1992)

There were major flaws nonetheless. HRM's ambiguity caused much worry. The more work that was done, the more it emerged that there was a massive gap between the rhetoric and the reality of HRM. Not only were relatively few organizations pursuing the practices, as the first findings of the 1998 WERS (Cully *et al.*, 1998) have emphatically confirmed, ironically it was mostly unionized companies that were doing so. Most SMEs showed no signs of a clear-cut approach of any description; if they did, it was mostly associated with Charles Dickens's *Bleak House* (see, for example, Sisson, 1995), judging by the grievances being raised with ACAS and Citizens Advice Bureaux.

Critically, HRM overestimated the ability of managers to respond to their environment by moving upmarket into quality products and by bringing about the associated changes in employment relations. Faced with the relatively poor take-up of the model in the USA, two of the key figures central to their propagation had to recognize that

'strategic' human resource management models of the 1980s were too limited . . . because they depended so heavily on the values, strategies and support of top executives . . . While we see [these] as necessary conditions, we do not see them as sufficient to support the transformational process. A model capable of achieving sustained and transformational change will, therefore, need to incorporate more active roles of other stakeholders in the employment relationship, including

27

government, employees and union representatives as well as line managers.

(Kochan and Dyer, 1992: 1)

The key point that most commentators missed is that strategic choices are not made in a vacuum. The structures within which this choice is exercised, for example the corporate governance arrangements described earlier, are profoundly important: they can support or hinder the approach. Moreover, such structures are deeply rooted. They are not easily changed and decision-makers may even fight shy of trying to do so, preferring instead to argue that there is no alternative to reducing costs. There is no simple model of the factors that support the development of so-called strategic HRM. It seems clear, however, in Streeck's (1992: 10) words, that a 'regime of free markets and private hierarchies is not enough to generate and support a pattern of . . . quality production'. It is those countries, such as Germany and Japan, with regimes characterized by interlocking and mutually reinforcing institutional arrangements and processes, which seem to offer the most favourable environment for this kind of approach for managing employment relations.

A new agenda?

Although the full impact of the developments described here, notably those outlined in the first findings of the 1998 WERS (Cully *et al.*, 1998), have yet to be absorbed, there has already been a significant shift of mood reflecting experience of the last decade. Thus, while many pundits continue to be extremely upbeat and to proclaim a set of nostrums about the 'hypertext organization', 'agile production' and the 'open-book' company, there is a much greater note of caution, indeed humility, on the part of more serious commentators. Typically, these either are reluctant to speculate about the future or, more honestly, admit to being undecided. Significantly, faced with a not dissimilar pattern of developments in the USA, this is exactly what erstwhile leading proponents of the 'transformation thesis', including Cappelli, Katz and Osterman, have recently done (Cappelli *et al.*, 1997: 226).

Some issues are becoming clearer, however, which give us greater confidence in our approach to the subject matter of later chapters. Most critically, there is a growing consensus, in the USA (Cappelli *et al.*, 1997: 226) as well as the UK (Sisson and Marginson, 1995: 117) and Europe (CEC, 1997), about the major challenge facing management for the foreseeable future, even if there is no easy answer. To paraphrase Herriot *et al.* (1998), given the intensifying competition and/or pressure on scarce resources, management has to reconcile two seemingly conflicting requirements: to cut costs to the bone and yet at the same time promote the security, autonomy and teamwork, which are the conditions for innovation into new markets, products and services. The European Commission's Green Paper *Partnership for a New Organization of Work* (CEC, 1997: 5) puts it nicely in suggesting that the policy challenges could be 'summarised in one question: how to reconcile security for workers with the flexibility which firms need'.

The introduction of the third and critical stage of economic and monetary union (EMU) at the beginning of 1999 (the setting up of the European Central Bank with responsibility for EU-wide monetary policy and the timetable for the introduction of a single currency) is likely to be especially important here. Regardless of its adoption of the euro, the UK is unlikely to escape the significant pressure for restructuring that the greater transparency of prices and costs, coupled with the development of a single capital market, will generate. Indeed, there are strong grounds for suggesting that the pressure in the UK is likely to be greater than in most other countries because of the presence of a large number of MNCs (see below), one of the loosest set of arrangements governing closures and the relatively low levels of productivity (see, on this point, Cressey, 1998).

Also clear is that, with the UK's signature of the 'social chapter' and its incorporation into the Treaty of Amsterdam in 1997, the future direction of the European social dimension is also likely to have a profound effect on employment relations in the UK. In particular, it is difficult to escape the conclusion that, whatever else happens, the European connection signals the end of the 'voluntarism' that has characterized UK employment

29

relations for a century. This is because our European partners have much stronger traditions of regulation in employment relations than the UK (for further details, see CEC, 1989: 8–12). In the early days of the European Community, the 'Roman-Germanic system' associated with the original six members of the European Economic Community was dominant. This tended to prioritize statutory regulation. In recent years, however, as the number of EU members has increased and concerns about subsidiarity have grown, the so-called 'Nordic system' of Denmark and Sweden has become more prominent. This puts the emphasis on collective agreements, which are subsequently made legally enforceable. Good examples would be the agreements on parental leave and equality of treatment for part-time workers reached under the social policy protocol process. These were negotiated by the European social partner organizations and subsequently given legal force by the European Commission in the form of directives requiring their implementation by member states.

Significant, too, is that much of the recent legislation provides for information and consultation through employee representatives from trade unions or some form of works council, reflecting the importance attached by our EU partners to both representative (i.e. collective) and direct (i.e. individual) participation. As well as the specific arrangements covering information and consultation in MNCs, there are general provisions in such areas as collective redundancies and transfers of undertakings, health and safety, and working time. So far, the UK government, while giving strong support to the notion of 'partnership' at workplace level, has opposed the introduction of a universal right to representation, preferring the approach of providing for issue-specific employee representation in each of the areas. This cannot go on for ever, though. Indeed, the European Commission has a draft directive on national-level information and consultation to go alongside that dealing with multinational companies. UK management, it seems, is going to have to get used to the idea of managing individually *and* collectively as we have previously argued (Storey and Sisson, 1993: 231–2).

A third issue likely to be of increasing importance in both the theory and practice of employment relations is that of integration.

Historically, there has been a tendency to put the main emphasis on 'best practice' in the individual areas of employment relations – the 'best' payment system, the 'best' performance appraisal system and so on. Yet there is a growing body of evidence reviewed in later chapters to suggest that it is not 'best practice' which is important. Indeed, its pursuit can be counterproductive, encouraging the mistaken belief that practices have automatic effect and promoting cynicism when things go wrong. Rather it is the way that practices are configured, i.e. fit together and make sense to employees in the particular situation, that creates the added value. Given the importance of the particular situation, it is difficult to draw up hard-and-fast rules governing integration, although key pointers are given in Chapter 10. An important implication, however, is that improving the management of employment relations is within the grasp of any organization and not just larger ones.

The rest of the book

As well as reviewing the latest thinking and developments, the rest of the book tries to show how the management of employment relations can be improved despite the very real obstacles to be found in the UK. It begins by tackling the issue of managing strategically. Various models are discussed and there are suggestions on how an organization might go about developing a more strategic approach. Chapters 3 and 4 deal with the relatively novel topics (novel in HR/IR texts) of managing restructuring and involvement and participation. Chapter 5 focuses on two issues at the heart of the employment relationship: pay and working time. Chapters 6 and 7 are concerned with improving the organization's competences and capabilities; Chapter 6 is concerned with training and development, and Chapter 7 with recruitment and selection. Chapter 8 focuses on managing with trade unions and, in particular, considers the much-heralded trend towards 'partnership'. Chapter 9 deals with another issue rarely receiving attention: the management of the HR/IR function and how its contribution might be realized and organized. The final chapter returns to the issues of the new agenda and discusses the practical implications.

Suggested further reading

Chapters 1–3 of *Managing Human Resources and Industrial Relations* (Storey and Sisson, 1993) carries much more detail on the historical and institutional background. For changes in the nature of work, see the report of Gallie and his colleagues (1998) *Employment in Britain Survey*. Strongly recommended are the two volumes dealing with the detailed reporting of the findings of the 1998 Workplace Employee Relations Survey (Cully *et al.*, 1999; Millward *et al.*, 2000).

2

MANAGING STRATEGICALLY

It is now a commonplace to suggest that organizations need to adopt a more *strategic* approach to the management of people (see, for example, the review in Mabey *et al.*, 1998a). Typically, a more *strategic* approach is seen as embracing the following:

1 Regarding people as a strategic resource for achieving competitive advantage.
2 The use of planning.
3 A coherent approach to employment policies and practices (internal integration).
4 The integration of employment policies and practices with business strategy (external integration).
5 Proactive not reactive management.
6 Action on employment issues at the most senior management levels.

Our aims in this chapter, which are reflected in the structure, are threefold. The first is to consider the arguments underpinning the view that people are a strategic resource for achieving competitive advantage. An appreciation of these is essential if the presentation in later chapters is to make sense. The second is to outline the main types of overall model or approach that have emerged. Some of these models may seem to be unrealistic in the light of the UK business context, yet they continue to exert a profound influence on people's thinking and so it is important to understand what they involve. The third, and much more pragmatic, aim is to show how it is possible for managers, notwithstanding the problems, to develop a strategic approach appropriate to their situation. The reason for introducing this topic at an early stage in the book is that the disciplinary framework outlined is as relevant to managing the specific areas of employment relations discussed in other chapters as it is to their integration in an overall approach.

The resource-based view

The resource-based view has its origins in the new business strategy literature and has very quickly become influential, giving rise to developments in pay systems and training as well as overall models or approaches. Put simply, the argument is that all organizations comprise unique bundles of assets and that their access to these, plus their ability to make effective use of them, provides the essential source of a firm's competitive advantage (Barney, 1991; Grant, 1991, 1995). Such an approach to understanding strategy places managers' role in identifying, utilizing and renewing such assets centre-stage.

There are variants in the resource-based view, but in essence proponents suggest that sustained competitive advantage derives from an astute use of a firm's internal resources. For these to offer ongoing advantage, the valued resources must have four qualities: they must add value, be unique or at least be rare, be difficult for competitors to imitate, and be non-substitutable (e.g. by technology). As is increasingly being noted, human capital resources can fit this demanding list of requirements rather well. This type of resource can embody intangible assets such as unique combinations of complementary skills and tacit knowledge accumulated over a lengthy period of time.

Hamel and Prahalad (1994) suggest that the nature of the basis of competition is changing and that critical to future competitive success will be the levering of 'core competences'. Under new conditions, business strategy necessitates 'thinking differently'. Old-style notions of strategy such as portfolio management or formal forward planning would be unable to keep pace with the leaders who are creating new products and even new industries at an ever-accelerating rate. Sustainable competitive advantage requires close attention to a firm's capabilities – their identification, utilization, development and renewal. The new competition involves not simply competition in the market for goods and services but, more importantly and underpinning this, competition for 'foresight, competition to build competences and competition to build industry evolution' (Hamel and Prahalad, 1994: 274). The focus, they imply, should therefore be upon why and how do some companies seem able to continually create new forms of competitive advantage? 'Foresight, stretch and leverage provide the energy and rationale for proactive advantage building and industry reengineering' (p. 277).

According to this perspective, therefore, the problem is not with 'strategy' but with the particular notion of strategy that predominates. What is being rejected, suggest Hamel and Prahalad, 'is not strategy in the sense that we define it but strategy as a pedantic planning ritual on the one hand or a speculative and open-ended investment commitment on the other' (1994: 281).

Strategic planning it is argued, usually fails to spark the necessary debates about 'who we are as a company and what we want to be'. Hamel and Prahalad critique the traditional planning approach while extolling what they term the 'crafting strategic architecture' model. The contrast between these two can be readily seen in Figure 2.1.

In sum, the key elements are: long-term focus; stretching goals built around shared strategic intent; levering key resources across organizational boundaries; and a commitment to safeguarding and building key resources. The crucial implication for HR arising from this perspective of strategic management can be summarized as follows. First, the truly strategic contribution of the HR function is the *recognition* of a firm's core capabilities and a *building of organizational capability*. Second, this means that not all HRM functions can be devolved to business units. Organization-wide capabilities must be renewed so that they are sustainable and they must be used flexibly across the organization when new ventures are being pursued. Interlinkages across units to add value to the business as a whole are necessary. Third, formal HR policies in

	Strategic planning	*Crafting strategic architecture*
Planning goal	• Incremental improvement in market share and position	• Rewriting industry rules and creating new competitive space
Planning process	• Formulaic and ritualistic	• Exploratory and open-ended
	• Existing industry and market structure as the base line	• An understanding of discontinuities and competences as the base line
	• Industry structure analysis (segmentation analysis, value chain analysis, cost structure analysis, competitor benchmarking, etc.)	• A search for new functionalities or new ways of delivering traditional functionalities
	• Tests for fit between resources and plans	• Enlarging opportunity horizons
	• Capital budgeting and allocation of resources among competing projects	• Tests for significance and timeliness of new opportunities
	• Individual businesses as the unit of analysis	• Development of plans for competence acquisition and migration
		• Development of opportunity approach plans
		• The corporation as the unit of analysis
Planning resources	• Business unit executives	• Many managers
	• Few experts	• The collective wisdom of the company
	• Staff driven	• Line and staff driven

Figure 2.1 Strategic planning versus crafting strategic architecture
Source: Hamel and Prahalad, 1994

themselves are unlikely truly to represent scarce and inimitable resources. Hence what is required in addition is the higher-order capability of evaluating the policies' potential contribution to performance and acting accordingly. Fourth, this perspective places massive emphasis on *learning* and indeed especially so on the *capacity to learn*. This latter point is the key to the idea of the learning organization discussed in Chapter 6. Some even claim that the only true source of sustained competitive advantage in the future will be the capacity to learn fast and effectively. Enabling this would be the central role of the HR function.

An array of models

A number of models or approaches have emerged reflecting the kind of thinking associated with the resource-based view. For the purposes of presentation, these can be divided into two main types: universal and contingency. Implicit in the notion of best practice in Chapter 1 is that there is an approach, coupled with a set of policies and practices, which is universally appropriate to managing employment relations in order to achieve superior performance, regardless of the specific circumstances of the organization. In contrast, the contingency models discussed later put the emphasis on adopting policies and practices to fit specific circumstances such as the stage in the organization's business life cycle.

Universal models

The HRM model
The influential idea of 'strategic HRM' came to prominence in the 1980s in the USA. As Chapter 1 outlined, central to the idea is a more strategic and all-embracing approach to the management of people than traditional personnel management or industrial relations seemed to offer. This meant planning resources not only in quantitative terms, which tended to be the main preoccupation with manpower planning, but in qualitative terms as well. It meant seeking to integrate the full range of policies with one another and with business planning. An ever-increasing number

of books and articles in the UK have proclaimed these features (see, for example, Armstrong, 1992a, b).

One of the most popular formulations in the UK (see, for example, Guest, 1987, 1998; Boxall, 1992) has been the Harvard model (Beer *et al.*, 1985). This suggests that HRM policy choices will be influenced by a set of stakeholders (shareholders, government, trade unions and so on) and by the particular set of situational factors which surround any particular case (such as product market conditions, the production technology and so on). Management's strategic task is to make certain fundamental policy choices in the light of these factors. Four clusters of choices are seen as especially important. These relate to the degree and nature of influence which employees will have; decisions about resourcing, through-flow and outflow of personnel; reward systems, and the organization of work.

Ostensibly the Harvard model allows for considerable variation and appears to contrast itself with situational determinism. In fact, the model posits what Guest (1987: 510) has termed an 'implicit theory'. In other words, the analysis of strategic choice contained herein has a strong prescriptive overtone. The specified desirable outcomes of commitment, competence and the like can be seen as the elevation of one particular strategic approach over all others. This model appears to suggest that there is one preferred and superior set of HR 'policy choices'. Although there is no 'official' version, the policies and practices typically associated with the model are shown in Table 2.1. Many of the ideas are deeply rooted in the so-called neo-human relations thinking of people such as Herzberg, Maslow and McGregor.

The 'partnership' model
Like the 'HRM' version, there is no clear definition of the 'partnership' model. Especially controversial is whether partnership is in essence about the relationship between the organization and the individual or the organization and the trade union. Some organizations in the UK claiming to be partnership companies, such as Motorola and Unipart, do not recognize trade unions. Significantly, too, a report from the UK's Department of Trade and Industry/Department for Education and Employment, reckoned to be highly regarded by ministers and those close to the Prime

Table 2.1 The HRM model

Policy area	Policy choice/practice
Beliefs and assumptions	Business and customer (internal and external) needs are main referent
	Search for excellence and quality and continuous improvement are dominant values
	Aim to go 'beyond contract'; emphasis on 'can do' outlook and high energy
	Widespread use of team analogy and metaphors
	High levels of trust. HRM central to business strategy
Managerial role	Top managers are highly visible and provide a vision for the future that employees can share; they also offer transformational 'leadership' setting the mission and values of the organization
	Middle managers inspire, encourage, enable and facilitate change by harnessing commitment and co-operation of employees; they also see developing employees as a primary role
Organization design	'Federal', highly decentralized, 'flat' organization structures
	Job design congruent with organization structure, technology and personnel policies
	'Cross-functional' project teams and informal groups responsible for particular products or services or customers; they 'contract' contribution to organization with jobs defined in terms of team role
	Teams enjoy large measure of autonomy and there is great deal of 'task' flexibility, if not interchangeability, between members
HR policies	Numerical flexibility, i.e. core and periphery workforce
	Time flexibility, e.g. annual hours. Single status, i.e. reward etc. of core employees reflects contribution
	Selection – emphasis on attitudes as well as skills

Table 2.1 Continued

Policy area	Policy choice/practice
	Appraisal – open and participative with emphasis on two-way feedback
	Training – learning, growth and development of core employees are fundamental values; lateral as well as upward career advancement with emphasis on 'general' as well as 'specific' employability
	Equal opportunities
	Reward systems – individual and group performance pay; skill-based pay; profit and gain sharing; share ownership; flexible benefits package, e.g. 'cafeteria' principle
	Participation and involvement – extensive use of two-way communication and problem-solving groups

Source: Based on Sisson (1994c)

Minister, extols the virtues of *Partnerships with People* (DTI/DfEE, 1997) but makes no mention of trade unions, albeit employees are expected mostly to be working 'collectively' in teams.

Even so, partnership agreements, along with the wider notion of partnership, have come to imply something like the HRM model combined with some form of collective employee representation or 'voice'. A TUC publication (1999: 13) draws on the earlier work of the Involvement and Participation Association (IPA, 1992) in identifying six key principles that it believes should underpin the model:

1 A shared commitment to the success of enterprise, including support for flexibility and the replacement of adversarial relations.
2 A recognition that interests of the partners may legitimately differ.
3 Employment security, including measures to improve the employability of staff as well as limit the use of compulsory redundancy.

4 A focus on the quality of working life.
5 A commitment to transparency, including a real sharing of 'hard, unvarnished information', an openness to discussing plans for the future, genuine consultation and a preparedness to listen to the business case for alternative strategies.
6 Adding value – the 'hallmark of an effective partnership is that it taps into sources of commitment and/or resources that were not accessed by previous arrangements' (IPA, 1992).

Further details of this model can be found in Chapter 8.

Contingency models

The models in the second group emphasize the variability of policy choices under different business conditions. Three main types of contingency model have so far predominated. One links HR strategic choices to different stages in the business life cycle; a second relates them to different strategy/structure configurations; and the third links HR strategies to different business strategies of the type identified by Porter (1980, 1985).

Business life cycle
The first of these approaches, the business life cycle approach seeks to link HR policy choices to the varying requirements of a firm at different stages of its life cycle, i.e. from business start-up, through early growth and maturity and eventually on to business decline. At each stage a business might be hypothesized to have different priorities. These different priorities in turn require their own HR strategies. There are a number of examples of the 'stages' approach (Kochan and Barocci, 1985; Baird and Meshoulam, 1988; Lengnick-Hall and Lengnick-Hall, 1988).

As Table 2.2 suggests, at the start-up stage a business is posited as requiring the following: recruitment and selection strategies which quickly attract the best talent; a reward strategy which supports this by paying highly competitive rates; a training and development strategy which builds the foundations for the future, and an employee relations strategy which draws the basic architecture and puts in place the underlying philosophy for the new business.

Under mature conditions the emphasis is upon control and

Table 2.2 Critical human resource activities at different organizational or business unit stages

Human resource functions	Life cycle stages			
	Start-up	*Growth*	*Maturity*	*Decline*
Recruitment, selection and staffing	Attract best technical/professional talent	Recruit adequate numbers and mix of qualified workers. Management succession planning. Manage rapid internal labour market movements	Encourage sufficient turnover to minimize lay-offs and provide new openings. Encourage mobility as re-organizations shift jobs around	Plan and implement workforce reductions and reallocation
Compensation and benefits	Meet or exceed labour market rates to attract needed talent	Meet external market but consider internal equity effects. Establish formal compensation structures	Control compensation	Tighter cost control
Employee training and development	Define future skill requirements and begin establishing career ladders	Mould effective management team through management development and organizational development	Maintain flexibility and skills of an ageing workforce	Implement retraining and career consulting services
Labour/employee relations	Set basic employee relations philosophy and organization	Maintain labour peace and employee motivation and morale	Control labour costs and maintain labour peace. Improve productivity	Maintain peace

Source: Kochan and Barocci (1985: 104)

maintenance of costs and resources. Hence, the recruitment and selection stance might be geared to trickle-feed new blood into vacant positions created by retirements. There might also be a policy of encouraging enough labour turnover so as to minimize the need for compulsory lay-offs. Meanwhile the pay and benefits policy is likely to be geared to a keen control over costs. Training and development might be expected to have as their priority the maintenance of flexibility and the adequate provision of skill levels in an ageing workforce.

Strategy and structure

The most noted example of the strategy/structure linkage of contingency theory is the work of Fombrun *et al.* (1984). Their model shows a range of 'appropriate' HR choices suited to five different strategy/structure types ranging from single-product businesses with functional structures, through diversified product strategies allied to multidivisional organizational forms and on to multiproduct companies operating globally. For each of the five types of situation the key HR policy choices in the spheres of selection, appraisal, reward and development are delineated (see Table 2.3).

For instance, for a company following a single-product strategy with an associated functional structure the HRM strategy is likely to be traditional in appearance. Selection and appraisal may well be conducted in a subjective fashion and reward and development practices may veer to the unsystematic and the paternalistic.

By way of contrast, a company pursuing a diversification strategy with a multidivisional structure is likely to be characterized by an HRM strategy which is driven by impersonal, systematic devices which are, however, adaptable to the different parts of the organization. Reward systems are likely to be formula-based with a tendency towards a built-in response to return on investment and profitability. Selection and even appraisal may be found to vary between the constituent business divisions. Where the multidivisional strategy is, however, accompanied by a business strategy built around interrelated, interdependent businesses, it is postulated that it is more likely in these circumstances that the HRM strategy will foster and take advantage of that interrelationship.

Table 2.3 Human resources management links to strategy and structure

Strategy	Structure	Human resource management			
		Selection	Appraisal	Rewards	Development
1 Single product	Functional	Functionally oriented: subjective criteria used	Subjective measure via personal contact	Unsystematic and allocated in a paternalistic manner	Unsystematic largely job experiences: single function focus
2 Single product (vertically integrated)	Functional	Functionally oriented: standardized criteria used	Impersonal: based on cost and productivity data	Related to performance and productivity	Functional specialists with some generalists: largely rotation
3 Growth by acquisition (holding company) of unrelated businesses	Separate self-contained businesses	Functionally oriented, but varies from business to business in terms of how systematic	Impersonal: based on return on investment and profitability	Formula-based includes return on investment and profitability	Cross-functional but not cross-business
4 Related diversification of product lines through internal growth and acquisition	Multidivisional	Functionally and generalist oriented: systematic criteria used	Impersonal: based on return on investment, productivity, and subjective assessment of contribution to company	Large bonuses: based on profitability and subjective assessment of contribution to overall company	Cross-functional, cross-divisional, and cross-corporate/divisional formal

Table 2.3 Continued

Strategy	Structure	Human resource management			
		Selection	*Appraisal*	*Rewards*	*Development*
5 Multiple products in multiple countries	Global organization (geographic centre and worldwide)	Functionally and generalists oriented: systematic criteria used	Impersonal: based on multiple goals such as return on investment, profit tailored to product and country	Bonuses: based on multiple planned goals with moderate top management discretion	Cross-divisional and cross-subsidiary to corporate: formal and systematic

Source: Adapted from Fombrun *et al.* (1984)

Matching business strategy and HRM strategy

The third type of contingency model links employment policy choices with different types of business strategy. Arguably, the most explicit example is that of Miller (1989). He seeks to tighten up what he sees as the rather loose usage of the term 'HR strategy' by suggesting that a HR approach is strategic only if it 'fits' with the organization's product market strategy and if it is proactive in this regard. Most of the theorists in this category draw on Porter's distinction among innovation, quality-enhancement and cost-reduction strategies (for example, Schuler and Jackson, 1987) or on Miles and Snow (1984).

Schuler and Jackson's (1987) model in Table 2.4 suggests that where a firm has opted for innovation as a means to gain competitive advantage this sets up certain predictable required patterns of behaviour. Prime among these requisite 'role behaviours' are creativity, a capacity and willingness to focus on longer-term goals, a relatively high level of collaborative action, a high tolerance of ambiguity and a high degree of readiness to take risks. On the other hand, concern for quality and for achieving output need only be at moderate levels. As a way of illustrating the contrasts with other strategic choices one might note that where a cost-reduction business strategy is chosen then the behaviour patterns at a premium will conversely hinge around a short-term focus and a willingness to perform and tolerate repetitive and predictable job cycles in a standardized undeviating way. The associated HRM policy choices to encourage this set of behaviours will include job design principles, close monitoring and control, and an appraisal system which rewards and punishes in accord with short-term results.

Developing a strategic approach

Valuable though the various models discussed above are in drawing attention to some of the fundamental issues, our experience is that most managers see them as remote and unrealistic. Important, too, is that no model is automatic: how it is applied is critical. Many of the elements of best practice are necessary but not sufficient. It is how they are 'configured', to use the jargon, that

Table 2.4 Business strategy and HRM policy choices. Employee role behaviour and HRM policies associated with particular business strategies

Strategy	Employee role behaviour	HRM policies
1 *Innovation*	A high degree of creative behaviour	Jobs that require close interaction and coordination among groups of individuals
	Longer-term focus	Performance appraisals that are more likely to reflect longer term and group-based achievements
	A relatively high level of cooperative, interdependent behaviour	Jobs that allow employees to develop skills that can be used in other positions in the firm
		Compensation systems that emphasize internal equity rather than external or market-based equity
	A moderate degree of concern for quality	Pay rates that tend to be low, but that allow employees to be stockholders and have more freedom to choose the mix of components that make up their pay package
	A moderate concern for quantity	
	An equal degree of concern for process and results	Broad career paths to reinforce the development of a broad range of skills
	A greater degree of risk taking	
	A high tolerance of ambiguity and unpredictability	

Table 2.4 Continued

Strategy	Employee role behaviour	HRM policies
2 *Quality enhancement*	Relatively repetitive and predictable behaviours	Relatively fixed and explicit job descriptions
	A more long term or intermediate focus	High levels of employee participation in decisions relevant to immediate work conditions and the job itself
	A moderate amount of cooperative interdependent behaviour	A mix of individual and group criteria for performance appraisal that is mostly short term and results orientated
	A high concern for quality	A relatively egalitarian treatment of employees and some guarantees of employment security
	A modest concern for quality of output	Extensive and continuous training and development of employees
	High concern for process	
	Low risk-taking activity	
	Commitment to the goals of the organization	
3 *Cost reduction*	Relatively repetitive and predictable behaviour	Relatively fixed and explicit job descriptions that allow little room for ambiguity
	A rather short-term focus	Narrowly designed jobs and narrowly defined career paths that encourage specialization, expertise and efficiency
	Primarily autonomous or individual activity	Short-term results orientated performance appraisals

Table 2.4 Continued

Strategy	Employee role behaviour	HRM policies
	Moderate concern for quality	Close monitoring of market pay levels for use in making compensation decisions
	High concern for quantity of output	Minimal levels of employee training and development
	Primary concern for results	
	Low risk-taking activity	
	Relatively high degree of comfort with stability	

Source: Schuler and Jackson (1987: 209–13)

makes the difference. In the words of Becker and Huselid (1998: 85), 'without the proper firm specific alignment of these policies with one another and the firm's strategic objectives, the full benefits will not be observed'. For these reasons, our attention now turns to how management can begin to develop a strategic approach which emphasizes the disciplines of planning rather than the properties of a particular model, taking into account the organization's own unique human resources.

Identifying strengths and weaknesses

The first step is to establish the strengths and weaknesses of the current approach to managing employment relations. Obvious sources of information are customers and employees. Most organizations typically have a range of means to elicit the views of these groups, although they may not currently be making use of them. For example, increases in customer complaints and employee turnover are sure signs that something is wrong. The importance of senior managers themselves undertaking a regular review across the full range of policies and practices cannot be exaggerated.

A number of approaches have emerged in the USA, notably Kaplan and Norton's (1992) 'balanced scorecard', which takes into account four main perspectives: the shareholder's; the customer's; the internal (i.e. cost, quality, response time); and the employee's. In our opinion, however, two very practical UK guides remain the most useful. The first, *Strategic Planning for People*, was produced by a working party of the National Economic Development Office and the Manpower Services Commission in 1987 as part of the People: The Key Success initiative (NEDO/MSC, 1987). This is a simple diagnostic exercise which involves asking four main questions:

1 What are our strategic objectives?
2 What strengths in our approach to people may help achievement?
3 What weaknesses in our approach to people may hinder achievement?
4 What action is indicated to build on strengths or to correct weaknesses in our approach to people?

The exercise then involves the identification of the improvements needed under headings such as 'leadership', 'involvement and communications', 'training and development', 'performance management', and 'pay and conditions'. For each area, there is encouragement to spell out what improvements are required, by when and by whom. ACAS (1998a) provides up-to-date checklists covering many of the topics that organizations need to think about in its guide *Employment Policies*.

The second, *Human Resource Management Audit* (Collins, 1991), is a much more detailed guide intended to provide managers with a framework to be adapted to suit their particular circumstances. Again, the focus is a series of questions. Each of the main areas of employment relations is covered and for each significant activity or process, paired statements are prepared which describe the potential extremes of a performance range. Performance is then rated using a numbered scale, so that an average standard of performance can be identified. One example, dealing with human resource planning, is shown in Figure 2.2 and is taken from full lists of over 15 questions.

In some cases, it is possible to assess effectiveness by setting

The ability of managers to plan the current and future use of human resources is an integral part of their performance review	1 2 3 4 5 6 7	Little account is taken of human resource planning in performance review

Figure 2.2 Human resource planning – example question
Source: Collins (1991)

objectives in quantifiable terms and measuring achievement against target. This can even be done in the relatively 'soft' area of communications where, for example, the frequency of team briefing, the timeliness of written reports and their quality as measured by employee complaints or queries can be measured.

For present purposes, however, it is the first step – establishing how far the organization has to go in developing an overall approach – which is most relevant. It will be seen from Figure 2.3 that, in this case, the questions touch on not only the quantitative dimension of strategy development, in the form of human resource planning, but also the qualitative – there is emphasis on the need for policies and practices to be integrated and mutually supportive and for the values of the strategy to be consistent with those of the organization's mission. Fundamentally important too is that attention is drawn to the role both of senior managers and of any specialist HR function. Each of these are issues to which we return later in the book.

Closing the information gap

Ensuring that the right people are in place at the right time is one of the basic building blocks of a more strategic approach. In the case of groups of employees, this means applying some of the techniques of human resource planning (HRP). In the case of individual employees, the equivalent is known as succession planning.

Figure 2.4 summarizes the sequence of activities involved in HRP. Three phases are involved. The *calculation of the demand for labour* starts with the organization's business plan and, from this, seeks to derive the HR implications of the projected nature and scale of operations over a stipulated period using a range of

The realities of human resource management

Questionnaire	Yes	No
1. Is there a clearly understood HRM strategy?	☐	☐
1.1 Is this strategy known and understood by all managers?	☐	☐
1.2 Does this strategy support and fit in with the business strategy?	☐	☐
1.3 Is the HRM strategy regularly reviewed?	☐	☐
1.4 Is the strategy consistent with the organization mission?	☐	☐
1.5 Are the values associated with the strategy consistent with the values of the organization's mission?	☐	☐
1.6 Is the HRM strategy consistent with other functional strategies?	☐	☐
2. Are people seen as a strategic resource by senior management?	☐	☐
2.1 Does the business plan demonstrate a belief that human resources are a valuable source of competitive advantage?	☐	☐
2.2 Do managers at all levels manage their staff in a way that recognizes their role in strategy implementation?	☐	☐
2.3 Do management training and development programmes take account of the need for all managers to think and behave strategically?	☐	☐
2.4 Does senior management take a long-term view of human resource issues?	☐	☐
3. Are there clearly understood strategies for the main elements of HRM?	☐	☐
3.1 Are these strategies integrated and mutually supportive?	☐	☐
3.2 Do these strategies focus on improving individual and organizational performance?	☐	☐
3.3 Have strategies been formulated for all the main elements of HRM?	☐	☐

	Yes	No
3.4 Are the values of these strategies consistent with the values of the overall HRM strategy?	☐	☐
3.5 Are these strategies tested by developing feasible implementation plans?	☐	☐
3.6 Are these strategies consistent with other functional strategies?	☐	☐
4. Does human resource planning (HRP) take account of internal and external environmental factors?	☐	☐
4.1 During the business planning process is a SWOT analysis carried out on human resources?	☐	☐
4.2 Does HRP take account of long-term environmental trends?	☐	☐
4.3 Are short- and medium-term HR plans consistent with longer term plans and forecasts?	☐	☐
4.4 Are appropriate forecasting techniques used in HRP?	☐	☐
4.5 Does HRP represent a proactive, as well as reactive, approach to the future?	☐	☐
5. Does the personnel function have a strategic role in HRM?	☐	☐
5.1 Does the most senior personnel manager help formulate business strategy?	☐	☐
5.2 Does the personnel department have a strategy for the delivery of its services?	☐	☐
5.3 Is the strategic role of the personnel department understood by both personnel staff and the line managers?	☐	☐
5.4 Does the personnel department's strategy focus on ensuring successful implementation of the organization's HRM strategies?	☐	☐

Figure 2.3 Strategic human resource management audit
Source: Collins (1991)

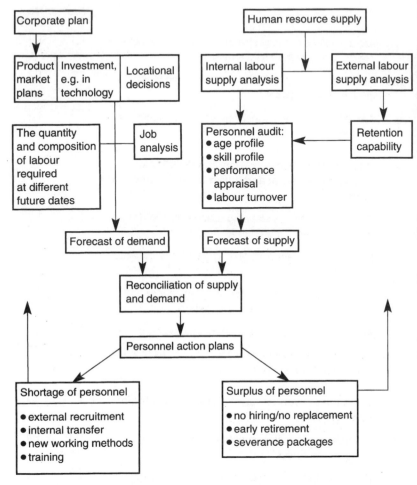

Figure 2.4 An idealized HRP model

forecasting methods such as current-base-plus forecasts, ratio-trend analysis and regression analysis. *Planning for labour supply* involves what is known as stocks and flows analysis, i.e. an audit of the current composition of the labour force tracking various movements such as people leaving the organization, being promoted or simply undergoing internal transfer. The *matching process* seeks to reconcile the supply and demand processes. Assuming a less than perfect fit between the two sets of forecast, a gap analysis can be made and policy options reviewed.

For SMEs in general and for large organizations in the case of key personnel, planning for individual employees is likely to be priority rather than planning for groups. This means succession planning. Here the basic instruments are a manpower audit sheet and management succession plan. Figures 2.5 and 2.6 show examples of these.

Figure 2.5 succinctly captures the basic data on key individuals and scores them in terms of current performance, personal qualities and assessment of potential. In the illustration it may be seen that Lee had an excellent performance rating and a good scoring also across all dimensions of perceived personal qualities. This person was also given the highest ranking on assessed future potential. On the basis of this analysis the management succession plan in Figure 2.6 was constructed.

The ACAS guide *Recruitment Policies for the 1990s* provides further basic details of these techniques (ACAS, 1997a). More comprehensive treatment can be found in Mayo (1991).

The discussion so far makes two assumptions which at first sight appear eminently reasonable. The first is that the organization possesses the necessary personnel information to engage in meaningful HRP and succession planning; the second is that there are operational plans flowing from the business strategy to enable this to be done. Each of these assumptions is in reality highly questionable. A major task facing the would-be planner is to close the information gap that currently exists in most organizations.

Securing adequate personnel data
As the Department of Employment recognized a quarter of a century ago, the quality of any human resources planning depends on the 'adequacy of ... personnel records and statistics' (DoE, 1968: 11). Ideally, the planner needs not only quantitative information about numbers of employees and their rate of turnover, but qualitative information as well about their competences, their career preferences and aspirations and so on. Figure 2.7, which is taken from Andrew Mayo, a former HR director of ICL, offers an idea of how this might be approached.

Manpower audit sheet

Key: 1 = High 5 = Low

Name	Job title	Age	Grade	Performance rating	Job knowledge	Planning/organization	Creativity/initiative	Ability to get results	Acceptability to others	Financial awareness	Development of subordinates	Assessment of potential
A. Smith	Production Manager	50	M2	Adequate to above average	2	4	4	3	3	4	4	Potential list 'D'
G. Dawson	Manager Site Services	58	M3	Adequate to above average	3	3	4	3	3	3	3	Potential list 'C'
B. Lee	Engineering Manager	38	M2	Exceptional	1	2	1	1	3	3	1	Potential list 'A'
J. Brown	P & MC Manager	40	M3	Adequate to above average	3	3	5	5	3	5	5	Potential list 'C'
B. Jones	Process Engineer	41	M2	Adequate to above average	2	2	3	3	3	4	3	Potential list 'D'

Figure 2.5 Manpower audit sheet

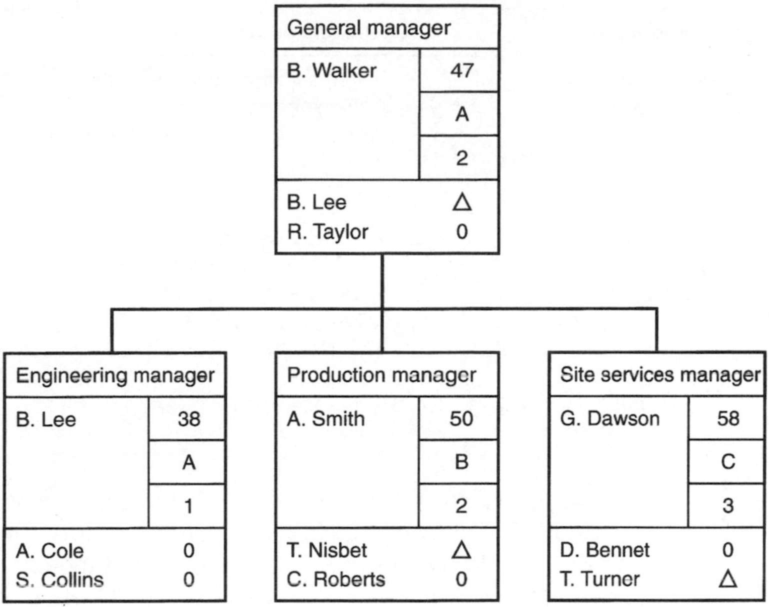

General manager	
B. Walker	47
	A
	2
B. Lee △	
R. Taylor 0	

Engineering manager			Production manager			Site services manager	
B. Lee	38		A. Smith	50		G. Dawson	58
	A			B			C
	1			2			3
A. Cole	0		T. Nisbet	△		D. Bennet	0
S. Collins	0		C. Roberts	0		T. Turner	△

Key

38   Age

Present performance
A.   Outstanding
B.   Satisfactory
C.   Needs improvement
D.   Unsatisfactory, replace when possible

Promotion status
△   Ready now
0   Almost ready

Potential
1.   Excellent
2.   Promising
3.   Doubtful
4.   Not to be promoted

Figure 2.6 Management succession chart

The problem is that much of this information, especially that which appears in the right-hand column, is rarely available in UK organizations because employment practices are too often rudimentary, as the previous chapter has already suggested. UK

The organization	The individual
• Strategic plan	• Personal information records
• Operating plan	• Training records
• Organization structure	• Appraisal and development reviews
• Organization demographics	• CVs
• Job grades/categories	
• Person specifications	• Personal growth profiles
• Career structures	• Career development plans
• Career bridges	• Test and assessment results
• Development positions	• Language capability
	• Career history dynamics

Figure 2.7 Sources of data for personnel planning
Source: Mayo (1991: 201)

managers have also been slow to make best use of the latest available management information technology, for example, in matching CVs to skills (Welch and John, 1998). Even in blue-chip organizations such as IBM, NatWest Bank and the Post Office, it seems, there are difficulties in carrying out skills-based planning because of the lack of information (for further details see Hirsch and Reilly, 1998). Needless to say, if the application forms used in selection are inadequate, the danger is that much information will be unavailable. If there is no appraisal system, the organization has in effect cut itself off from the major source of information about individuals. If the organization does little or no training, it will not have the information from skills audits that are to be found in large companies in some other countries. The answer is implicit in the analysis. The organization has to improve its practices in order to improve the quality of its personnel information. ACAS publishes a useful guide to setting up and running a records system covering application forms, employment history, assessment of employee performance, disciplinary action, absence, and analysis of employment and turnover (ACAS, 1997b).

Shifting the focus of business planning
A second major problem that has to be addressed as a matter of priority is the nature of the business planning process. It has to be

accepted that, as various analyses have shown (see, for example, Mintzberg, 1978, 1985; Quinn, 1980; Johnson, 1987; Pettigrew and Whipp, 1991), rather than occurring in linear fashion, the formulation and implementation of business strategy is best understood in terms of 'processual' and 'incremental' models. Strategy, in Mintzberg's (1978) classic formulation, may be best seen as 'a pattern in a stream of decisions'. Strategy, in the words of other well known commentators (see, for example, Johnson, 1987; Whittington, 1989), is also 'interpreted', i.e. it is to be seen as a social outcome shaped by the prevailing ideologies, rituals, myths and symbols of the organizational culture. Changing the strategy entails an exercise in the manipulation or management of meaning. Effecting such a shift is difficult because managers and employees operate within deeply embedded 'causal maps', 'scripts' or 'ideologies' which may be hardly perceived at the conscious level.

The implication is that the would-be HR planner will never have the neat and tidy business plans that much of the prescriptive literature takes for granted. Even so, pressure has to be applied to secure operational plans, however rudimentary, if there is to be any sensible attempt to forecast the number of employees and their skills.

Also complicating matters is the dominant approach to business planning of the 1980s and 1990s. Known as portfolio planning, this sees strategy as making decisions about the mix (portfolio) of businesses or activities and the allocation of capital among them. Important implications, as Purcell (1989) and Sisson (1994c: 174–7) point out, are that the enterprise is seen not as a unified business but as a collection of businesses; there is a limited role for headquarters in setting goals, values and missions; and planning in the sense of the medium- and long-term direction, including the area of HR/IR, is delegated to the management of individual businesses. Especially important is that financial performance controls tend to replace administrative controls. Typically, the management of individual units have to work to extremely challenging and regularly monitored financial targets, with strict short-term payback criteria of two to four years applied to investment decisions. The net result is that, even in many large organizations, there is likely to be little remotely resembling the business planning that is assumed in many of the prescriptive texts. Everyone is too pre-occupied with short-term financial results.

Again, the message is simple. The business plan has to be trans-lated into operational plans if there is to be a strategic approach to managing employment relations. Those developing the employ-ment relations strategy must also have the necessary organiz-ational power to make these fundamental decisions. This is why, to go back to the earlier discussion, those who draw up the busi-ness plan, i.e. the organizations' senior managers, cannot escape the responsibility for developing the employment relations strat-egy as well. Indeed, if senior managers now genuinely believe that the challenges facing business today involve building HR capa-bilities and competences, employment relations and business strategies have to be drawn up simultaneously, instead of the former being 'downstream' of the latter.

Vision and mission

The importance of vision and mission in developing a strategic approach to managing employment relations has been empha-sized by those policy-makers grappling with the day-to-day real-ities of realizing it (see, for example, Connock, 1991). The concept of 'vision' can be understood as the overarching view of where the organization could, and perhaps should, be heading. 'Mission' can be thought of as a rather more firmly agreed set of ideas (pos-sibly in the form of a formal statement) concerning what the organization is trying to do in a relatively enduring way. This may be expected to cover the scope of the organization's operations and its distinctive focus. Both a vision and a mission are necessary to establishing the values that underpin both the choice of specific approaches and policies and their expression in practice.

The process of developing a vision and a mission arises from continual questioning of, and active listening to, all the major stakeholders – customers, employees, suppliers, and so on. Indeed, the vision can only be kept alive by continual questioning of this kind. A useful technique in aiding the process is 'culture mapping'. This juxtaposes the cultural values that one is seeking to establish with the employment practices that actually prevail. For example, in Figure 2.8 the cultural values being sought are listed

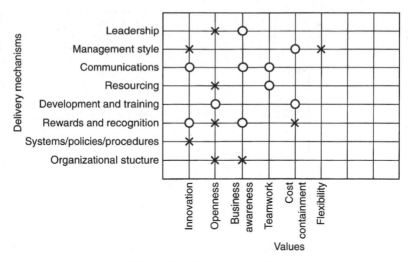

Figure 2.8 Culture mapping

on the horizontal axis: innovation, openness, business awareness, teamwork, cost containment and flexibility. Key employment practices are listed along the vertical axis: recruitment and selection methods, the rewards system, appraisal criteria, training practices and so on. The culture map allows one systematically to evaluate the extent to which prevailing employment practices actually support or militate against the proselytized culture.

Considerable care needs to be taken in drawing up mission statements if they not to be dismissed by employees. Many statements are shaped around the idea of 'serving customers'. But, having a mission statement of this kind will not be enough if there are too few means to accomplish it. Moreover, a 'market orientation' forced on a rigid organization and an uncommitted or fearful workforce is unlikely to lead very far. Another problem is that 'enterprise' missions have been found not to penetrate very deeply into organizations. Indeed, a significant proportion of executives do not feel accountable for the missions which have been promulgated by their enterprises. All this points up the fact that the production of mission statements can all too easily be cynically viewed (even by those involved in devising them) as merely a formal exercise.

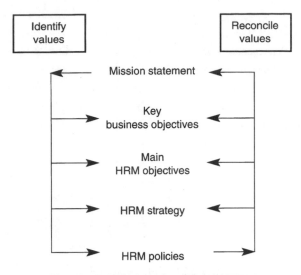

Figure 2.9 Values and policies in HRM
Source: Collins (1991)

Critically, there is also a need to recognize that it is not enough to come up with a 'wish list'. The values in the mission statement have to be reconciled with the other elements as Figure 2.9 suggests to ensure that they are both integrated and complementary. The process, it will be seen, is two-way. The implication is that there is a need to accept that employment relations objectives, strategies and policies have to be drivers of as well as driven by the values, mission and business objectives.

Changing the culture

Throughout the 1980s and 1990s there was an unusual, not to say extraordinary, upsurge in the number of managers seeking, quite consciously and deliberately, to shape, control and manage their organizations' culture, values and norms. Previously peripheral organizational development (OD) notions of visioning and culture change came decidedly centre-stage. It became commonplace for senior managers, in just about all sectors, to talk routinely about their role in driving or desiring culture change and likewise to be engaged in constructing organizational mission statements. The attempted reconstruction of 'mental sets' and the associated reshaping of behavioural patterns are built around the interlocking concepts of vision, mission, values, customer-orientation and quality. The management of these became an issue high on many an executive's agenda. Expectations about what they can deliver often run extremely high. Reactions in other parts of the organization (at managerial as well as non-managerial levels) are increasingly likely to be deeply cynical.

For those managers who are serious about developing a strategic approach to managing employment relations, this kind of campaign has to be directed above all towards themselves. As the following chapters spell out, it is, on the whole, management, not employees and trade unions, that is the major barrier to change. It is not just the roles and behaviour of many first line and middle managers that have to change – blaming them may offer some solace, as did blaming employees and unions – but also those of their senior colleagues. In our experience, the single most important influence on the roles and behaviour of first line and middle managers is their own appraisal and reward system; if these put a premium on short-term results, it is hardly surprising that managers take their cue from them, whatever the rhetoric of human resource management. Similarly, how senior managers themselves behave sets powerful role models for their colleagues. Is it any wonder that telling middle and first line managers that they have to develop and involve their staff is likely to fall on deaf ears if senior managers do little or nothing themselves to support their immediate colleagues in this regard. Communication by example is, after all, the most powerful form of learning there is.

There is an array of techniques (or, as management consultants in the organizational development tradition prefer to call them, 'interventions') which can be brought to bear to help illuminate an individual's readiness or resistance to change; to highlight preferred managerial style; and to uncover and bring into the open for discussion and analysis many other attributes which can be useful in preparing the ground for instigating a change in behaviour, attitudes and assumptions. Indeed, the various steps outlined above can play a key role here. Sooner or later, however, there will have to be some kind of 'commitment mapping'. This involves considering

Key players	No commitment	Let it happen	Help it happen	Make it happen
1.		X———————————►O		
2.			XO	
3.	X———►O			
4.	X———►O			
5.				XO
6.	X———————————————►O			
7.		O◄———————————X		
8.				
9.				

Figure 2.10 Commitment mapping

the position of the key individuals whose behaviour is likely to be influential in determining the fate of the culture change attempt. As is shown graphically in Figure 2.10, a judgement has to be made about the extent to which each individual is lacking in commitment to the change, is willing to acquiesce and let it happen, is more supportive and hence willing to help it happen, or is fired-up and eager to make it happen.

On the figure, X indicates the level of commitment which the individual is judged to have currently and O the desired level. Typically, the aim would be to notch-up commitment by moving individuals towards the right-side of this figure. However, this would not necessarily be so in every case. There could be instances where, perhaps for micro-political reasons, it is actually unhelpful to the cause to have a particular person openly championing the change. In such a case the diagnosis might lead one to seek to reposition such a person so that he or she merely becomes willing to let it happen rather than be seen as promoting the change (see person number 7 on the example shown in figure 2.10). For the rest, the harsh reality is that they are helped to change, if necessary with training and/or a job move, or are asked to leave.

Conclusions

A strategic approach to managing employment relations can mean two main things. The first is the pursuit of particular models. Two main types of universal or best practice model have been identified in this chapter: the HRM and the partnership. In addition, the chapter outlined and discussed a variety of contingent models related, for example, to the particular phase in the business cycle or organizational structure or to a particular business strategy. The key message, in each case, is the critical importance of integration – of business strategy with HR/IR strategy and of HR/IR policies and practices with one another (see, for example, Storey, 1998a and Schuler *et al.*, 2000).

While this first approach is valuable in drawing attention to the importance of the need for integration, it is the second which is likely to be of most practical relevance, above all to managers in SMEs. This sees strategy in terms not so much of a specific model as of a set of disciplines, making it possible to configure or tailor an approach suitable to their circumstances. These are relatively commonplace in other areas of activity and yet are rarely applied in managing employment relations. Regular stocktaking, simple scenario planning and regular monitoring and control are examples. A clear allocation of responsibilities and a basic personnel database make up the portfolio, together with a need to express business plans in terms of their human resource implications. Underpinning these is the need for an awareness of a sense of values and direction. Put like this, the approach appears somewhat banal. In practice, however, such a disciplined approach to managing employment relations is rare, which helps to explain why the landscape described in Chapter 1 looks as it does.

Chapter 10 returns to the issue of integration and its key role in delivering a strategic approach. In the meantime, our focus shifts to some important issues and elements in managing employment relations. Each of these is important in its own right and has to be treated in some detail if there is to be a proper appreciation of what is involved. The approach to managing strategically advocated here is nonetheless as relevant to managing these issues and areas as it is to their integration.

Suggested further reading

Hamal and Prahalad (1994) is a 'must' for the background to the development of the resource-based view, while Mabey *et al.* (1998a) is a major source for the debates over strategic HRM and its applications more generally. Studies of attempts to apply a strategic approach in practice are rare; by far the best is Clark's (1995) highly readable account of the Pirelli management's experience in setting up a 'green-field' cable plant in South Wales. Excellent sources of practical advice are NEDO/MSC (1987), Collins (1991) and ACAS (1998a).

MANAGING FOR HIGH PERFORMANCE:
Organizational structures and processes

The ways in which tasks are divided, activities coordinated and decisions taken within organizations, together with the monitoring and control of performance, are the basic building blocks for managing employment relations. These issues are often ignored, however, in discussions of employment relations. If not ignored, they tend to take second place to questions of 'culture'. In McKinsey's famous 7S framework, for example, structure is deemed to be only one of seven factors contributing to effective management (see, for example, Peters and Waterman, 1982). It is also seen as part of the 'cold triangle', along with strategy and systems, rather than the 'warm square' of style, skills, staff and subordinate goals.

One erroneous assumption is that organizational structure and processes are a 'given' rather than something that managers can decide. Another, and even worse, mistake is to assume that they have automatic effects which exonerate managers from having to pay attention to the way they are managed.

Apart from their intrinsic importance, the particular reason for the focus on organizational structures and processes here is that, under the pressure of increasingly competitive environments and the shifting nature of competitive advantage, major changes are taking place. As Chapter 1 suggested, these embrace both the external face and internal structure of organizations. Businesses and public service organizations alike have been changing the way that they allocate and organize work in significant ways and these carry wide-ranging implications for employment relations. The search for adaptable, lean and responsive organizational forms has been hotly pursued. High on the agenda of many managers have been the issues of 'de-layering', 'downsizing', 'flexibility', 'teamworking', 'service level agreements', 'high performance work systems', 'strategic business units', 'core and periphery', 'teleworking', 'franchising' and other similar organizational devices and issues. There is bewildering talk of an array of supposedly new forms which provide the answers to our problems. They include 'federal' organizations (Handy, 1984), 'network' organizations (Miles and Snow, 1986; Powell, 1990), 'cluster' organizations (Quinn, 1992), 'horizontal' organizations, 'hypertext' organizations (Nonaka and Takeuchi, 1995), 'virtual' organizations (Byrne, 1993; Wally et al., 1995), with 'agile production' vying to take over from 'lean production' (IRS, 1998n).

According to some commentators, these changes herald the dawn of a new era. They bring not only a shift from the bureaucratic organization of the past, but also greater individual responsibility or 'empowerment'. Seemingly the benefits make it possible to square the circle – to meet the demands for greater economic efficiency and yet at the same time make a significant contribution to improving the quality of working life.

From the employee's perspective, many of these developments have appeared very differently (see, for example, Edwards, 2000). It is not so much the much-vaunted empowerment which has impressed them, although any greater autonomy has been generally welcomed, rather it is redundancy, the end of career opportunities, work intensification and massive insecurity which have left their mark.

In the circumstances, understanding of the key underlying assumptions is vital as is an appreciation of the implications, negative as well as positive, for employment relations. Equally important to appreciate is that the changes do not have automatic effects: they have to be managed. A failure to recognize this has been perhaps the biggest single cause of personnel problems. Overall, our argument is that the managing of the restructuring is likely to be the major challenge facing the management of employment relations. How managers cope with it is likely to be critical in competitive performance.

The structure of the chapter is as follows. The first section offers an overview of the main changes taking place, the key underpinning developments, namely, divisionalization, devolved budgeting and 'marketization' (i.e. the application of market principles to decision-making) and their implications. The second and third sections highlight the two areas which, in our experience, are likely to be of most relevance to managers in large and small organizations alike: the why and wherefore of the flexible organization (sometimes known as the 'extended organization' and the 'core/periphery' model) and the 'lean organization'. The fourth focuses on the issue of performance appraisal and where it fits in. The fifth and final section highlights what is the most difficult task facing managers: the need to balance flexibility of operations with security of employees.

The underlying developments

Changes in the structure and systems of organizations have been wide-ranging as well as fundamental and go far beyond the 'rightsizing' euphemistically associated with closures and redundancies (see Figure 3.1). One group of changes reflects a move away from hierarchy with the reduction or de-layering of a number of tiers of management. Another involves the organization of work. Specialization, in which tasks, jobs and functions are broken down and defined as narrowly as possible, is giving way to work organized into cells, groups and teams. A further two groups reflect similar processes at higher levels of the organization. In the case of national companies and organizations, these involve the regrouping of activities on the basis of products or services rather than functions and include 'businesses within a business' as well as strategic business units (SBUs), divisions, sectors and streams. In the case of international companies, the changes involve the regrouping of

---

- Decentralized – 'divisionalization' and devolution of responsibility
- Flat – de-layering of management tiers
- Flexible – opening up of specialized roles
- Laterally-communicating – internal market and de-emphasizing functional hierarchies
- Cross-boundary – increasing permeability of internal and external borders
- Self-organizing – teamwork, and training and development
- Customer-responsive – empowerment of front-line employees

Figure 3.1 Key features of the 'new' forms of organization
Source: Based on Storey (1998b,c)

activities on the basis of products or services at the territorial level, such as Europe, or North America or the Far East, rather than on the basis of individual national company subsidiaries.

Perhaps the most important group of changes involves the break-up of the large-scale hierarchical organization into a number of semi-autonomous or 'quasi' businesses responsible for most, if not all, activities within their jurisdiction. In the case of many companies, and public sector organizations such as the Post Office, it has involved the creation of a number of 'businesses' or 'divisions'. In the civil service and NHS, it has involved the creation of 'executive agencies' and 'trusts'. In the case of companies such as Courtaulds and ICI, there has been a literal break-up: there has been a demerger of what, in each case, was a single entity into two separate and independent companies.

It is important to emphasize that these developments are affecting not just manufacturing organizations. Teamworking, for example, is now more likely to be found in the service sectors, public and private, than in manufacturing (European Foundation for the Improvement of Living and Working Conditions, 1997: 60–3). UK service organizations recently introducing teamworking include the Nationwide Building Society (see Scott and Harrison, 1997) and Do It All, the DIY chain (IRS, 1998l).

Three common developments underpin what might appear to be a range of apparently unrelated changes. One is divisionalization, the second budgetary devolution and the third 'marketization'. Each of these is considered here with the aim of getting behind the labels and the rhetoric to discuss what is actually involved. Two figures show diagrammatically what has been happening. Figure 3.2 shows structural changes within organizations, while Figure 3.3 classifies changes beyond organizational boundaries.

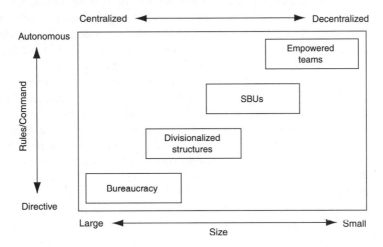

Figure 3.2 Types of restructuring within organizational boundaries

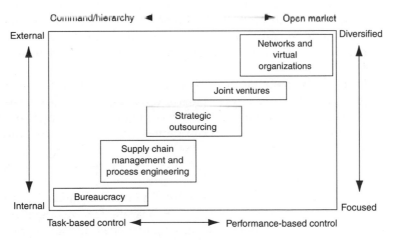

Figure 3.3 A spectrum of relationship structures beyond conventional organizational boundaries

Divisionalization

Divisionalization can take many forms: as well as division, for example, the terms SBUs, sectors, streams, not to mention executive agencies and trusts might be used. In practice, however, divisionalization involves a number of major organization changes which are more-or-less common. One is the disaggregation of the organization into quasi-independent units. Such divisions may embrace the activities of individuals or of units or groups of units or even of groups of companies. The principle of their organization can be business activity or territory or some combination of business activity and territory. In the case of Lucas Varity, for example, many of the teams working under cellular manufacturing are quasi-businesses as are the diesel systems division and the automotive sector, both of which are organized on a worldwide basis. Examples of divisionalization based on business activity would be the executive agencies in the civil service. Examples of divisionalization based on territory would be the multiple retailers such as Marks & Spencer and Sainsbury or the main clearing banks, where individual retail stores and branches service specific geographical localities. An example of divisionalization based on business activity and territory would be NHS Trusts. Typically, NHS Trusts organize the provision of health care by broad activity such as acute services or ambulance or mental health within the geographical area which is roughly the equivalent of the former district or regional health authority of which they were a part.

In the case of many multinational companies, such as Nestlé or Unilever, divisionalization operates at the international as well as the domestic level. Historically, such companies were organized around functions and national companies. Increasingly, however, the key decision-making unit is the international division which has responsibility for individual products or related products either on a European or worldwide basis.

The second and third changes involved in divisionalization are closely related. They are the separation of strategic from operating management and the decentralization of responsibility for operating management to individual divisions. That is to say, strategic management (certainly in the sense of deciding the composition of the portfolio of the business) remains at the centre as does, in most cases, responsibility for the selection, development and reward of senior managers in the individual divisions. Day-to-day operation (and, in some cases, responsibility for strategic management in the sense of medium- and long-term planning) is devolved to the divisions. In a phrase, the divisionalized organization is 'decentralized operationally, but centralized strategically' (Whittington and Mayer, 1994).

Whereas divisionalization is a relatively recent departure in the civil service and the NHS, most large companies in the UK have long been run on some form of divisionalized lines (see, for example Hill and Pickering, 1986). The Warwick Company Level Industrial Relations (CLIRS) results not only confirm the widespread coverage of divisionalization but also offer further details on its nature (Marginson et al., 1993, 1995). Just over half of the 176 companies in the survey reported that business activity was the basis of division, with the remainder split between territory and a mixture of business activity and territory as the basis. To illustrate the complexity of what can be involved, about 60 per cent also reported that they had intermediate divisions between the headquarters and the individual divisions. Most (70 per cent) individual divisions were 'mainly single site' rather than 'mainly multi-site' (13 per cent) with the balance reporting a mixture.

CLIRS also confirms the importance of the developments associated with divisionalization in accounting for the changes taking place in many large UK companies. Over the five years up to 1992 more than half of the companies had given increased accountability to the individual division (business unit), just over one-third had introduced some form of delayering and about one-quarter had moved in the direction of further decentralization. Significantly, two-thirds of the 176 companies said that they had introduced at least one of the three developments associated with divisionalization (Marginson et al., 1995: 5).

Of course, divisionalization is not a new concept. Senior managers of such companies as General Motors and DuPont pioneered divisionalization more than seventy years ago (Chandler, 1962). The reasons why they have been taken up so enthusiastically in recent years are twofold. One is the pressure of competition. In the private sector, this comes from increasing globalization and puts pressure simultaneously on costs, reliability and quality. In the public sector, it is competition for scarce resources which is leading to the same outcome. In these circumstances, traditional organizational structures rooted in the hierarchy, bureaucracy and task specialization associated with so-called Fordist or Taylorist systems have proved not only to be costly and inefficient but also a major barrier to the flexibility increasingly required. The second is the revolution in information processing facilities made possible by the coming of the microchip and associated developments in computer software. These facilities have produced instruments of management control and coordination that are far more effective and efficient than hierarchy and bureaucracy. An organization that can obtain data on sales and costs on a daily basis, for example, is in a position to do a number of things for which it previously needed substantial numbers of expensive managers – these range from sending further supplies, to making comparisons between divisions as a means of improving performance. No self-respecting senior manager in the mid-1990s has to issue an instruction to get his or her way as in the old days. Subordinates take heed of the implications of the performance information with which they are deluged, or take the consequences.

Budgetary devolution

This is where budgetary devolution comes in. Budgetary devolution involves the allocation of responsibility for managing activities within financial resources or targets. Like divisionalization, with which it almost invariably goes hand-in-hand, budgetary devolution can operate at a number of levels. It can relate to the SBU within a company or a trust within the NHS or an executive agency within the civil service. It can also relate to the internal units within such divisions and even bundles of activities. Individual cells or teams in manufacturing, for example, may have budgets devolved to them as may the different clinical directorates in an NHS Trust or a social services department within a local authority. Budgetary devolution can also vary in its scope. It can cover some or all items of income and expenditure. While managers of individual departments in the local authority case described below, for example, had responsibility for keeping within staff budgets, they did not themselves set these budgets. Evidently, too, the make-up of budgets can vary from situation to situation.

The operation of budgetary devolution also depends on whether the division is seen as a cost or a profit centre. Individual divisions within an organization, such as a cell or team or a department in a local authority, are typically cost centres, whereas an SBU within a company is usually a profit centre. It is not always as straightforward as this, however: in some companies, individual SBUs may be cost rather than profit centres. An example would be a motor manufacturer, such as Ford, which produces major components in several factories and assembles them in others: each of the factories, which may have thousands of employees, is in essence a cost rather than a profit centre. Arguably, even the individual outlets of some multiple retailers, such as Marks & Spencer and Sainsbury, which have highly centralized merchandising, are best seen as cost rather than profit centres: the local store manager has little control over many of the key elements which go into profit such as type of goods and their price, let alone the decision about the location of the store, and is accountable mainly for running the store as efficiently as possible. The CLIRS found that most business units (85 per cent) were designated as profit centres (Marginson *et al.*, 1995: 6).

To anticipate the point that will be developed later, it is important to note that, paradoxical as it may seem, budgetary devolution is perhaps the most potent instrument of the centralization of strategic control within organizations. Targets involve significant constraints as well as freedoms. Failure to keep within budgets or achieve targets can have the most drastic consequences. Respondents in 60 per cent of the CLIRS companies were able to recall at least one occasion when an individual division had been significantly off target. Asked what happened to the manager who was responsible,

Forty-four per cent of the interviewees mentioned the removal, demotion, retirement or 'disappearance' of business unit managers, as against 24 per cent who referred to some form of support, such as revised objectives or new reporting requirements. Some or all the workforce lost their jobs in 53 per cent of the cases . . .

75

Apart from the raw figures, the tone of many of the replies indicates that the headquarters of many of Britain's large companies has only limited tolerance of failure to meet targets. Perhaps the reply 'divisions failing to perform are sold', with its overtones of dispassionate routine, best exemplifies the attitude of our interviewees.

(Marginson *et al.*, 1993: 23)

Marketization

In practice, marketization takes two main forms. The first, which might be labelled *externalization*, involves the subcontracting or outsourcing of activities previously performed inside the organization. It is closely associated in many people's minds with the exposure of managerial decision-making in the public services to competition after the Conservative governments of the 1980s and early 1990s introduced compulsory competitive tendering (CCT) and 'market testing' for a wide range of activities. Managers, first in the civil service and NHS, and then in local authorities, were obliged to allow private sector organizations to bid for contracts to do work previously done by the organization's direct employees. Initially, so-called ancillary services such as cleaning, catering, laundry, refuse and ground maintenance were targeted. Subsequently, the net widened to include professional services such as the work of architects, lawyers and solicitors, finance and personnel specialists in local authorities, and the collection of statistics and the management of information technology in central government (for further details, see Colling and Ferner, 1995).

Many organizations in the private sector have also put out to contract these and other activities. The reasoning that led them to do so typically followed from a review of their 'core' activities, in some cases in the wake of relatively disastrous overdiversification in the 1970s and early 1980s, and a determination to get 'back to basics' and to concentrate on 'core competences' (Peters and Waterman, 1982). The organization had little or no expertise, it was argued, in carrying out many of the ancillary or professional services described above. Not only that, it also had very little idea of the market rate for such activities. In practice, it had tended to relate what it paid to its employees doing these activities to the arrangements for the 'core' staff. At the very least, continued the argument, the organization should put the activities out to tender to establish their true market cost. Other things being equal, the organization should subcontract these activities to the 'specialists', who would be responsible for any research and development in their area, and concentrate its own energies and resources on the 'core' products or services. In this respect, the thinking has close affinity with that of the so-called flexible organization model discussed below.

A much more fundamental theoretical underpinning, rarely mentioned in prescriptive texts recommending it, is to be found in the developing branch of economics known as transaction costs analysis. This approach sees there being two ways to get something done: one is through the market and the other through hierarchy, i.e. organization. Other things being equal, goes the argument, the market is the most efficient instrument. In a number of cases, for example, where specific skills are involved, the market does not work so effectively and so hierarchy may be more appropriate. In practice, it is possible to envisage a number of possible types of relationship. These range from the 'pure' market relationship, which can involve long-term relationships such as Marks & Spencer or the Japanese car manufacturers have sought to establish with their suppliers as well as single so-called spot market transactions associated with CCT, through partnership and joint ventures to different forms of hierarchy (intra-firm trading and direct internal control), which is the subject of a later section (for further details, see Williamson, 1975, 1985; Colling, 2000).

The second main form which marketization takes, internal markets, is a variant of the first. It involves a critical distinction between the purchasers and the providers of services within the organization. This distinction is to be found in its most obvious form in the internal market of the NHS. The district health authorities, which were formerly responsible for total health care provision within a given area, were split into two: the authorities or commissions, which are responsible for purchasing services from the most effective source available, and the trusts, which provided the services, in effect, to whichever authority would buy them. An internal market does not have to take such an extreme form, however. Many organizations practising an internal market do not necessarily require the activities of 'providers' to be put out to subcontract or even market testing. They do nonetheless expect services to be traded and may give the purchasers the freedom to buy in services from outside agencies. In this way, so supporters argue, providers become more responsive to the needs of their internal customers and have to ensure that the activity is cost-effective. Again, other things being equal, it enables the organization to establish the cost of various activities.

New structures, new problems

A reading of many of the texts dealing with restructuring gives the impression that the changes are automatic in effect. Nothing could be further from the truth. Everything depends on how they are managed. It is important to recognize too that they bring intrinsic problems of their own which have to be dealt with.

In a detailed study of the operation of budgetary devolution in one of the UK's largest local authorities, Keen (1995) identifies two problems which managers need to be aware of. One is the relationship between purchaser managers and provider managers. The problem is the competitive element that the changes encourage. This may be important in the short run in helping to deal with some of the problems of traditional organizational structure, such as the inflexibility between functions. The danger is, however, that the participants quickly adjust to the rules of the new game. Individual managers become even more protective of their positions than under old-style hierarchy with the result that individual departments and businesses may be performing well but only at the expense of the organization as a whole.

The other was a failure on the part of very senior managers responsible for the changes to distinguish clearly between devolution of budget responsibility to middle managers and the devolution or delegation of decision-making authority, which may or may not form part of devolved budgetary process. In practice, the expectation of middle managers that budgetary devolution would mean greater autonomy was massively qualified; senior management, under pressure from increasingly rigorous external funding and regulatory constraints, used it to increase levels of centralized control over resource management and utilization. The disillusionment and cynicism comes through in the following comments, first from one of the highways managers, and second from a social services manager:

> In theory there is devolution down, but the reality is that devolution doesn't really exist at this level. It is really very cosmetic. There is very little equipment on my budget, my cost centre is effectively staff, and that is dictated . . . If I was, say, underspending on that budget, then in theory I have the ability to spend that money on additional staff or some bits and pieces. But the reality is that the group manager would want my underspend to balance someone else's overspend. Profits too – if my team was doing well and making an income, then the income wasn't mine to spend because that was wanted for the department generally.
>
> (Quoted in Keen, 1995: 92)

> You're told you're autonomous, that you've got responsibility but the reality is very different. I always feel a bit like Gulliver – you know – sort of pinned down. I don't feel that they've delivered what they promised . . . They don't actually trust us – it's an insult to our intelligence . . . .
>
> (ibid.)

More fundamentally, as Purcell (1989) has forcibly argued, the widespread adoption of divisionalization, devolved budgeting and internal markets poses serious questions about the ability of organizations to develop and maintain a strategic response to HRM. For the human resource function is itself being crucially affected by the developments taking place. As Chapter 9 shows in greater detail, there is a considerable devolution of the special-ist function from headquarters to divisions and the passing of responsibilities for HRM to line managers. On the face of it, both are to be welcomed, if they encourage greater local 'ownership' of the issues. There are inherent dangers, however. The rundown in the number of HR specialists at headquarters potentially denies the organization strategic capacity. In theory, specialists at local level can do what is required in close cooperation with line managers who have been convinced that HRM is the key to business success. Even other things being equal, however, it is a moot point if local managers will have the time or expertise to develop the kind of integrated approach to employment relations that is needed. Especially difficult is maintaining an adequate supply of managerial talent. Unless careful steps are taken to avoid it, the natural tendency is for individual 'barons' to hold onto their bright young managers rather than releasing them to the organization as a whole.

Critically, too, there is a need to have the strategic capacity to think through the employment relations implications of the 'extended organization' which is being brought about by the substantial subcontracting and outsourcing of activities. Externalizing the problems associated with managing the employment relationship does not mean that the problems disappear. Issues such as performance and quality, training and development, and health and safety, remain fundamentally important. If the organization itself does possess specialists with skills and expertise in these areas, it is very difficult to see how they will be able to help the subcontractors to develop them. Who, in this event, takes responsibility for training or health and safety is a worrying issue for all concerned.

Significantly, a number of organizations have begun to realize that the process of divisionalization may have gone too far. One case is ICL reported in Arkin (1998). After operating as autonomous units for more than a decade, the various businesses are now being brought back together again. The talk is of a process of 'defragmentation' to emphasize the point that many of the synergies of the large organization have been lost.

A focus on the 'flexible' organization

Our reason for singling out for special attention the 'flexible firm' model devised by the Institute for Manpower Studies (Atkinson, 1984; Atkinson and Meager, 1986) is not only that it has provoked extensive interest in managerial circles, but also that it became *de facto* government policy in the 1980s and 1990s. The analysis suggests that in order to be adaptable to market changes and to hold labour costs down, three different types of labour flexibility are being simultaneously pursued:

1 Functional flexibility refers to the capability of employees to switch between different tasks. It includes, for example, multi-skilled craftspeople moving across mechanical and electrical job boundaries and workers switching between indirect and direct production jobs.
2 Numerical flexibility is the term used to denote the employer's scope to adjust easily labour supply to meet immediate needs. It includes freer use of hire-and-fire as well as various forms of so-called atypical or non-standard forms of contracts such as temporary working.
3 Financial flexibility is pursued so that pay costs for various groups of workers can more freely reflect current external labour market conditions. It implies a switch away from collective negotiations based on cost of living and indeed away from across-the-board rate for the job, towards new pay systems which take account of immediate local conditions.

Atkinson goes on to suggest that these different dimensions to flexibility can be brought together in the concept of the flexible firm. It is suggested that, in the 1980s, 'many UK firms are trying to introduce' (1984: 29) a new organizational structure which involves the break-up of the workforce into a series of 'peripheral', therefore numerically flexible, groups of workers clustered around a numerically stable 'core' which performs the organization's critical firm-specific activities in a functionally flexible manner. Figure 3.4 shows the lay-out of these groups. Under conditions of market growth the periphery expands; under reverse conditions the periphery contracts. The core workforce by contrast is shielded from market fluctuations.

The first periphery group shown in the figure are also full-time employees and are likely to include secretarial, clerical and assembly workers. They have less access to career opportunities, however, and, although not numerically flexible in the full sense, these jobs are likely to be filled on the open labour market and may involve a quite high degree of turnover. The second peripheral group is a catch-all and includes part-time employees, short-term contract staff and similar categories. Job security and career

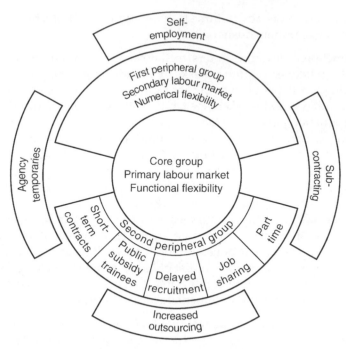

Figure 3.4 The flexible firm
Source: Atkinson (1984: 29)

development for these subgroups will be slight, as it is for the third set which includes agency temporaries, self-employed workers and subcontractors.

There are significant managerial implications arising from the adoption of such a strategy. Figure 3.5 gives a brief summary. For the core, the focus of attention is arguably the person rather than the job, whereas for the external groups the situation is reversed. The core group employees are measured against cooperation and progress; the external groups are evaluated against timely delivery to specification. A participative management style for the one is contrasted with a directive style for the other. The core are employed on an incremental salary basis, whereas those on the periphery are likely to be paid for units of work completed to standard.

	Core workers	Periphery
Focus for management	Employee	Job
Instrument of control	Effecting deployment	Delivery against specification
Management style	Participative	Directive
Remuneration system	Wage for time worked	Fee for work done
Incentive system	Performance appraisal	Delivery on schedule
Supply	Recruitment and training	Competitive tender and severance

Figure 3.5 Managing the flexible firm
Source: Atkinson (1984: 31)

The flexible firm model is intuitively appealing. As well as the obvious attractions, it would also seem to offer a 'cut price' way of achieving the HRM model discussed in Chapter 2. It has, however, been extremely controversial. As well as debates about its status (descriptive or prescriptive) and take-up, more fundamental problems have emerged. Deciding who the core workers are is not always easy and can change; none of the large food retailers, for example, would regard the vast armies of part-time employees as peripheral. The introduction of such an obvious status divide also runs counter to the trend towards teamworking and can be bad for performance. Peripheral workers have a lesser reason to show commitment to the organization and may, in consequence, require greater degrees of supervision and control than other staff, which sits uneasily with the desire to shift away from traditional control mechanisms. 'A critical HR management issue', in Storey's words, 'is the potential loss of expertise in certain areas which may be difficult to recover. Outsourcing may "hollow out" the organization, threatening any aspirations towards organizational learning, corporate culture and shared vision' (Storey, 1998b: 41). Like so many of the seeming panaceas, the flexible firm model should never be introduced without careful consideration and adaptation to specific circumstances.

A focus on the 'lean' organization

Our second focus of attention is on the 'lean organization' which became extremely popular in the first half of the 1990s. The use of the adjective 'lean' to describe an organization has come to be associated with downsizing and de-layering or, even more graphically with the 'slash and burn' exercises in cost reduction associated with corporate restructuring in the USA and, to a lesser extent, in the UK in the early to mid-1990s. This is unfortunate because a more fundamental set of ideas is involved. By general agreement, these have come to be associated in the first instance with Womack and his colleagues and their book *The Machine that Changed the World* published in 1990. To paraphrase the authors, organizations could dramatically improve their performance, by embracing the new set of working methods pioneered by Toyota in Japan. The essential changes required were as follows:

1 Eliminating unnecessary activities
2 Aligning all steps in an activity in a continuous flow
3 Recombining labour into cross-functional teams dedicated to a given product or activity
4 Continuously striving for improvement.

Aware of the danger of people arriving at a simplistic association between these changes and improved performance, two of the authors (Womack and Jones, 1994) went on to emphasize that 'lean production' was in itself not sufficient. An integrated sequence of improvements was required throughout the value stream from design to aftersales and service.

The point was illustrated by reference to the experience of Lucas. The company itself had made considerable progress in improving quality and delivery times, but momentum evaporated because many of its customers had not adopted the logic of the lean organization. The placing of orders in unpredictable ways, for example, forced Lucas plants to maintain high stocks; the more that employees relied on these buffer stocks, the more the 'lean factory began to gain weight', leading to pressure to shrink the product range and cut staff.

The significance of these points was given a further fillip with the popularization of business process reengineering (BPR) associated with Davenport (1993) and Hammer and Champy (1993). Storey (1998b: 31) summarizes the main ideas as follows:

1 A 'fresh start' review
2 A process rather than a functional view of the organization
3 Cross-functional solutions
4 Step change
5 The exploitation of information technology
6 Attention to work activities on and off the shopfloor
7 Producing value for the customer
8 Processes must have owners.

Yet another source of ideas was total quality management (TQM) which is seen to have three fundamental principles: customer orientation, process orientation and continuous improvement (Hill and Wilkinson, 1995). A helpful definition given by Dale and his colleagues is:

> Put simply, TQM is the mutual co-operation of everyone in an organization and associated business processes to produce products and services which meet the needs and expectations of customers. TQM is both a philosophy and a set of guiding principles for managing an organization.
>
> (1994: 10)

A useful summary of the changes and techniques typically associated with the lean organization is given in Figure 3.6. The approach is valuable in highlighting not only the linkages between the various structures and processes, but also the contribution of personnel policy which is all too often forgotten.

Both the positive and negative potential outcomes are also outlined in the figure. Rees *et al.* remind us that most of the latter are unintended and reflect the lack of attention paid to personnel policies (IPD, 1997a: 72). The dilemma for management is nicely summed up in the following quotation:

> Developing and maintaining a lean organization might be likened to walking a tightrope. Just as the high-wire acrobat has to perform a balancing act, so those managing this change have to be aware of the costs and benefits of leanness. If the perceived costs of downsizing, delayering and

work intensification become too high to offset the perceived benefits of increased operational autonomy, some skill-enhancement, and more extensive communications, then the employee commitment, desirable to buttress the fragility of lean systems, is unlikely to develop or survive.

(Legge, 2000: 63)

TQM	BPR	HRM
Quality procedures	Information flow	Commitment + involvement

LEAN ORGANIZATION
Minimizing waste:
materials, time, space, people = added value

Operating systems   *Work practices*

Just-in-time   De-layering
Statistical process control   Teamworking
Supply chain management   Functional flexibility
Total productive maintenance   Job rotation
Material resources planning   Quality circles
Right first time   Involvement and participation
Benchmarking   Communication

Organizational principles

Continuous improvement   Employee development
Flexible work organization   New work skills
Customer satisfaction   Self-regulation

Cultural change

Control systems   *Human costs*

Monitoring and measurement   Stress and pressure
Surveillance of work   Individual scrutiny
Workflow change   Effort intensification
Routinization of tasks   Reduction in discretion
Peer group pressure   Feelings of blame

Figure 3.6 The 'hardware' and 'software' of a lean organization
Source: Based on Rees *et al.* (IPD, 1997a)

Managing employee performance

Managing employee performance took on a new significance in the late 1980s and early 1990s in the light of the developments described above. Indeed, the expression 'performance management' sometimes came to be used to refer to the totality of employment relations practices embracing planning, target-setting, training, coaching, customer care, total quality and reward. For present purposes, performance management is best seen as an interlocking set of policies and practices which have as their focus the enhanced achievement of organizational objectives through a concentration on individual performance. The key elements may be identified as:

1 The setting of clear objectives for individual employees derived from the organization's strategy and a series of departmental purpose analyses.
2 Formal monitoring and review of progress towards meeting objectives.
3 Utilization of the outcomes of the review process to reinforce desired behaviour through differential rewards and to identify training and development needs.

Two features are especially noteworthy. First, attention to the management of individual performance is elevated to a higher plane: it comes to be regarded as an issue of strategic importance. Indeed, arguably the whole point about the concept of performance is that it promises or offers a way to link the micro activities of managing individuals and groups to the macro issue of corporate objectives. Secondly, while few if any of its constituent elements are new, it is the way in which they are placed together into an interlocking whole which is claimed to make the difference. In effect therefore, most commentators when talking of performance management are by implication referring to a performance management system (PMS).

Sheard (1992) describes the system introduced in ICI Pharmaceuticals as part of a wide-reaching culture change. Previous ways of managing, she claims, were ill-suited to the increasingly competitive environment facing ICI at the end of the 1980s and early 1990s. An internal review revealed a situation where four problems were endemic: decisions were being taken at too high a level and were thus out of touch with the marketplace and customer needs; the culture was task-oriented in the sense that people concentrated on task inputs and methods rather than being output-oriented; people-management skills were under-valued and therefore undeveloped; and employees were discon-nected from the business.

Sheard, who was a training and development consultant at ICI Pharmaceuticals, describes how performance management was used to tackle these four problems. She reports how the chief executive led the way to a new performance improvement. This entailed the communication of strategic objectives throughout the business. Explicit mention was made of the importance of people in attaining those objectives. People at every level be-came familiar with the objectives. There was a cascade process so that managers at every level were asked to review their own and their unit's objectives and to place these within the frame of the corporate objectives. Departmental purpose analyses were conducted and objectives were explicitly stated for units and departments for the next 12 to 24 months.

Employees were then fed business results and these were debated with employees 'in a way which encouraged interaction and debate by relating them to their own areas, supplemented with a review of departmental activities' (Sheard, 1992: 40).

Integral also was the introduction of a new 'development of people, work and reward' system. Crucially, for ICI, the perform-ance management system focused on *developing* people rather than assessment. As part of this, line managers were involved in coaching, encouragement and motivation. Thus, Sheard claims, ICI focused on a development-driven model, although a more performance-related reward system was also introduced.

A further feature of the ICI case worth noting is that the per-formance-related pay that did accompany the PMS was itself decentralized. Each department devised its own reward plan reflecting its priorities and business goals. Implementation was also managed locally within agreed budget constraints. Local managers therefore were encouraged to use this discretion to determine the type, scale and timing of the rewards.

In key respects – the focus on clear objectives, an emphasis upon contribution not task, agreed individual targets, development plans based on these targets, and the involvement of individuals in setting objectives – this summary describes the essence of an ideal PMS. Interestingly, it seems that many more organizations have been going down the same road, according to the most recent Institute of Personnel and Development (IPD) survey of the practice of performance management (see Armstrong and Baron, 1998a,b). When the Institute of Personnel Management (now IPD) did its original survey of the area in 1991, performance management was very much associated with individual performance pay. Seven years on, say Armstrong and Baron, the picture is very different. The process has become much more linked to development and many organizations are trying to distance it from pay decisions.

Such arrangements are likely to be beyond the ambition of many UK organizations, however, and SMEs in particular. For them, the critical consideration is likely to be an effective appraisal system, which most commentators agree should be at the heart of any serious attempt to improve individual performance. Figure 3.7 outlines the main types. Appraisal serves two main purposes:

1 *Performance review* – to give managers and employees opportunities to discuss how employees are progressing and to see what sort of improvements can be made or help given to build on their strengths and enable them to perform more effectively.
2 *Potential review* – to predict the level and type of work that employees will be capable of doing in the future and how they can best be developed for the sake of their own career and to maximize their contribution to the organization (ACAS, 1998c: 3).

For many people there is a third purpose of appraisal, namely a reward review to determine the basis of individual performance pay; this is discussed in the next chapter. Indeed, such has been the pressure of this view that many texts are equivocal about having separate processes or a single process: it is often presented as a matter of preference or convenience. In our view, an organization which is serious about performance management will keep the reviews of performance and potential separate from any reward review. If the three processes are mixed up, there is an inevitable danger that none will be done properly.

- *Rating* – a number of factors, such as quality and output of work, are rated on a numerical scale according to the level of performance, e.g. outstanding; exceeds requirements of the job; meets the requirements of the job; shows minor weaknesses; shows some significant weaknesses; unacceptable

- *Comparison with objectives* – the manager and the employee agree objectives at the beginning of the appraisal period and the appraisal is based on how far these objectives have been met

- *Critical incidents* – the appraiser records incidents of the employee's positive and negative behaviour during the appraisal period and the record forms the basis of the appraisal report

- *Narrative report* – the appraiser describes the employee's work performance in his or her own words in the form either of an open narrative or of answers to certain questions or guidelines

- *Behaviourally anchored rating scales* – the appraiser uses a custom-built set of characteristics or 'anchors' derived from analysis of the particular job to rate the performance of the employee

---

Figure 3.7 Types of appraisal system
Source: ACAS (1998c: 12–18)

The need to balance flexibility and security

Our final comments in this chapter are reserved for what is likely to be the critical issue in the ongoing management of restructuring. It is, in the words of the European Commission's 1997 Green Paper *Partnership for a New Organization of Work* (CEC, 1997), the need to balance flexibility and security. Much of the emphasis in the UK in recent years has been on external flexibility, i.e. the ability of the organization to vary its commitments through reductions in the number of employees or changes in their status (for example from permanent to temporary) or through subcontracting. The problem, as Collinson and her colleagues (1998) found in their study of TQM, is that it is difficult to maintain the credibility of, let alone the commitment to attempts to promote improvements in the quality of the goods or services if the only way in which management seems capable of managing the turbulence in its environment is through redundancy.

Significantly, managements in a number of organizations have begun to recognize this. A key feature of some 'partnership' agreements discussed in more detail in Chapter 8 is an explicit trade-off between far-ranging internal flexibility and a measure of employment security. Organizations which have introduced so-called flexicurity arrangements include Blue Circle, Halifax, Lloyds/TSB, Rover, Welsh Water (Hyder), and United Distillers. Further details of the arrangements can be found in IRS (1992, 1997d,f; Welch, 1998).

It is also important to emphasize that the flexibility that managers supposedly need has been massively overdone. Indeed, there is a growing body of evidence to suggest that managers need at the very least a measure of certainty – about working time patterns, for example, and about competences to perform particular skills, which comes from some specialization and ongoing training and development. This point emerges most forcibly from Clark's detailed study of the Italian-owned Pirelli plant at Aberdare in South Wales. Specifically, he found that 'under conditions that were highly favourable to full flexibility – contractual requirement, high level of automation, greenfield site – it has been neither required nor used' (Clark, 1993: 128). He gives six reasons why management sought limited rather than full flexibility which are profoundly important in helping to develop a more realistic perspective on the potential of many of the new working arrangements:

1 The 'horses for courses' principle – many employees were more suited to, and interested in, certain tasks than others.
2 Specialist knowledge – there were significant advantages in employees being specialized and 'knowing what their job is'.
3 Ownership – employees given responsibility for a particular area were more likely to be committed to the achievement of high quality work.
4 Training – there was a substantial requirement for on-the-job training of new recruits requiring existing employees to be fully up to date with their particular process.
5 Skill retention – employees could not use skills adequately if they were not given regular opportunity to practise them.
6 Tight staffing levels – whereas these made for functional flexibility in areas such as maintenance, in others, for example administration, they led to very low levels of flexibility because employees in one area could not be spared for training.

Suggested further reading

For studies of the detailed application of many of the developments discussed in this chapter, see IPD (1997a) and Collinson *et al.* (1998). For a
critical review, see Legge (2000). For further information on performance
management, see Armstrong and Baron (1998a,b) and the ACAS guides
cited in the text.

4

INVOLVEMENT AND PARTICIPATION: THE KEY TO SUCCESS?

Central to many of the new forms of organizational structure and processes is the importance of employee involvement and participation. The idea, and indeed various manifest forms, of participation have been around for a long time. Greater participation or industrial democracy has been one of the fundamental goals of trade unions. This helps to explain why, although most managers use the terms 'involvement' and 'participation' interchangeably, some insist on reserving 'participation' to describe more structured (and, by implication, less desirable) forms giving employees 'rights' in decision-making. The novelty, however, is the unprecedented widespread management interest in using direct participation to improve business performance (Marchington and Wilkinson, 2000). In the words of one commentator (Osterman, 1994: 173), the need for direct participation in the organization of work has become a 'new conventional wisdom'. Involvement and participation are increasingly characterized by being management rather than union driven and by the underlying aim of increasing commitment and seeking competitive advantage. Indeed, it can be argued that involvement and participation are no longer optional, but are a functional necessity given the rise of the new 'knowledge' workers and technological and organizational restructuring which puts a premium on adaptability, spontaneity and commitment. Critically, there is a growing body of research evidence for Europe, Japan, the USA and the UK showing that organizations which take involvement and participation seriously are reaping a significant dividend in terms of productivity and performance.

Our aims in this chapter are reflected in its structure. The chapter begins by reviewing the many forms that involvement and participation can take: communications, direct participation, indirect participation and financial participation. The intention is not to suggest that there is a menu from which managers can choose – ideally, organizations should be looking to an integrated approach rather than, as so often happens, firing on one or two cylinders only – but to make sure that it is clear what is involved. The second section explores in more detail the managerial logic of involvement and participation. Involvement and participation can look like a loss of authority and status as well as being personally uncomfortable. The third section draws on the evidence of practice to discuss some of the issues and problems that management is experiencing in introducing involvement and participation. In general, it appears that management is losing much of the advantage of the new forms of organization because it is not practising what it preaches. Understanding why is fundamental to further progress.

Types of involvement and participation

Involvement and participation come in a variety of forms and there have been many attempts to categorize them. Our preferred framework, which appears in Figure 4.1, is that developed for the European Foundation for the Improvement of Living and Working Conditions' EPOC project investigating the nature and extent of direct participation in organization (Geary and Sisson, 1994). Along with information disclosure or communications, it distinguishes three main forms of participation: direct participation involving individual employees; indirect or representative participation through the intermediary of employee representative bodies, such as works councils or trade unions; and financial participation. Each of these forms is discussed in more detail below.

Communications (information disclosure)

Direct participation
- consultative
- delegative

Indirect or representative participation
- joint consultation
- co-determination
- collective bargaining
- worker directors

Financial participation
- profit-sharing
- share ownership

Figure 4.1 Types of involvement and participation

Communications (information disclosure)

Communications can, of course, be two-way. Sometimes the terms 'top-down' and 'bottom-up' communications are used. For the purposes of analysis and exposition, however, it makes sense to use the term 'communications or information disclosure' to describe the former and 'consultation' the latter. It is appreciated that the latter term may frighten some managers: 'listening to employees' smacks largely of a symbolic gesture, whereas consultation sounds much more meaningful (and threatening?). It is important to face up to the reality, however, if there is to be any serious understanding of what is required. Figure 4.2 lists the main channels of communications or information disclosure identified by ACAS (1998b) in its guide *Employee Communications and Consultation*.

The importance of communications hardly needs emphasizing. Lack of understanding is a major source of inefficiency and lack of motivation. More worrying from a management perspective is that, in the absence of clear information, the infamous 'grapevine' takes over. The mess that results in the celebrated John Cleese video of the same name is no caricature. This is what happens when managers remain silent.

Face-to-face methods
- Group meetings (e.g. team briefing)
- Cascade networks
- Large-scale meetings
- Interdepartmental meetings

Written methods
- Company handbooks
- Employee information notes
- House journals and newsletters
- Departmental bulletins
- Noticeboards
- Individual letters

Other methods
- Information points
- Audiovisual aids
- E-mail

Figure 4.2 Channels for communicating with employees
Source: ACAS (1998b: 22–7)

More positively, as ACAS (1998b: 10) suggests, good communications can improve organizational performance, management performance and decision-making, and employee's performance and commitment; help develop greater trust; and increase job satisfaction.

Direct participation

Direct participation is a term often used but rarely clearly defined. Following the conceptual framework of the EPOC project, it can be seen as taking two main forms:

1 *Consultative participation* – management encourages employees to make their views known on work-related matters, but retains the right to take action or not.
2 *Delegative participation* – management gives employees increased discretion and responsibility to organize and do their jobs without reference back.

Both consultative and delegative participation can involve individual employees or groups of employees. The two forms of

---

Individual consultation
- *Face-to-face* – arrangements involving discussions between individual employee and immediate manager, such as regular performance reviews, regular training and development reviews and '360 degree' appraisal
- *Arm's-length* – arrangements not involving discussions between individual employee and immediate manager, such as a 'speak-up' scheme with 'counsellor' or 'ombudsman', attitude surveys and suggestion schemes

Group consultation
- *Temporary groups* – groups of employees who come together for a specific purpose and for a limited period of time, e.g. 'project groups' or taskforces and focus groups
- *Permanent groups* – groups of employees that discuss various work-related topics on an ongoing basis, such as quality circles

Individual delegation
- Individual employees are granted extended rights and responsibilities to carry out their work without constant reference back to managers – sometimes known as job enrichment

Group delegation
- Rights and responsibilities are granted to groups of employees to carry out their common tasks without constant reference back to managers – most often known as group work

---

Figure 4.3 The main forms of direct participation

consultative participation can be further subdivided. Individual consultation can be face-to-face or arm's-length; group consultation can involve temporary or permanent groups. This gives us six main forms of direct participation regardless of the particular label applied. The six forms are set out in Figure 4.3, together with examples of relevant practices from EPOC's literature review (Fröhlich and Pekruhl, 1996) and round-table discussions.

The EPOC literature study suggested that the delegative forms of direct participation had been prioritized in both the policy and scientific debates. Group work in particular was seen as the 'dominating concept' and the 'core element of new forms of work organization' (Fröhlich and Pekruhl, 1996: 79). Yet the term was being used in very different ways. At the risk of oversimplification, two extreme types of a continuum were being referred to: the so-called Scandinavian model associated with some of the early

Table 4.1 Types of group work

Dimensions	'Scandinavian'	'Toyota'/lean production
Membership	Voluntary	Mandatory
Selection of group members	By the group	By management
Selection of group leader	By the group	By management
Qualifications	Mixed	Generalists
Reward	Skill-dependent	Uniform (seniority)
Task	Complex	Simple
Technology	Independent of pace	Dependent on pace
Autonomy	Large	Narrow
Internal division of labour	Voluntary	Largely prescribed

Source: Based on Fröhlich and Pekruhl (1996).

experiments in semi-autonomous group involving organizations such as Saab and Volvo; and the 'Toyota' or lean production model, which is generally applied in Japan and often in European and American 'greenfield sites'. As the ideal-typical expression of them in Table 4.1 suggests, the two models have very different implications in terms of the relative degree of management control and employee autonomy. The first has been described as 'flexible Taylorism' (Berggren, 1993), while the second equates with the semi-autonomous workgroup which many European policy-makers aspire to. Both models are said to have their strengths and weaknesses. The Scandinavian model is often seen as not sufficiently productive, whereas the Toyota model is considered too rigid and too mean (rather than lean) to employees.

Indirect or representative participation

Of the forms listed under indirect or representative participation in Figure 4.1, two need not concern us greatly. Co-determination applies to the rights of works councils in some EU countries, notably Germany, to make decisions jointly with management in areas such as social policy, while worker director participation is also relatively limited in its coverage – Germany and Sweden are the countries mainly affected (for further details, see Carly, 1998).

Collective bargaining and joint consultation are the two forms of indirect participation relevant to the UK. Collective bargaining, for which Flanders (1970) suggested a better description would be *joint regulation*, makes it possible to agree the key procedural as well as substantive rules governing the employment relationship. It can, therefore – as it has in many EU countries and at the EU level itself – be a substitute for legal regulation. An added advantage is that it enables workers themselves to shape the decisions affecting them through democratic activity within the trade union. Here the implication is that the outcome of the process is an explicit agreement between the two parties. If the union withholds its agreement, management does not proceed. If it does insist on proceeding then it recognizes that it may face industrial action.

The other form of indirect participation is joint consultation. Here the implication is that the management will seek the views of employee representatives and take them into account in making its decision. It may go ahead with a decision, however, even if these representatives express their opposition.

In most other EU member states other than the UK, the two processes are separate. The most obvious example of such a dual system is to be found in Germany where it is enshrined in the legal framework. Joint regulation is largely the responsibility of the employers' organizations and trade unions and takes place outside the workplace at the level of the industry or the *Land*. Inside the workplace, the task of representing the interests of employees is taken over by the statutory works councils, which have limited rights of joint regulation but extensive powers of joint consultation as well as information, which means a much wider range of issues is discussed between management and employee representatives.

As Chapter 1 has observed, both trade unionism and collective bargaining are in decline in the UK. It will be recalled that, according to the first findings of the 1998 Workplace Employee Relations Survey (WERS), union recognition had fallen from 66 per cent in 1984 to 53 per cent in 1990; between 1990 and 1998 it fell a further eight points to 45 per cent (Cully *et al.*, 1998: 28).

Although some companies, such as Sainsbury, the major food multiple retailer, have recently introduced non-union works councils, there is no statistical evidence that UK management as a whole are embracing joint consultation with employee representatives.

The first findings of the 1998 WERS suggest that no more than 28 per cent of workplaces had a joint consultative committee at that level, which in effective means no change since 1990 (Cully *et al.*, 1998: 12).

Financial participation

There are two main forms of financial participation: profit-sharing and share ownership. Both have a long history in the UK. The John Lewis Partnership, for example, which embraces Waitrose, the multiple food retailer, as well as the John Lewis department stores, has long been a strong advocate of profit-sharing. Both forms have also received considerable support from the government in the form of tax incentives through the Financial Acts, above all under the Conservative governments of the 1980s and 1990s.

Although a regular feature in the remuneration of many managers, profit-sharing and share ownership have relatively limited application. According to the first findings of the 1998 WERS, the number of workplaces with a employee share ownership scheme for non-managerial employees amounted to no more than 15 per cent, while that for a profit-sharing scheme was 30 per cent (Cully *et al.*, 1998). Typically, too, the amounts of money involved in profit-sharing or the number of holdings in share ownership are quite small.

In these circumstances, the extent to which financial partnership is or can be a serious form of involvement and participation has to be a matter of debate. Our own view is that, in practice, it is probably best to look upon financial participation as a communications device. Profit-sharing and share ownership can be very useful in sensitizing employees to the state of the business; it is a moot point, however, whether they do a great deal for involvement and participation on a day-to-day basis. Arguably, they need to be raised to the levels available to senior managers to have a serious impact in this respect.

The case for involvement and participation

The main reasons for the interest in involvement and participation are easy enough to identify. If all workers are to be pulling in the same direction, they need to be aware of the key objectives, the prime considerations, priorities, threats and opportunities and so on. To some extent, therefore, there is a single communication issue underlying the involvement theme. Clear communication could, however, be pursued even under highly directive managerial styles. In circumstances where there are attempts to install devolved forms of organization of the types discussed in the previous chapter, the need to involve employees rather more fully in the logistics of the task become more sharply apparent. In fact, it could be said that employee involvement is a necessary corollary of team forms of work organization in marked contrast to Tayloristic forms where strict conformance to assigned standardized tasks was the requirement and 'all' that was asked.

Although involvement and participation have a long history, and a basic rationale, it is the severe economic pressures confronting most industrialized countries in recent years that lie behind the present interest. Lack of stable markets, coupled with the continuous erosion of competitive positions in key sectors, has set the context. In particular, the speed with which Japanese enterprises have successfully penetrated world markets for motor vehicles and electronics using direct participation to both improve quality and reduce costs has led to a fundamental reappraisal of traditional work organization.

A key distinguishing element of the new thinking is its view of the main source of competitive advantage in this rapidly changing environment. Costs are of course important, but developed economies, it is argued, cannot hope to compete solely in terms of cost with competitors in Eastern Europe and the Far East, let alone the third world. Instead, the emphasis needs to be on quality products and services. Not only will these satisfy the growing demand for more specialized niche goods but also, and more fundamentally, they make it possible to build on employees' longstanding demands for more challenging and rewarding jobs and 'exploit their higher education and skills to contribute to the process of continuous improvement' (see also ACAS, 1997b). For some, therefore, management support for involvement and participation has been seen, more cynically, as devices 'designed to elicit employee's ideas while retaining control over decision making' (Applebaum and Batt, 1994: 75).

Another respect in which the thinking differs from received wisdom involves the type of flexibility being sought. Most recent attention has been on external flexibility, i.e. the ability of the organization to vary its commitments through reductions in the number of employees or changes in their status (for example from permanent to temporary) or through subcontracting. The real advances, it is argued, are much more likely to come from internal flexibility leading to improved organizational capacity. In the words of the European Commission's Green Paper *Partnership for a New Organization of Work*:

> It is about the scope for improving employment and competitiveness through a better organization of work at the workplace, based on high skill, high trust and high quality. It is about the will and ability of management and workers to take initiatives, to improve the quality of goods and services, to make innovations and to develop the production process and consumer relations.
>
> (CEC, 1997: 5)

For many organizations there is an even more basic reason for going down the involvement and participation route: they cannot afford the managerial hierarchies, whose primary responsibility was to make sure 'subordinates' did what they were paid to do anyway. In an article for *People Management*, for example, appropriately titled 'Delayering to fire steel profits drive', Overell (1998) describes the situation confronting British Steel. Output levels have improved nearly five times since 1977 with substantial and regular job losses and yet still the pressure to do better mounts, fuelled by the substantial rise in the value of the pound in 1997 and 1998, which threatened to price the company out of many markets. The cornerstone of the survival strategy is de-layering and teamwork. Already in many units, fifteen levels have been cut back to one with managers themselves being absorbed into teams.

The promotion of communications and direct participation of employees will probably not raise too many management hackles, although the nature and extent of the changes proposed may frighten some. The notion that management should positively promote some form of indirect or representative collective voice for employees, however, either in the form of a works council or local trade union representatives, is likely to be received very differently. Surely, it might be argued, it is the individual who should be the focus of management attention; trade unions and collective bargaining are withering on the vine. Even if they are not, employee representation is a matter for trade unions and governments. It is not something that managers should encourage.

Managers have to recognize the validity of the argument that the individual employee needs representation to help balance the inequality of power with the employer. Yet the case for doing so is as much managerial as it is a question of rights. The views of employees, most commentators agree, are vital to the success of changes in work organization. In the absence of a representative voice, there is a danger that these views are either not expressed, for fear of antagonizing managers, or are simply ignored.

The insecurity that much of the de-layering and downsizing of recent years has produced, it is also argued, is proving to be counterproductive. There is little or none of the trust that managers are encouraged to seek as the basis for a new 'psychological contract'. One way of improving the situation is to recognize that trust depends on the legitimacy of decisions and that joint regulation is one of the most tangible ways of expressing such legitimacy.

Put negatively, managers who do not involve employee representatives run the risk of giving the impression they have something to hide. Seen from the shop or office floor, claims to be a participative organization are hardly credible unless management is willing to embrace collective as well as individual forms of involvement.

Perhaps even more to the point, the speed of change is nowhere near fast enough and the main reason is the unwillingness not so much of employees or their representatives to move but of managers. Certainly the reality of change in the 1980s and 1990s in key areas such as work organization does not match the level of management rhetoric. In effect, advocates of the new thinking argue, a coalition for change is required which involves all the major stakeholders and not just management.

103

The evidence of practice

Our attention now turns to the evidence of the practice of involvement and participation as revealed in the growing body of case study and survey material available in the area. There is 'good' and 'not so good' news. Involvement and participation clearly 'work' in the sense of making a contribution to improved performance. Yet the practice of involvement and participation remains limited. Also important, in suggesting that there are two possible explanations for this, the evidence produces a number of valuable insights and implications.

Good news, bad news

Involvement and participation 'work'
There is a growing body of empirical evidence to suggest that involvement and participation make management sense. In a first wave came the evidence collected by Womack *et al.* (1990) covering the automotive industry. The team-based lean production methods associated in particular with Toyota appeared to be far superior in performance terms to traditional forms of work organization, requiring

> half the human effort . . . half the manufacturing space, half the investment in tools, half the engineering hours to develop a new product in half the time. Also, it requires keeping far less than half the needed inventory on site resulting in many fewer defects, and produces a greater and ever growing variety of products.
>
> (Womack *et al.*, 1990: 13–14)

In terms of the standard measure of the number of direct labour hours used in body construction, paint and assembly, the results are shown in Table 4.2. In terms of quality, measured as the number of defects per 100 cars traceable to the assembly plant reported in the first three months of use, the results appeared to be equally impressive (Table 4.3).

Although the findings have not been without their critics (see, for example, Berggren, 1993), the experience of Japanese transplants in other countries such as the UK and the USA would nonetheless

104

Table 4.2 Comparison of direct labour hours used in automotive manufacture under different forms of organization

	Best	*Worst*	*Weighted average*
Japan	13.2	25.0	16.8
North America	18.6	30.7	24.9
Europe	22.8	55.7	35.5

Source: Womack *et al*. (1990: 85)

Table 4.3 Comparison of quality of output in the automotive industry under different forms of organization (number of defects per 100 cars)

	Best	*Worst*	*Weighted average*
Japan	37.6	88.4	52.1
North America	35.1	168.6	78.4
Europe	63.9	123.8	76.4

Source: Womack *et al*. (1990: 86)

appear to confirm the main thrust. The Japanese approach to manufacturing cars, even though it involved only limited direct participation, did apparently produce 'better' results.

In the USA, more systematic evidence supporting the case for the involvement and participation of employees in work organization comes from the detailed enquiries of a number of scholars (see, for example, Huselid, 1995; Becker and Gerhart, 1996; Koch and McGrath, 1996; Pil and MacDuffie, 1996; Ichinowski *et al.*, 1997; Becker and Huselid, 1998). The adoption of high-involvement work practices, albeit accompanied by a number of mutually reinforcing changes in pay systems and other personnel arrangements, has been shown to be positively associated with improvements in performance outcomes.

In the case of the UK, further support comes from five recent sources: the EPOC survey of ten EU countries on the role of direct participation in organizational change, sponsored by the European Foundation for the Improvement of Living and Working

Conditions (1997); the research by Patterson and his colleagues sponsored by the IPD (1997b) covering 67 manufacturing plants; the survey carried out by Guest and Peccei of some 300 member companies of the Involvement and Participation Association (IPA, 1998); Sako's (1998) investigation into the nature and impact of employee voice in the European car components industry; and the first findings of the 1998 Workplace Employee Relations Survey reported in Chapter 1 (Cully *et al.*, 1998).

In the case of the EPOC survey, all forms of direct participation were judged to have a strong impact on a range of indicators of economic performance, as the summary in Figure 4.4 shows. Even more significantly, the more forms that were used, the greater the reported effects. Also, the greater the scope of the form (i.e. the range of issues on which employees were consulted or given rights to make decisions), the greater the reported effects.

Especially intriguing, the data from the EPOC survey represent a considerable body of evidence to question conventional wisdom on the relative significance of consultation and delegation in the new forms of work organization. It is not just that a majority of respondents, including many of those who practised delegation, regarded the consultative forms to be more important than the delegative, but also that the effects of the consultative forms were

---

- All forms were shown to have a strong impact on economic performance
- The more forms were used, the greater the reported effects
- The greater the scope of the form, the greater the reported effects

The significance of education and training
- The higher the qualification of employees, the greater the effects of direct participation
- The more substantial the training for direct participation, the greater the effects of direct participation

The significance of employee representative involvement
- The effects of direct participation increased with the degree of employee representative involvement in its introduction
- The more extensively employee representatives were involved, the more successful direct participation was deemed to be in the view of managers

---

Figure 4.4 The effects of direct participation

found to be at least as strong as those of the delegative on a range of indicators of performance. Indeed, it often needed the more intense application of the delegative forms to achieve similar effects to those of the consultative of lesser scope. The consultative forms, in particular face-to-face consultation, showed a more positive relationship with employment: the more intensively managers consulted employees, the more likely there was to be an increase in employment and the less likely a decrease (Sisson and Fröhlich, 1998).

It will also be seen from the summary in Figure 4.4 that two ingredients of the 'success' of involvement and participation are confirmed. Involvement and participation go hand-in-hand with qualification and training. The greater the scope of direct participation, the greater the associated qualification and training required. Also qualification and training were reckoned to be significant influences on the economic effects of direct participation. High employee qualification and high-intensity training for teamwork, for example, made it much more likely that direct participation was regarded by managers as successful and that various economic benefits of direct participation were attained.

Strong forms of employee representative involvement in the introduction of the various forms of direct participation were also found to go together with the practice of a wide scope of these forms, whereas a narrow scope was most frequent in workplaces without such involvement. Employee representatives were, in most cases, regarded as agents of change rather than barriers to progress. The extent of employee representative involvement, in the opinion of managers, was also positive so far as the effect of the introduction of direct participation on the economic performance was concerned. This also extended to reducing employment in the short-term.

Involvement and participation are not practised extensively
Evidently, direct participation would seem to 'work': it is something that makes sense not just theoretically but also practically. At first sight, the results of the EPOC survey on the practice of direct participation look promising: something like four out of five workplaces in the ten countries had at least one form of direct participation. Closer inspection suggests that there is a considerable

gap between the rhetoric and the reality of new forms of work organization, however. Figure 4.5 gives a summary of the main findings on the practice of direct participation.

The results were not dramatically different by sector. Significantly, in view of the interest that it has attracted in this sector, industry was not the 'leader' in matters of direct participation. The incidence, coverage and scope of direct participation was greater in services and, especially, public services. Construction came bottom on most dimensions.

Any expectation that recent developments, notably the decline in collective bargaining, might have led to above-average levels of direct participation in the UK does not appear to be substantiated. The UK was above average for face-to-face and permanent group consultation, and for the incidence of multiple forms, but only around the average so far as the two forms of delegation were concerned, with the same being true for the coverage of the

---

- Five of the six forms were practised by a minority of workplaces (around one-third); only in the case of individual delegation did the proportion of workplaces exceed 50 per cent of workplaces.
- Less than one in seven workplaces had five or six forms, i.e. very few could be said to have something approximating to an integrated approach.
- The coverage of the three group forms was less than 50 per cent of the largest occupational group in the majority of workplaces.
- The scope in terms of number of issues involved was limited for each of the forms – the proportion of workplaces with a wide scope for any of the practices reached double figures in the case of individual delegation only.
- The proportion of workplaces with semi-autonomous group work approximating to the Scandinavian model (i.e. extensive delegation + high qualification + high training intensity) was less than 2 per cent; most cases seem to have been positioned between the Scandinavian and Toyota models with a tendency towards the Toyota (i.e. low-intensity delegation + medium or low employee skills + low training intensity).
- A significant proportion of workplaces (around one-quarter) did not involve employee representatives in the introduction of direct participation – half of these reflecting the lack of employee representatives and half the lack of their involvement where they were present.
- Only about one in ten workplaces might be said to have been skills-oriented in as much as the level of qualification required was high or very high and there was fairly intensive training of managers and workers for direct participation.

Figure 4.5 The practice of direct participation

group activities. The UK was also below the ten-country average for the scope of the four consultative forms of direct participation and only slightly above for the two forms of delegation. On the face of it, like most of the other countries, the direct participation taking place appears to be limited.

A question of process?

One explanation for the gap between the rhetoric and reality of involvement and participation emphasizes process. Most commentators, it can be argued, have considerably underestimated the problems that organizations have in introducing 'quality' work organization; the practice of direct participation is relatively new and it will take time to learn the lessons. It is not so much a question of divergent interests or lack of knowledge of alternative arrangements – although these themselves can be barriers to change in certain cases. A major problem, as the recent literature on innovation (see, for example, Pil and MacDuffie, 1996) reminds us, is that there is a strong temptation for managers to prefer the incremental path to change, i.e. to try one or two elements and assess their impact before going further, reflecting worries about the costs associated with abandoning old practices and introducing new ones. Yet the incremental path, much of the recent research evidence cited above suggests, is likely to mean failure and disappointment. One of the key findings of this research is that it is 'bundles' of complementary practices which have the greatest impact on success and failure. As is shown below, these include focused training, pay systems to promote teamworking and flexibility, careful appraisal and realistic targets, effective systems of information and consultation and a measure of job security, backed up by an adequately staffed personnel function.

The second and perhaps more uncomfortable finding is that managers themselves have to change as part of the learning process. Indeed, after a detailed study for the IPD of the research evidence relating to involvement and participation in the lean organization and their own studies in a number of companies, Rees and his colleagues (IPD, 1997a: 96) are forced to come to the conclusion that the attitudes and prejudices of UK managers themselves are a major consideration. Thus, they put to their respondents one of the findings to emerge from a study of management attitudes in Japanese transplants in the UK (Broad, 1994), namely that, compared with their Japanese counterparts, UK managers were obsessed with 'prerogative and secrecy', which they saw as a way of retaining their hierarchical power. There was an acceptance that this was the case. It found particular expression in both a reluctance to share information openly with junior colleagues (as in the case of NatWest Bank) and in a feeling that UK firms could never go as far as their Japanese counterparts in conceding autonomy to teams (as was the case with Rover).

The way these two issues interact is revealed in three sets of case studies. The first set involves quality circles. Adverse reactions from middle managers is a constant refrain in studies of the trials and tribulations of quality circles in the 1980s (see, for example, Carrington, 1991a,b). Hill's (1991) comparison of the way in which quality circles were introduced in a UK and a US company offers useful insight, however. In the former, the initial enthusiasm quickly waned. In particular, there were complaints from circle members that managers were refusing to implement their suggestions. In the latter, things were very different. Managers were much more cooperative and quality circles were generally regarded as a major success by all concerned.

The key to the fate of quality circles seemed to lie at the door of middle managers in both companies. The reason for the very different reaction in the two companies, suggested Hill, was perfectly understandable in the circumstances. In the UK company, quality circles had been bolted onto the workloads of middle managers with little or no preparation and without any change in their own appraisal and reward systems. In short, they were expected to make a success of quality circles and carry on managing as if they were not there. Not surprisingly, as well as seeing quality circles as extra work, they saw their own positions threatened. In the US company, by contrast, great care was taken to prepare middle managers for quality circles. They were to be seen as an intrinsic part of a change in the role of managers who were to become more involved in development activities. Not only that: their own appraisal and reward system was changed to reflect the importance that senior managers attached to quality.

Disillusionment and cynicism is also a not uncommon finding

in situations where teamworking is not fully followed through and supported by the wider personnel systems. Buchanan and Preston's (1992) report of the results of a study into cell operations in a British aero-engine components manufacturer is a case in point. The company had introduced cells as part of its drive towards manufacturing systems engineering. This involved changes to production control, to organization and to materials flow. The operation of the cells was found to be deficient in a number of respects. Morale was low – it seemed that expectations had been raised which had not been met. Flexible working was inhibited, in part because the company's centralized payment system did not allow for cross-skills working and additionally because cell members were not permitted to make adjustments to computer numerical control (CNC) programs to resolve minor equipment problems. Although the researchers found some positive consequences arising from the move to 'autonomous' cells, the most crucial finding was the extent to which unrevised HR policies and practices served to undermine the initiative. They highlight five key aspects of the company's employment relations policy which were deficient:

1 The absence of managers with personnel skills on the taskforce responsible for implementing the project.
2 Ineffective training for new shopfloor and supervisory roles.
3 A rigid and centralized collective bargaining machinery.
4 A central job evaluation structure inhibiting local adjustment and flexibility.
5 An inability to devise and implement local reward systems.

Our third set of case studies concerns total quality management (TQM) and was undertaken for the Department of Trade and Industry by colleagues in the Industrial Relations Research Unit (IRRU) (Collinson et al., 1998). Organizations as diverse as Severn Trent Water, Halifax Building Society, the London Borough of Lewisham, South Warwickshire NHS Trust, British Steel (Shotton) and Philips Domestic Appliances (Hastings) were involved. Employees, the research suggests, were very much in favour of the core idea of quality and working to improve it; the organizations also gained considerable benefits from the programmes including the achievement of recognized public standards such as ISO 9001 and the smoothing of the path to privatization (in the case of Severn Trent). As well as a careful appraisal of the project, the extent of the success depended on five key employment relations benchmarks, which were only present to varying extents:

1 *Provision of training linked to quality*. There was a strong tendency for employees most favourable to quality programmes to be those who said that they had been trained specifically in quality ideas and teamwork. By contrast, other forms of training, and the total amount of training, had little or no effect. Significantly, too, only one-fifth of the overall sample saw quality or teamwork as the main purpose of their training, which suggests that much of this training might have been insufficiently focused.

2 *An effective relationship with the customer*. In the Halifax, for example, the relationship with the customer was direct and so it was much easier to argue the case for quality of service. In the manufacturing companies, by contrast, it was more difficult, even though in some cases great emphasis was put on seeing other departments and units contributing to the final product as 'internal customers'.

3 *The ability to keep short-term pressures in check*. In the Philips case, acceptance of quality principles was qualified by continuing problems of product design stemming from the very short timescale within which new products had to be developed.

4 *Employment security*. The contrast between the Halifax and the local authority is instructive. In the former a guarantee of employment security was seen as a crucial foundation for the success of TQM; in the latter, intense budgetary pressures leading to redundancies and revisions in terms and conditions of employment undermined the changes involving the group which had only recently been publicly proclaimed to be the flagship department.

5 *Effective employee representation*. Each of the six organizations was unionized. Two were characterized by a strong management/union relationship, two by the marginalization of unions, and two by a more anti-union stance. The success of TQM declined across the these three categories. The absence of a good working

relationship between the management and union made it harder to communicate the messages of TQM effectively as well as to win the trust of individual employees.

A particular point emerging from both the TQM and lean production studies anticipates the argument of the next section. It is that, even though many of the organizations were facing similar competitive pressures and were adopting similar solutions, the details of the immediate context were extremely important. It was not a question of adopting a blueprint and implementing it. Rather it was resolving the specific problems and challenges which the management of change generated that were the most difficult to deal with.

A question of choice?

As well as shedding light on the ingredients of success, recent research is also valuable in drawing our attention to the uncomfortable conclusion that the so-called transformation thesis which has informed so much of our thinking in the area of work organization is seriously flawed. Far too many commentators make the mistake of assuming that the new forms of work organization supposedly emerging are inevitable and universal in their application. To quote from the comments submitted by IRRU (1997) in its response to the European Commission's Green Paper *Partnership for a New Organization of Work*:

1 The manufacturing sector is treated as the paradigm for the economy as a whole at a time when its significance is decreasing in employment terms. Many parts of the service sector, along with much of manufacturing, remain largely insulated from the international competition which is held to be one of the main drivers of change.
2 The thesis of mass production economy in crisis is suspect within its own terms: the notion that economic activity was once driven by mass consumer goods markets which are now experiencing saturation and fragmentation is at best impressionistic and at worst plain wrong.
3 It is dangerously simplistic to counterpose a model of multipurpose machines/differentiated products/short production

runs against one of dedicated machines/standardized products/long production runs: it exaggerates considerably the flexibility of the former and the inflexibility of the latter – the strategy of market segmentation, for example, is longstanding in the automobile industry, while many new domestic and leisure electronic products are as standardized as their predecessors.

4 Competitive success based on quality and up-skilling is only one of a number of strategies available to organizations. Others include seeking protected or monopoly markets; growth through takeover and joint venture; shifting operations overseas; cost-cutting and new forms of Taylorism and Fordism.

In the case of work organization, to develop the last point, it is possible to identify a number of trajectories besides what might be described as the 'quality option' at the heart of the emerging European social model. Each of these trajectories starts from the same point – the questioning of traditional forms of work organization in the light of intensifying competition. In each case, however, the outcome is very different, reflecting specific products and services, market position, cost pressures, technology and management frames of reference. It may take the form, for example, of straightforward work intensification or some of the leaner (and 'meaner') forms of teamworking, i.e. the Toyota rather than the Scandinavian or Volvo model set out in Table 4.1, p. 98.

The major banks in the UK provide a good example of the complexity of response within even the same organization. Faced with an increasingly competitive and oversaturated market, most banks are pursuing a combination of strategies. Takeover or the threat of takeover is an ever-present option depending on position – today's takeover predator can become tomorrow's victim. There is a constant search for new markets both at home (for example investment banking) and overseas (for example ill-fated forays into the USA). Similarly, the approach to work organization combines the new and the old. The introduction of business centres and an increasing focus on customer care, coupled with the introduction of new technology, are creating demands for new skills. There have also been programmes in job redesign and teamworking. Simultaneously, however, much of the work previously undertaken in the branch offices has been shifted to so-called office factories and telephone call centres, where the organization is extremely Taylorist and the range of skills much narrower than before. The prospect of the transfer of much of this work overseas, where it could be undertaken at a fraction of even UK labour costs, is also ever present (for further details, see Terry and Newell, 1996; Storey *et al.*, 1999).

Conclusions

Perhaps the most important point to be taken from this chapter is that there is a substantial body of evidence which backs up the conceptual point. Involvement and participation, it seems, work. Obviously, they are not a panacea for all the organization's ills. The finest programmes of involvement and participation are no substitute for the right products and adequate investment. Other things being equal, however, involvement and participation pay dividends. Not only that, but also the more forms of involvement and participation which are applied and the more extensively they are applied, the greater the return.

Equally clear, however, should be that the effects of involvement and participation are not automatic. Involvement and participation need to be properly managed like everything else. The policy is not for the faint-hearted: it requires substantial investments in the training and development of managers and employees. It means too that the supporting practices have to be in place, including appropriate pay and working time arrangements. These are the subject of the next chapter.

Suggested further reading

The findings of the ten-country EPOC survey (European Foundation for the Improvement of Living and Working Conditions, 1997) put the UK into perspective. The report for the DTI on organizations' experience in implementing TQM by Collinson and her colleagues is also strongly recommended. The two volumes reporting the findings of the 1998

Workplace Employee Relations Survey (Cully *et al.*, 1999: Millward *et al.*, 2000) contain much useful up-to-date information on involvement and participation and their links with business performance. The various ACAS guides cited are the best source of practical advice.

5

RESHAPING THE WAGE/WORK BARGAIN:
Pay and working time

In this chapter, our focus is on two issues at the heart of the employment relationship: pay and working time. To paraphrase Brown and Walsh (1994: 437), being quantifiable, and thus generalizable across all manner of jobs and employees, pay and working time are the common focus and language of policy-makers, practitioners and commentators alike. Not only that, but the management of pay and working time is also fundamental to productivity, motivation and performance. For employers, pay is the price of labour and the arrangement of working time patterns helps to determine the way in which goods and services can be provided. For employees, pay is a measure of self-esteem as well as the means to livelihood, while working time patterns shape the very experience of work – its intensity and how it fits with domestic and social life – as well as being a major factor in compensation. It is therefore no surprise that pay and working time are major sources of conflict with a significant bearing on the job satisfaction, motivation and retention of employees (Cully *et al.*, 1998: 21–2).

Sadly, in recent years, pay has become inextricably tied up with the debate over individual performance-related pay (IPRP) to the

117

neglect of the wider issues that need to be addressed. Working time has tended to be ignored almost entirely, being treated as a received framework devoid of scope for strategic choice and rarely getting a mention in most texts dealing with employment relations.

Our starting point in this chapter is that there is considerable scope for improvement in both areas. The first half of the chapter reviews the issues that need to be taken into account in the effective management of pay. The second reviews the options for change in working time arrangements, bearing in mind that the implementation of EU directives dealing with working time, parental leave and equality of treatment for part-time employees offers a unique opportunity for reform.

Key issues in the effective management of pay

There is no dispute about the overall significance of the reward system in performance management. The reward system is important in attracting and retaining employees of the required quality, underpinning the drive to improve performance and supporting the ability to change. However, as will be clear from reading any standard textbook, one of the great debates in personnel management is whether the system of rewards, in Herzberg's (1966) terms, is to be seen as a 'motivator' or a 'hygiene' factor. In other words, is the system of rewards to be seen primarily as a positive incentive to greater performance or, if employees feel that it is unfair, as a source of disincentive? Our view is that it is sensible to start from the second position. This is because, in the headlong rush to IPRP, there has been a tendency in many UK organizations to neglect other key components of reward systems.

Pay has two main aspects. One is the pay system. This is best understood in terms of the set of rules linking reward to effort or to status in work or both. The second is the pattern of pay relationships or pay structure. Typically, setting the relationship between jobs as the basis for payment has involved, on the one hand, some form of job evaluation to help establish a perceived fairness in internal pay relationships and, on the other, external comparability to help ensure that the organizational rate does not fall behind the market rate. Also important is the issue of status, which affects how payment is made as well as other financial rewards from employment such as pensions and sick pay.

Selecting a pay system

Three main types of system can be identified for the purposes of analysis, although they are often combined in practice. Under the first, the employee is paid by time, typically for hours of attendance but increasingly for availability. Here the expectation is that a combination of moral obligation and management discipline will help to ensure that the employee contributes a fair day's work. Under the second, the employee is paid for performance. In this case, pay can be related in some way to relatively objective results such as physical productivity or sales or, in the case of senior managers, financial results more generally. Alternatively, it can be related to a largely subjective managerial assessment of the contribution that the individual is making (see Figure 5.1).

The third is a competence-based system. Here too there can be a similar distinction between objective and subjective criteria. Employees can be paid on the basis of clearly identifiable competences. Alternatively, the basis can be a behavioural dimension.

---

1 Fixed incremental scales with limited flexibility, i.e. there is a standard increase for the majority of staff, but the manager can increase payments for exceptionally effective staff or reduce the increase for poor performers
2 Performance pay linked to an incremental scale, i.e. attainment of the next point on the scale is dependent on the employee reaching a satisfactory performance rating
3 Pay increase based on performance rating and awarded by a series of fixed percentage points, for example:

	% increase
Unsatisfactory	0
Satisfactory	2.0
Above average	3.5
Excellent	5.0

Figure 5.1 Examples of individual performance-related pay
Source: Based on ACAS (1997c: 31)

119

		Job	**Role**	**Person**
Method of linkage	**Evaluation**	Factor plans (e.g. Portsmouth Housing Trust)	Classification systems (e.g. Guinness)	Life cycle stage model (e.g. Lex Services)
	Pay adjustment	Skill/competence pay steps in ranges; formula-based increase (e.g. VW)	Pay increases based on assessments of results and competences (e.g. Woolwich)	Pay increases based wholly/largely on competences (e.g. ICL)

Figure 5.2 Typology of competence-related pay
Source: Brown and Armstrong (1997)

Another important distinguishing feature is the balance between the acquisition and the effective use of competences. Depending on these features, competence pay is hardly different from payment by time (objective criteria plus acquisition) or payment by performance (subjective criteria plus use). A typology of competence-related pay systems is shown in Figure 5.2.

Historically, there was a major division in the UK between manual employees, on the one hand, and non-manual, on the other. Many manual workers, notably in key sectors such as engineering, were paid an hourly rate to which was added some form of payment by results related to physical productivity, such as piecework (i.e. payment by item) or measured daywork involving the techniques of work study to establish standard times. Most non-manual workers were paid an annual salary for a fixed working week plus an annual increment for each year of service.

Two major trends may be identified. The first, in the case of manual workers, is a shift away from payment by results towards greater emphasis on the acquisition of new skills. The second, which primarily affects non-manual employees, is the introduction of IPRP largely dependent on the judgement of managers. Unlike some previous trends in pay systems, the public sector as well as the private sector is affected; for example, among the 500,000 non-industrial civil servants, assessed performance is now integral to salary progression for most grades (Kessler, 1994:

471–2). Even so, it is important to keep things in perspective. According to the first findings of the 1998 Workplace Employee Relations Survey reported in Chapter 1 (Cully *et al.*, 1998), while non-managerial employees had some form of appraisal in just over a half of workplaces, in only one in ten were these employees on IPRP schemes.

The pros and cons of performance-related pay
The appropriateness of different pay systems is a never-ending topic of debate in the UK, reflecting changing circumstances and deeply held views. If one ignores for the moment the substantial body of evidence which casts doubt on the links between pay and performance, the case for IPRP sounds very plausible. It is difficult to quarrel with the overall objective, which has been described as 'to improve performance by converting the paybill from an indiscriminate machine to a more finely-tuned mechanism, sensitive and responsive to a company's and employees' needs' (Brading and Wright, 1990: 1). Equally, there appears to be nothing exceptional about the kinds of specific objectives which organizations are said to be looking for in introducing IPRP (see Figure 5.3), especially if the possibility of group as opposed to individual PRP is taken into account.

However, despite the quantity of advice and consultancy available, the signs are that in many organizations IPRP has led to major problems. As Kessler's (1994) review of the research

---

1 It focuses effort where the organizational wants it (specified in performance plans, objectives or targets)
2 It supports a performance-oriented culture (pay for results not effort)
3 It emphasizes individual performance or teamwork as appropriate (group-based schemes foster cooperation; personal schemes focus on individual contribution)
4 It strengthens the performance-planning process (the setting of objectives and performance standards will carry more weight)
5 It rewards the right people (high rewards to those whose performance is commensurately high)
6 It can motivate all the people (a well designed scheme will be motivating to all participants)

Figure 5.3 The logic of performance pay
Source: Brading and Wright (1990: 1)

evidence suggested, there has often been a significant gap between assumptions and reality in those many organizations which have introduced IPRP. A common feature has been a failure to think through the introduction of IPRP in a coherent manner. Thus, in many cases the establishment of formal performance criteria leaves a great deal to be desired – 'objectives' and 'behaviours' which bear little relationship to work practice are being engineered purely for the purposes of having an IPRP scheme. In the performance assessment process, which lies at the heart of IPRP, there are complaints about subjectivity and inconsistency which are often compounded by lack of attention to the training of managers in carrying out appraisal and to the administrative procedures for monitoring arrangements. The links between performance and the level of pay are not always clear and effective – in many cases, it is argued, the amount of the incentive element is far too small to make any material difference. Few organizations, it seems, have built in arrangements to monitor the impact of IPRP on productivity, or indeed to estimate how much such schemes cost to run (see also Marsden and French (1998) for further evidence on many of these points).

It has also long been noted that excessive emphasis on extrinsic motivation in the form of pay can result in damage to intrinsic motivation (Deci, 1975). Motivation which comes from pride in work may be undermined, with the arrangements often being disliked by those carrying out the appraisals and those who are appraised. Ted Riley, a principal adviser in the ACAS Work Research Unit observed that in some specific instances performance-related pay can be successful, for example, 'In a small organization with highly dynamic whizz-kids it might work . . . But most organizations are not like that' (Riley, 1992).

Perhaps the most worrying aspect, however, is that IPRP would seem to contradict or sit uneasily with a number of other policies and objectives which managers profess themselves to be pursuing. One of these is the emphasis which many organizations are putting on teamwork. In many cases, notably where operations are interlinked, IPRP would appear to be totally inappropriate. Focusing on individual performance goals in such situations can undermine team spirit and cooperation. At the very least, employees may focus their attention on individual targets (especially if they are artificially contrived for the pay system) at the expense of the performance of the unit. Even so, there appears to have been a widespread insistence on having IPRP, come what may. Arguably, this clamour is as good an example as any of the kind of *lack* of strategic thinking in HR and IR which we comment upon throughout this book.

Kessler (1994, 1999) is extremely helpful in understanding why there has been a headlong rush towards IPRP. He identifies two analytical approaches to understanding managers' choices of pay systems which draw attention to the confusion of motives that appear to be present in many organizations. The first approach sees the choice of pay system as part of a relatively ordered and rational process in which managers pick the scheme which is appropriate to their needs. This, the contingency approach, has a long tradition in writing about pay systems in the UK (Lupton and Gowler's, *Selecting a Wage Payment System*, which was published as long ago as 1969, is a well known example and is still probably the best guide there is). The second approach sees the choice of the payment system as a far less ordered or rational management process. Rather, it is a largely political or ideological process acquiring symbolic value to support particular interests or values. In this case the details of the scheme, and how it is introduced and monitored, are likely to be seen as largely irrelevant by decision-makers: it is the message sent by the introduction of the scheme that matters most.

It is difficult to escape the conclusion that it is the second view that it is most appropriate to adopt, namely that IPRP has been introduced for largely ideological reasons. The messages which senior managers would appear to be wishing to give are also fairly clear. First, there is to be a change in the culture of the organization. It is no accident, for example, that some of the most publicized IPRP schemes were in the newly privatized public utilities – senior managers were as anxious to impress the stock market analysts with their commitment to the commercialism of the private sector as they were their own employees. Secondly, managers must manage. A key implication of IPRP is that managers have to take responsibility for performance management: requiring them to take tough decisions about the payments that are going to be made to individual employees is seen as a critical element in the process. Thirdly, and perhaps most importantly, there is the focus on the individual; the implication, at the very least, is that trade unions and collective bargaining will play a lesser role in pay determination. Indeed, in some well publicized cases, for example management grades in British Rail and BT, the introduction of IPRP was directly associated with the withdrawal of collective bargaining rights over pay.

Teamworking equals team pay?
The coming of teamwork inevitably raises the question of the form of the pay system. Other things being equal, it might be expected that teamwork would automatically equal team pay. Certainly, there are organizations introducing team pay and in doing so are aiming to deliver three key objectives: (1) to support teamworking arrangements, encourage cooperative behaviour and underline the importance of effective teamwork; (2) to provide incentives and a method of rewarding improved team performance; and (3) to relate team reward to the completion of clear, agreed targets and standards of performance.

However, the incidence of team pay remains relatively low. Recent Industrial Society surveys suggest that just one in ten organizations paid a bonus based on team performance, despite the fact that the vast majority (86 per cent) had increased their use of teamworking over the past two years (Industrial Society, 1998c). According to the Industrial Society, the experience to date suggests that few organizations are prepared to support the development of teamworking with team-based reward, even though it predicts that team pay will become more common over the next two years.

The uncertainty of many organizations about the relative merits of team pay is reflected in Figure 5.4 which reproduces the list of advantages and disadvantages of team pay as seen by the Institute of Personnel and Development. It is interesting to note that a number of the disadvantages appear to have more to do with teamworking itself than team pay. Many organizations, it seems, remain nervous about some of the implications of teamworking and (true to form perhaps) look to some form of individual pay system as one of the instruments of controlling them.

Advantages	Disadvantages
• Encourages teamworking and cooperative behaviour	• Effectiveness depends on the existence of well managed and mature teams which may be hard to identify and may not be best motivated by purely financial reward
• Clarifies team goals and priorities and provides for the integration of organizational and team objectives	• It is not easy to get people to think in terms of how their performance impacts on other people
• Reinforces organizational change in the direction of an increased emphasis on teams in flatter and process-based organizations	• Identifying what individual team members contribute may be a problem, which might demotivate individual contributors
• Acts as a lever for cultural change in the directions of, for example, quality and customer care	• Peer pressure which compels individuals to conform to group norms could be undesirable and appear oppressive
• Enhances flexible working within teams and encourages multiskilling	• Pressure to conform, which is heightened by team pay, could result in the team maintaining its output at lowest common denominator levels
• Provides an incentive for the group collectively to improve performance and team process	• It can be difficult to develop performance measures and a method of rating team performance which are seen to be fair
• Encourages less effective performers to improve in order to meet team standards	• Problems of uncooperative behaviour may be shifted from individuals to the relationship between teams
• Serves as a means of developing self-directed teams and encourages multiskilling	• Organizational flexibility may be prejudiced – people in cohesive, high-performing and well rewarded teams may be unwilling to move, and it could be difficult to reassign work between teams or to break up teams altogether

Figure 5.4 Benefits and drawbacks of team pay
Source: IPD (1996)

125

An appropriate pay structure

Two main aspects are involved in creating a pay structure. One is internal pay relationships or differentials; the other is external pay relationships or relativities. Both are fundamentally important because they are inextricably tied up with notions of fairness. The problem is that fairness is a not an absolute but a relative concept. Pay relationships provide the critical measure of the worth or status which the individual is accorded in the organization and in society more generally; their fairness is judged in comparison to others. If they are felt to be unfair, they can be a major disincentive. In Brown's words:

> The most ingenious of bonus systems and the best of supervision are of little use if the underlying pay structure is felt to be unfair. Consequently, the prudent personnel manager devotes far less time to devising new pay incentives than to tending old notions of fairness.
>
> (Brown, 1989: 252–3)

The recommended method of setting the basis for pay differentials which are felt to be fair is job evaluation. This is simply a procedure for allowing systematic comparisons between jobs. A variety of methods is available, but four main types can be found: ranking; paired comparisons; grading or job classification; and points rating (ACAS, 1997d).

The starting point in each case is the preparation of a description of the jobs being compared using common headings or factors. The first three methods are often referred to as non-analytical. The simplest – ranking – is fairly rudimentary and involves a number of judgements: should job A be paid more than job B, C or D? Paired comparison is very similar, the difference is that each job is compared with every other job in turn. Grading reverses the process: a decision is taken to have a certain number of grades and then the jobs are allocated to the different grades. Points rating is referred to as an analytical method. This method involves deriving a number of factors and the relative weighting to be attached to each of them. Each job is then considered factor by factor to give a points total which can be used to determine the position in the job hierarchy.

Typically, UK companies have operated with a minimum of five or six grades. A number of the Japanese companies who have invested in the UK, notably Nissan, have chosen to work with only two major grades. If a major objective is to improve flexibility, it is argued, too many grades can present major obstacles – job evaluation, by definition, involves the preparation of job descriptions. The tighter these are drawn for the purposes of distinguishing one job from another, the greater the inflexibility. Some form of so-called broad-banding, it seems, is the answer, which is to have a smaller number of pay grades and greater overlap between them.

External pay relationships or relativities, the second aspect of pay structure, have in the past been an issue of considerable controversy especially during the periods of incomes policy in the 1960s and 1970s. Currently, to return to the point made earlier about the ideological explanation of management behaviour, they are supposed to be a 'non-issue'. The main considerations in pay determination, it is argued, ought to be the specific circumstances of the individual organization – the ability to pay, in other words, is of paramount importance. The problem is that the issue will not go away. Organizations have to be aware of what potential competitors for their employees are paying: otherwise, they risk losing their best people. In the main, they do this through market surveys. In the case of managers, for example, considerable use is made of the Hay system to judge the appropriateness of pay levels. In the case of manual workers, the local employers' organization is often the source of the data. In the public services, groups like the armed forces, senior civil servants, doctors, nurses and teachers have formal review bodies responsible for making recommendations on the basis of comparisons.

Regrettably, the good sense advocated by Brown in the earlier quotation was something many managers chose to ignore in the first half of the 1990s. They did, indeed, put their energies into the vain search for new forms of incentives. Job evaluation came to be seen as something bureaucratic and unnecessary. The market rate become the important benchmark.

Although job evaluation continues to have its critics, the signs are that there is growing recognition of a need for some form of systematic and defensible underpinning to pay relationships (see, for example, IRS, 1998m). One reason is legislation relating to equal pay for work of equal value; in the absence of job evaluation, or a satisfactory job evaluation system, the organization can be extremely vulnerable to claims from female employees. Another is the difficulty that many organizations have had in operationalizing the concept of the market rate. Comparing jobs with similar titles is pretty meaningless; there is no substitute for a firm basis of comparison, which means at least some rudimentary form of job evaluation (for further details, see Pickard and Fowler, 1999).

Single status?

It will be recalled from Chapter 1 that only four out of ten workplaces have single-status arrangements between managers and non-managerial employees. Most commentators accept that divisions like this – there are also very often status divisions between manual and non-manual and between hourly paid and monthly paid employees – cannot be justified and make little sense. Most are grounded in history and bear little relationship to the job. A key reason is that the very existence of these status differences makes it extremely difficult to win the kind of co-operation and commitment that organizations claim to be seeking. There is no defensible reason, for example, why a 50-year-old skilled craftsman, who has worked 30 years with an organization should have sick pay or pension arrangements inferior to those of his 18-year-old son or daughter who only recently joined as an office junior. A second reason is that in many organizations it is increasingly difficult to make an objective distinction between manual and non-manual jobs. A third reason is that, as the non-pay items increase in their cost, management wants greater return from them. Indeed, in the USA the so-called 'cafeteria' principle is becoming increasingly important: in the attempt to draw attention to the costs and benefits of these elements, employees are encouraged to choose between different combinations of non-pay benefits instead of taking them for granted.

Such concerns have not been translated into practice, however, despite predictions about the decline of the status gap (Price and Price, 1994). Certainly throughout the 1980s and 1990s there have been moves to harmonize some of the terms and conditions of manual and non-manual workers. Sick pay is a case in point. Examples of single-status arrangements, however, remain the exception rather than the rule. One of the most significant, in terms of coverage, is the single-status agreement reached in local authorities in 1997 which is described in detail in an IRS case study (IRS, 1997e).

Admittedly, there are some major problems in moving towards single-status arrangements. One is cost. Sizeable increases may be involved and many organizations are in no position to pay the bill. Especially important is the cost of security that would be involved in many organizations as a result of different notice provisions which would arise. Another is the opposition of non-manual employees who are afraid of losing their particular advantages or who fear that they will be held back while others catch up. In many cases, there is a suspicion that managers simply do not perceive the status divide to be a major cause for real concern. On the contrary, the divide could be seen as bringing positive advantages to management. Rightly or wrongly, managers in some organizations feel that it enables them to enjoy the tactical advantage of playing one group off against another.

Towards flexible working: an array of options

The Working Time Regulations implementing the EU Working Time Directive came into force on 1 October 1998 and are inevitably pushing working time to the top of the employment relations agenda for action. For the first time ever, UK management is obliged to comply with a wide range of detailed statutory rules covering minimum rest periods, night and shift work, maximum weekly working hours and paid annual leave. The regulations, which will be enforced via employment tribunal claims and action by the health and safety authorities, also involve a wide range of exclusions, 'derogations' and transitional arrangements, making this one of the most complex areas of employment law facing UK management. Along with the two other EU directives emanating from the Maastricht social policy process, dealing with parental leave and equality of treatment for part-time

129

workers, the Working Time Regulations add up to the biggest change ever seen in the regulatory framework of employment in the UK since the Industrial Relations Act 1971 (for further details see Hall *et al.*, 1998).

Although it will be the Regulations which prompt managers in many UK organizations to review their existing working time arrangements, there are a number of reasons why they should be putting the reform of working time arrangements at the top of their agenda in any event:

1 The intensification of competition in the private sector and scarcity of resources in the public sector are putting management under pressure to find ways to improve efficiency and minimize costs – developments in outsourcing, for example, are often an important catalyst for changes in in-house working time arrangements.
2 The need to respond to customer expectations of more extensive services, ranging from manufacturing companies competing in world markets having to meet ever tighter delivery deadlines, to service organizations in both the private and public sectors needing to respond to demands for longer hours of availability.
3 Investment in new technology is not only putting a premium on maximum utilization to justify costs, leading to longer working hours, but in many cases it also creates opportunities to develop fresh products and services involving different patterns of working time.
4 Employee demands for reductions in hours and more family-friendly working time arrangements are a source of pressure for change in their own right.

Much has been made of the flexibility of the UK labour market (see, for example, Beatson, 1995) and so it might be thought that the argument for radical change applied less to the UK than to other countries. Yet nothing could be further from the truth. The absence of regulation is not the same as flexibility. As Table 5.1 shows, far-reaching options, such as annual hours, affect only a small minority of the workforce in the UK, as do so-called family-friendly working arrangements (see Table 5.2). Few organizations, a recent Industrial Society (1998b) survey suggests, have a formal policy on flexible working.

Table 5.1 Percentage of employees by type of flexible work arrangement, spring 1997

	All	Men	Women
Employees with a flexible work arrangement[a]	22.0	18.0	26.3
Flexible working hours	10.0	8.8	11.5
Annualized hours contract	4.5	1.5	7.8
Term-time working	4.2	4.3	4.1
Job-sharing	2.1	2.7	1.5
Four-and-a-half-day week	0.9	0.2	1.7
Nine-day fortnight	0.8	0.8	0.9
Zero hours contract	0.3	0.5	0.1
Employees without a flexible work arrangement	78.0	82.0	73.7
Employees who gave a valid response ('000) (=100%)	21,250	11,127	10,124
Base: All employees who gave a valid response ('000)[b]	22,447	11,784	10,663

[a] Columns add up to more than 100% because respondents can cite more than one type of flexible arrangement.
[b] Percentages are based on those people who gave a valid response to the flexible working question. Estimates of levels can be obtained by multiplying the percentages by the base.
Source: Labour Market Trends LFS63 (December 1997).

Critically, there is the long-standing problem of long hours. In theory, long hours can be seen as evidence of a flexible labour market. Overtime working enables management to meet exceptional changes in demand without incurring the extra costs associated with additional employees. It is not to meet exceptional changes in demand, however, that overtime working is used in many UK organizations. Rather it is endemic – it is worked regularly and consistently. Moreover, the payment for overtime has become a key component of the regular weekly wage. Indeed, it is no exaggeration to suggest that, in many cases, the main rationale for overtime working is the maintenance of the regular weekly wage.

Table 5.2 Access to flexible and family-friendly working arrangements

| | Private sector | | Public sector | | All employees |
	Men % of employees	Women % of employees	Men % of employees	Women % of employees	% of employees
Flexitime	24	36	37	39	32
Job-sharing scheme	6	15	23	34	16
Parental leave	21	30	35	33	28
Working at/from home	10	6	13	9	9
Workplace nursery/child care subsidy	2	3	6	9	4
None of these	57	42	40	34	46

Base: All employees in workplaces with 25 or more employees.
Figures are weighted and based on responses from 25,491 employees.
Source: Cully *et al.* (1998: 20).

It may be argued that such overtime working can be justified on the grounds that it enables employers to get long hours on the cheap. Yet, as the reports of the Donovan Commission (1968) and the National Board for Prices and Incomes (1970) argued three decades ago, far from making for flexibility, the exact opposite is often the case. In practice, endemic overtime working can make for rigidity and be a major source of inefficiency. It is not just that it leads to health and stress problems (Institute of Management, 1995, 1996) and family dislocation (Ferri and Smith, 1996; National Work-life Forum, 1998), important though these are. It also encourages demarcation and resistance to technological change on the part of employees anxious to maintain their overtime earnings. Less obvious, but even more important, it fosters sloppy management: there is little incentive for managers to plan or to innovate if long hours of relatively cheap labour are so easily available. The experience of many of the organizations which have moved away from the basic working week to annual hours is that changes in working time are the key to changes in work organization more generally.

Changes in the duration of working time

The aim of this section is to offer a guide to the reform of working time arrangements in the UK. In keeping with the scope of the Regulations, the focus is on the duration and distribution of the working hours; the range of alternative options to the standard working week is reviewed and examples given throughout.

There have been three main types of change in the duration of working time in recent years. The first, 'compressed working weeks', has tended to exaggerate the long hours of full-time workers by concentrating working time into longer shifts. The second, predominantly but not exclusively in the service sectors, involves the break-up of working time into shorter blocks for part-time workers. The third relates to the duration of the contract for work rather than to the length of the working day or week itself.

The compressed week
A compressed week usually involves the reallocation of hours into fewer and longer blocks of time. For example, one reaction to

reductions in the working week in engineering at the beginning of the 1990s was to reorganize on the basis of four and a half days a week or nine days in a fortnight. Typically, this involves a Friday downtime so that employees get the benefit of a longer weekend. A number of organizations have also moved to 12-hour working as part of wider restructuring involving flexible rostering and annual hours arrangements discussed later. Examples which have been studied include BT (IRS, 1995), Rockware Glass (IRS, 1993) and Zeneca Agrochemicals (IRS, 1994).

Overall, however, the number of organizations with some form of compressed week in the UK is small. According to Labour Force Survey data for 1997 shown in Table 5.1, only 0.9 cent of employees worked a four-and-a-half-day week and only 0.8 per cent a nine-day fortnight. The engineering industry has the largest proportion of employees working a four-and-a-half-day week and transport and communications the largest proportion on a nine-day fortnight.

Part-time working
Part-time working is generally taken to mean hours less than the normal basic week, although official statistics often use a definition of thirty hours a week or less. Much of the growth in part-time working came in the late 1970s and early 1980s and reflected supply-side considerations – the wish of many employees, especially women, to work part-time rather than full-time. Employer demand was also important however, and has continued to fuel the growth of part-time work. According to the most recent WERS data, two in five workplaces reported an increase in the employment of part-timers over the previous five years (Cully *et al.*, 1998: 9). One of the main benefits of part-time working is increasingly seen to be the greater flexibility it makes possible, especially in covering so-called key periods of activity (ACAS, 1998d: 10–11). In a survey of nearly four hundred workplaces in 1995, for example, the Labour Research Department (1995: 7–12) found that just over one-fifth employed part-time workers at peak times. These so-called key-time workers were especially significant in energy and water supply, transport and communications, banking and finance, and the public sector.

Although part-time working has come to be associated with the service sector, it is not unknown in manufacturing. Table 5.3 shows that a majority of manufacturing workplaces employ at least some part-time workers, although in very few cases do they represent a majority of employees. In this sector, part-time working is most often associated with two main patterns which are particularly prevalent in food, drink and tobacco. The first is the so-called early riser shift, typically starting between 5.30am and 6am and going on to 1pm or 1.30pm. The second is known as the twilight shift. This is usually of between four and five hours duration and begins in the late afternoon or early evening (for further details, see Labour Research Department, 1996).

Temporary working
Temporary working enables employers to vary the total hours worked by changing the numbers employed on contracts of

Table 5.3 Use of part-time employees (under 30 hours per week), by industry

Industry	No part-time employees % of workplaces	Most employees part-time % of workplaces
Manufacturing	36	1
Electricity, gas and water	51	0
Construction	39	0
Wholesale and retail	14	43
Hotels and restaurants	3	55
Transport and communications	23	4
Financial services	20	5
Other business services	23	7
Public administration	9	1
Education	0	40
Health	1	50
Other community services	8	51
All workplaces	16	26

Base: all workplaces with 25 or more employees.
Figures are weighted and based on responses from 1914 managers.
Source: Cully *et al.* (1998: 7).

limited or predetermined duration. This can take the form of employing temporary agency workers ('temps') or workers on fixed-term contracts. Around two-thirds of all workplaces have used temporary agency workers or employed staff on fixed term contracts over the past five years (Cully *et al.*, 1998: 9). Of these, between one-quarter and one-third reported their use to have increased, compared with only one in ten which had decreased their use, with the rest remaining broadly the same. The most affected occupations are the clerical and professional groups, while only a small minority of other categories used either temps or people on fixed-term contracts.

The distribution of working time

Shift working

Shift working has been the main way in which employers have sought to improve the distribution of working time. Shift working involves the working of two or more periods within the same 24 hours by different employees usually organized in crews or teams. The aim is to increase the coverage of working time beyond the working day of the individual employee even taking into account overtime. *Continuous* systems provide cover for the full 24 hours throughout the week; *non-continuous* or *discontinuous* systems provide for lesser coverage than this – for example, it may be for 12 or 16 hours out of 24 each day and/or five days out of seven (for further details, see Hall *et al.*, 1998: 44–5; ACAS, 1998d).

Shift working has long been a feature in many sectors in the UK. Historically, shift working has been mainly associated with manual workers, above all in transport and manufacturing. Increasingly, however, its net has spread to include non-manual workers in services. Shift working is now common, for example, in sectors such as banking and finance and in retail; it has long been a feature in the NHS. Approximately 3.6 million people 'usually' worked shifts in 1997 according to *Labour Market Trends* (1997, LFS60). The largest numbers were involved in double-day shifts, followed by continuous three-shift systems. Four-shift systems were the rarest type.

From fixed to variable hours

The arrangements considered so far involve fixed hours worked on a weekly basis. Most recent attention, however, has focused on arrangements under which hours worked are variable over the day, week or year. It is the extra flexibility that variability brings which, in theory, management might be expected to find especially attractive.

Under *zero hours* arrangements, the employer calls in 'employees' at short notice as and when there is a need. Employees may even be asked to 'clock off' and so lose pay in quiet periods even though they are required to stay on the premises. The practice, which affected some 0.3 per cent of the workforce in 1997, came to prominence in the early 1990s in the retail and financial sectors especially (for further details, see Neathey and Hurstfield, 1996), and is in essence little different from the casual system prevalent in a wide range of industries in the nineteenth century. It has been widely condemned on the grounds that the individual 'employee' has no minimum employment rights whatsoever, and it demonstrates most explicitly the potential for abuse inherent in some forms of flexible working (NACAB, 1997). The government is currently seeking views (following its 1998 White Paper *Fairness at Work*, para. 3.16) on whether 'further action should be taken to address the potential abuse of zero hours contracts and, if so, how to take this forward without undermining labour market flexibility'.

There are two main forms of *flexible hours*. The first, popularly known as *flexitime*, exists mainly for the benefit of employees. Employees may choose to vary their working hours within set limits. Typically, there are core times when employees have to be present, say, between 10am and 12pm and 2pm and 4pm. Employees may vary their starting and finishing times, together with the time they take their lunch, provided that they work their total hours within a set accounting period of usually one month. According to the LFS data reproduced in Table 5.1, 10 per cent of employees worked under flexitime arrangements in 1997. The practice was most prevalent among clerical and secretarial groups, where it affected more than one-fifth of the total of employees, and other non-manual groups. By sector, the highest proportions were to be found in banking and financial services

137

and, in particular, public administration, where just over 40 per cent of employees were involved.

The second form of flexible hours primarily serves the employer rather than the employee. One variant, sometimes known as *minimum hours* or *mini-max hours*, is found primarily in retail and affects mainly part-time employees. Unlike zero hours, the employee has a contract for a fixed number of hours each week. By agreement with the employee, however, and subject to reasonable notice, the employer can increase the daily or weekly hours up to a preset maximum. For example, such arrangements have been introduced into multiple food retailing by Tesco: part-timers can opt to work a fixed core of 10–16 hours a week on the understanding that they may be asked to work up to 31 hours a week to cover sickness and other absence. This is subject to special provisions designed to safeguard against casualization, such as minimum guaranteed periods of work and notice required (for further details, see IRS, 1996a).

Another variation involves *flexible rostering*. Under these arrangements, the employer can vary the daily or weekly hours around a range. A recent and major example of flexible rostering would be the Customer Service Improvement Programme introduced in BT and covering its engineers servicing domestic customers. Employees in the large number of technical and engineering grades are rostered to attend according to four main patterns. In each case, management can adjust the starting and finishing times up to an hour each day with debits and credits of up to four hours being accrued (for further details, see IRS, 1995).

In the case of *seasonal hours*, employees work different hours depending on the time of year, with excess hours in one period 'banked' and taken off in lieu in another. Long a feature of agriculture, these have emerged in manufacturing and services more generally in recent years. In manufacturing, for example, Blyton (1994: 517–18) quotes in particular the example of Hitachi in South Wales. Since 1991 the standard working week of 39 hours has been modified to meet the extra demand in the run-up to Christmas. Employees work a 42 hour week between August and December and 37 hours at other times. Pay, however, remains standardized at 39 hours per week throughout the year.

Arguably, the *annual hours* system, which brings together a number of practices discussed above such as minimum hours, hours 'banking', and flexible rostering, represents the most advanced form of change to the management of working time. The basic principle is that working time is defined in terms of the year rather than the week. The employer is therefore better able to match working time to fluctuations in demand for products and services.

In its simplest form, the total number of annual hours is based on the number of weeks in the year multiplied by the number of working hours per week with a deduction for holidays. For example:

52.2 weeks × 39 hours = 2035.8 hours
less 25 days holiday at (39 hours ÷ by 5 days) = 195 hours
less 8 public holidays at (39 hours ÷ by 5 days) = 62.4 hours
Total = 1778.4 hours

Like shift working, annual hours arrangements differ significantly in the details. Following Blyton (1994: 515–16), however, they are typically one of two types. In the first, the emphasis is on the variability of weekly hours with work periods longer in busy times and shorter during slacker times as in seasonal hours. In the second, rostered hours are less than the agreed annual hours: workers are in effect on call for the non-rostered time and can be required to come into work to cover unforeseen circumstances.

The first type has been applied particularly in businesses with seasonal demand. The second type is found mainly in continuous process industries in both manufacturing and services (notably television, finance, education and local authorities, for further details, see IRS, 1998c,e). In finance, for example, NatWest Bank has announced that it is putting all its branch staff on annual hours (Whitehead, 1999).

Commentators have been predicting a significant take-up of the annual hours system for over a decade (see, for example, Brewster and Connock, 1985; Taylor, 1996). At first sight, there are major attractions in terms of flexibility, costs and productivity. First, an annualized hours system promises greater time flexibility – the closer matching of worked hours to service or production demands – whilst undermining the 'overtime culture'. Workers (and supervisors) are less likely to anticipate or contrive opportunities for 'extra hours' working once the direct link with pay is removed. Instead, there is a strong incentive to get work done within the allotted time in order to avoid drawing on any 'reserve' hours. It also facilitates easier cover for absence and holiday leave, and enables scheduling for maintenance work and employee training. Second, an annual hours system can deliver significant cost savings by reducing overtime working and the hiring of temporary staff. It can also facilitate a reduction in overall staffing levels for some categories of employees by its more precise matching of worked hours to demand. In addition, it offers employers the advantage of greater predictability in calculating their anticipated labour costs. Third, annual hours may have a beneficial productivity effect by reducing the underutilization of staff, particularly if the introduction of the scheme is designed to improve task flexibility and multiskilling at the same time, as has been the case in companies such as Rockware Glass and Zeneca Agrochemicals. There may also be gains in terms of employee attendance, motivation and reduced levels of turnover if the scheme is able to provide benefits for the workforce. These relate mainly to the possibility of more preferred working patterns, such as greater sequences of days off, being incorporated into the design and scheduling of work shifts and the greater stability which the system provides for employee earnings.

In terms of coverage, however, annual hours remains very much a minority practice. At first sight, the relatively poor take-up of annual hours arrangements is puzzling in view of the advantages they are supposed to bring. Evidently, there are situations where such arrangements are not appropriate, for example at the extremes of predictability and unpredictability of demand. Elsewhere, however, defining working time in terms of the year rather than the week would seem to be the obvious thing to do.

Obvious it may be. Yet it is difficult to escape the conclusion that, for many managements, assuming they are aware of the concept, the changes involved in annual hours arrangements pose particular problems. As Arrowsmith and Sisson (1999) point out, not only do they represent a radical departure in the working time arrangements for employees, but also a particularly marked change for management. Among the (dis)advantages listed by ACAS (1998d), for example, annual hours requires much more planning in general and of human resources in particular.

Arguably, neither is something that UK management, under pressure to work within relatively short-term financial constraints, has found it easy to do. In the circumstances, and bearing in mind the relative cheapness of labour in the UK, it has been easier to stick with overtime or go for forms of 'external' flexibility such as outsourcing.

Conclusions

In the case of pay, there are three main points to be borne in mind. First, the payment system, important though it is, constitutes only one element in the effective management of performance. All too often, it can be argued, UK management has relied exclusively on the payment system – be it payment by results in the 1950s and 1960s, or IPRP in the 1980s and the early 1990s.

Second, there is no such thing as a perfect pay system or a perfect pay structure. Certainly there are general considerations to be taken into account and many of them have been considered here. But there is really no alternative to deciding what is appropriate in the particular circumstances.

The third point is no less basic than the others. As circumstances change, so do the pressures. In other words, a pay system or pay structure is not for ever. Systems and structures which may seem highly appropriate in one period can be highly inappropriate in the next when products and services have changed or when new operating systems and technologies have been introduced. These and other elements in the performance management system, then, need constant review and the expectation must be that they will require substantial change at frequent intervals.

Turning to working time, the case for a radical overall change does not depend on the Working Time Regulations implementing the EU directives, though they may be the catalyst. Rather the contribution that changes in working time arrangements can make to performance is the main consideration. In this respect, if they encourage UK management to take the management of working time more seriously, the Regulations may turn out to be a blessing in disguise. A reliance on a standard working week plus overtime is hardly appropriate in the ever-intensifying competitive environment: such arrangements are costly and encourage sloppy management as well as have significant health and safety implications.

Suggested further reading

More detailed treatment of the material in this chapter will be found in Arrowsmith and Sisson (2000) and Kessler (2000). For analysis of the implications of the Working Time Regulations 1998, see Hall *et al.* (1998). The various ACAS guides cited are the best source of practical advice.

6

IMPROVING COMPETENCES AND CAPABILITIES I:
Training and development

In this and the next chapter our focus is on the spectrum of activities aimed at improving the human capital within an organization. In the preface, the significance of context was emphasized. Of no activity in the management of employment relations is this more true than vocational training and development, which is the focus of this chapter. The ability of organizations to develop the skills and knowledge to do present and future jobs (which, roughly translated, is what training and development is about) is critically affected by wider national education systems. Especially important are: (1) the variations between national systems in the legal framework – statutory industrial training boards and levy/grant arrangements were experimented with in the UK in the 1960s and 1970s; (2) the fiscal system – possibilities here include remissible tax systems, such as in France, or credits for lifelong learning; (3) the processes and procedures for acquiring and legitimating qualifications; (4) the extent to which academic disciplines are favoured as opposed to job-related knowledge; and (5) the overall philosophy or approach. The critical consideration is the extent to which vocational training and development are seen as a voluntary, market-based operation with the

143

key decisions reflecting immediate organizational decisions, or as an activity which involves state intervention.

The UK, along with the USA, has generally been characterized by an extensive form of voluntarism. Vocational training and development have been deemed to be the responsibility of employer and employee. The state's role has largely been seen as one of encouragement and facilitation. Such a view reached its apogee under the Conservative governments of 1979–97. The industrial training boards set up in the 1960s were closed down and policy was set firmly against any form of compulsion or use of the tax system.

In practice, however, things have never been this clear-cut. Even under the Conservative governments there was never a total withdrawal by the state. In essence, government policy-makers have wanted to have their cake and eat it. The Treasury in particular has been reluctant for the state to assume greater responsibility for fear of having to meet the costs. At the same time, however, there has been a recognition that even less would happen if the government absented itself altogether. It is in this connection that the setting-up of the Training and Enterprise Councils (TECs) by the Conservative government in 1990 is best understood. The intention was that these should comprise local business interests, who would be given the responsibility of promoting training and development within their area, with a limited amount of government pump-priming. Sheer necessity coupled with cajoling would do the trick.

In any event, the essentially voluntarist approach, coupled with other features discussed in Chapter 1, has been a major consideration in what has generally been accepted to have been one of the worst records of major developed economies (Lane, 1990; Noble, 1997). There is also a demonstrable link between training and the wider issues of industrial relations. The nature of this connection has been effectively explored by Lane (1990). She reveals how the vocational and educational training (VET) system in Germany forms a pivotal role in the virtuous circle of high investment in training, effective utilization of advanced technology, high levels of skill, high wages but low unit costs, and high levels of competitiveness, especially at the premium end of the market. These in turn are all linked with functional flexibility and low levels of labour conflict.

Justifying investment in intangibles, which is what training and development are, is difficult at the best of times. It is difficult to prove the benefits and there is always the fear in an area such as training and development that it will be the employees who will benefit, rather than the organization that pays the bill, because the skills make them a more marketable commodity in a free labour market.

The vacuum that has existed in the UK has made things even worse by creating something of a vicious circle which is akin to what economists term 'the prisoner's dilemma'. People do know they should train; they know too that everyone will benefit, including themselves, if everyone invests in training and development so that the stock of human capital is higher. Yet they tend not to train because they are worried that other employers, instead of doing their share, will poach the employees they have trained. In the circumstances, with short-term financial results so paramount, it is easy to persuade themselves that training and development are something of a luxury. More pragmatically, if they find they are short of a particular set of skills, they try to get by the best they can by seeking to buy-in, poach, outsource or use temporary workers, all of which are usually much easier to justify in a crisis situation than the original investment in training and development. In the case of most occupations, employers in the UK are also operating in a relatively low pay economy. These circumstances constitute the recipe for the 'low-skills equilibrium' that commentators have come to associate with the UK's training and development record (see, for example, Keep and Mayhew, 1998).

Against this background, the present chapter presents the case for training and development in order to underline the changing importance now being attached to them. It then goes on to review a range of initiatives and innovations in training and development which offer pointers to what might be done by managers in their own organizations. The third section draws on the results of recent research to highlight the fundamental barriers to progress that remain in many organizations, arguing that these have to be faced and surmounted if learning is to become a key ingredient of competitiveness.

The case for training and development

Let us begin with the negatives. The alternatives to training and development are nowhere near as effective or efficient as they may appear to be in the short-term. The costs of recruitment and selection, as the next chapter shows, are considerable. A wrong selection decision can be especially costly. Some of the other possibilities such as subcontracting are equally fraught with problems. Externalizing the management of employment relations does not mean that the problem goes away, as Chapter 3 has pointed out. On the contrary, it simply means a different form of relationship. Those managers who do not feel confident enough to train or cannot be bothered to do so would do well to reflect on this. Are they going to be any better at recruiting and selecting or managing the 'extended organization'? The answer is almost certainly no.

A second point to bear in mind is that it is likely that those organizations looking to recruitment to solve their problems will find it difficult to secure enough people with the requisite skills. It is not just that, with relatively little training going on, the people who might have these skills are likely to be at an expensive premium. The distinction between general and specific skills also comes into play again. A belief in the superiority of the recruitment route over training ignores one critical factor. More and more it is specific skills that the organization needs rather than general ones. Increasingly, for example, training and development are also being seen as important in improving attitudes and approaches to tasks. Increasing realization of the importance of tacit skills knowledge ought to point clearly to the significance of learning and development.

Customer care and total quality management (TQM), which have been considered in Chapters 3 and 4, are good examples. In the 1980s, organizations such as British Airways and British Rail pioneered 'customer care' and 'customer first' campaigns to bring about shifts in employee attitudes as part of their marketing strategies. In the case of British Airways, for example, it was claimed that every member of its staff attended a two-day workshop devoted to raising awareness of the importance of the customer and what could be done to improve performance in this area. In the 1990s a number of organizations sought to bring about more wide-ranging shifts in culture through TQM programmes. Here government pressure, notably in the form of the Patient's Charter and the Citizen's Charter was important (see, for example, Rainbird, 1994: 354–6).

The third point also picks up the rapid changes that have been highlighted in previous chapters. Such is the pace of change, in markets, technology, operating systems and the like, that organizations find it increasingly costly not to attend to organizational learning. Few organizations can realistically hope to replace its workforce overnight and repeatedly. Arguably, the only real decision is the approach that is going to be adopted to training. At one extreme, consciously or unconsciously, the organization can try to get by, hoping people will somehow or other pick things up by 'sitting next to Nellie' in time-honoured fashion. The corollary is that this is not the most effective or efficient way of doing things from a management point of view. At the other extreme, organizations can recognize the reality of their position, that training is going to take place one way or another, and make efforts to ensure that it is as systematic and effective as possible.

Most fundamentally, training and development are the basic building blocks of the 'learning organization' which many commentators see as the real key to developing competitive advantage, reflecting a number of interlinking trends said to be driving change in the way that organizations in the developed world operate and compete. Thus, to paraphrase Keep and Rainbird (2000), it is argued that in the global marketplace organizations in developed countries can no longer compete solely or even mainly on the basis of price. Instead, they must offer a range of customized products and services. At the same time, change in product ranges is massive and rapid. Organizations are ceaselessly having to learn to do new things, offer new services and to reorganize fundamentally the way they deliver service to their customers, not least because product development leadtimes and life cycles are apparently becoming ever shorter (the example of personal computers and other consumer electronics is frequently used here).

In the face of these changes, the argument goes on, the only viable response for organizations who want to be successful is to seek to make best use of the skills and knowledge of their employees. Their skills, viewed collectively, form the organization's core competences. In order to develop and enhance these core organizational competences, organizations need to go beyond seeing training as individuals learning things. The goals are organizational learning, where the organization as an entity starts to develop ways in which it can learn lessons collectively, and the 'learning organization', where the central organizational goal is systemic learning. In Senge's (1990: 4) words, the learning organization is one 'where people continually expand their capacity to create the results they truly desire, where new and expansive patterns of thinking are nurtured, where collective aspiration is set free, and where people are continually learning to learn together' (see also Mabey et al., 1998a: 310–15). Figures 6.1 and 6.2 give some idea of what is involved.

The idea of the learning organization in its full-blown sense can easily be criticized as utopian, above all in a context such as the UK's. Yet it does draw attention to the role which skills, training and development policies can play within a broader strategic framework. In Keep and Rainbird's (2000: 175) words, 'Instead of training and skills being a bolt-on extra, learning moves to centre stage and becomes the chief organizational principle around which business strategy and competitive advantage can be developed.' It also serves as a warning. There is no doubt that some major organizations see organizational learning as a potential trump card; such is the scope in this area that even a small improvement in the status quo could make a significant difference.

This brings us to the fourth and related consideration. Following Keep (1989), there are strong grounds for contending that training and development deserve to be viewed as the vital component in managing employment relations. If the approach is largely based on the treatment of labour as a strategic and valued resource rather than merely a cost, then it would seem to follow that training and development would offer the surest expression of the investment in, and nurturing of, that resource. Managerial commitment to training is significant, for example, in its symbolic value. Where managers fail to train they send a message which suggests that labour is easily dispensed with and of little value.

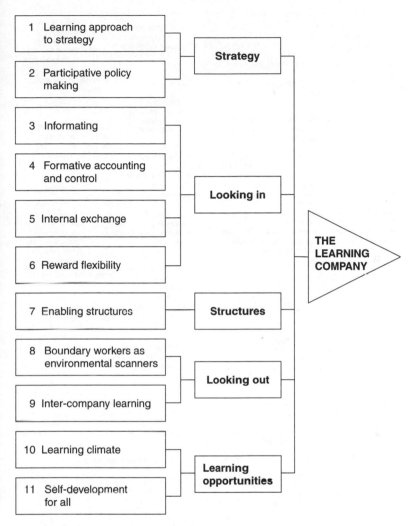

Figure 6.1 The blueprint of the learning organization
Source: Pedlar *et al.* (1991)

Where significant training is undertaken, it indicates a commitment to people and the recipients are more likely to feel valued.
Depending on its nature and extent, training may also signal the
choice of a value-added business strategy in place of a lowest-cost

The realities of human resource management

Company regularly takes stock and modifies direction and strategy as appropriate.

Policy and strategy formation structured as learning processes.

All members of the company take part in policy and strategy formation.

Policies are significantly influenced by the views of stakeholders.

1 The learning approach to strategy

2 Participative policy making

Managerial acts seen as conscious experiments.

Business plans are evolved and modified as we go along.

Commitment to airing differences and working through conflicts.

Company policies reflect the values of all members, not just those of top management.

1.

Deliberate small-scale experiments and feedback loops are built into the planning process to enable continuous improvement.

Appraisal and career planning discussions often generate visions that contribute to strategy and policy.

2.

Information is used for understanding, not for reward or punishment.

Information technology is used to create databases and communication systems that help everyone understand what is going on.

Systems of accounting, budgeting and reporting are structured to assist learning.

Everyone feels part of a department or unit responsible for its own resources.

3 Informating

4 Formative accounting and control

You can get feedback on how your section or department is doing at any time by pressing a button.

We really understand the nature and significance of variation in a system, and interpret data accordingly.

Accountants and finance people act as consultants and advisers *as well as* score-keepers and 'bean counters'.

Control systems are designed and run to delight their customers.

3.

Information technology is used to create databases, information and communication systems that help everyone to understand what is going on and to make sound decisions.

The financial system encourages departments and individuals to take risks with venture capital.

4.

Departments see each other as customers and suppliers, discuss and come to agreements on quality, cost, delivery.

Each department strives to delight its internal customers *and* remains aware of the needs of the company as a whole.

The basic assumptions and values underpinning reward systems are explored and shared.

The nature of 'reward' is examined in depth.

5 Internal exchange

6 Reward flexibility

Managers facilitate communication, negotiation and contracting, rather than exerting top-down control.

Alternative reward systems are examined, discussed, tried out.

6.

Departments speak freely and candidly with each other, both to challenge and to give help.

Departments, sections and units are able to act on their own initiatives.

5.

Flexible working patterns allow people to make different contributions and draw different rewards.

We are all involved in determining the nature and shape of reward systems.

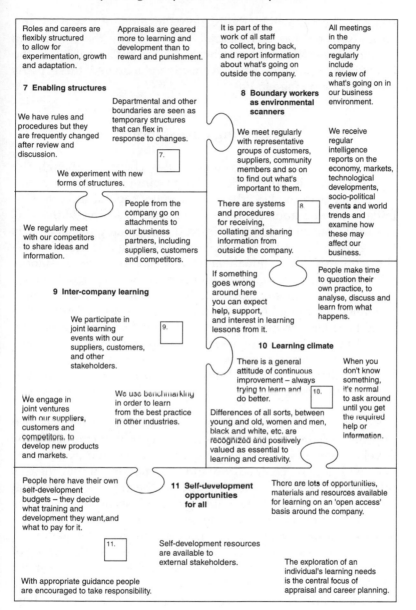

Figure 6.2 The learning organization profile
Source: Pedlar *et al.* (1991)

strategy. The research by the National Institute of Economic and Social Research has demonstrated very clearly the contrasting conditions, possibilities and consequences in Germany and the UK where companies have respectively followed these paths (Steedman and Wagner, 1987).

A training renaissance?

As we argued at the beginning of this chapter, although the national scene is not particularly propitious for training and development in the UK, there are certain hopeful indicators of initiatives being pursued. Indeed, the chief executive of the TEC National Council has even claimed that a training renaissance is taking place in the UK (Humphries, 1997). Paradoxically, recession and resultant rationalization have in some circumstances acted as catalysts for change which have had repercussions on training and development. Reductions in manpower have prompted the recombining of jobs in various ways. Craft differences have been reduced. Balanced labour force initiatives have sought to compensate for shortages in one craft area with surpluses in another; teamworking has led to a certain amount of interchangeability and flexibility; there has even been a diminished distinction between blue- and white-collar jobs especially at technician level.

Recession apart, increased international competition has also impelled certain changes which carry implications for employee development. New technology has often been introduced to keep pace with foreign competition and this may mean that there is little option other than to embark on the training of existing employees. In addition, the shifting of the basis of competition to areas of quality in product and service delivery has meant an increased need to train staff in customer care and total quality.

Several of these themes come through in the first IPD survey of training carried out in conjunction with the Centre for Labour Market Studies at Leicester University (see Cannell *et al.*, 1999). Using the budgets of training departments as a measure of how much money is going into the activity, it would seem that the size of investment in developing the workforce has been 'seriously underestimated'. Furthermore, the traditional view that expenditure on training declines during a downturn was challenged: over 40 per cent of respondents thought that spending on training would increase over the next twelve months, with most expecting it to stay the same. Importantly, too, linking training to business strategy had become a commonplace, with more than 60 per cent using an analysis of the business plan to identify training needs and a similar number having a training audit.

Further scope for optimism comes from the findings from a recent large, representative national survey management development in 904 organizations covering all the main industry groups and employment sizes. The survey was conducted by the Open University Business School in conjunction with the Department for Education and Employment (DfEE) and the Management Charter Initiative (Storey, 1997; Thomson *et al.*, 1997). Ten years previously the state of management development in the UK had been roundly condemned in a string of influential reports (Mangham and Silver, 1986; Constable and McCormick, 1987; Handy, 1987). When compared with its major industrial competitor countries, UK management training and development had been judged as typically 'too little, too late for too few'. However, the findings from the 1997 Open University Business School survey suggested that management training and development is now in a more robust state. The priority given to management development by top teams in the late 1990s was much higher and the amount of training and development provided had also increased. Many of the major targets set by the reports in 1987 had been met: the amount of training offered to managers had increased and the expansion in the number of MBA graduates had been achieved. By 1997, only 4 per cent of larger companies reported doing no training – compared with a situation ten years previously when, according to Constable and McCormick, 'somewhat over half of all UK companies appear to make no formal provision for the training of managers'. One of the significant findings was that the move towards a more rounded approach to management development went with a more balanced apportionment of responsibility between the organization and the individual. In sum, at least in so far as training and development provision for managers is concerned, this is a success story of some magnitude.

As well as the above, another domain of development has been the government-sponsored initiatives on the basis of which many of the organizational activities are taking place. Key areas are modern apprenticeships, National Vocational Qualifications (NVQs), lifelong learning and Investors in People. These are the focus of the following discussion.

Modern apprenticeships

The training of young workers in the UK has traditionally been associated with the craft apprenticeship system. Typically, this was exclusive and time-served. This meant that in the industries in which it predominated, notably construction, engineering and printing, if young workers did not gain access in their teens they were more-or-less condemned to semi-skilled or unskilled status for the rest of their lives. There was also no guarantee that even the privileged few had achieved any objective level of skill – it was enough to have served one's time. In the industries without such arrangements, i.e. the great majority, this meant that there was little or no training available at all. Young workers simply picked things up rather haphazardly as they worked. This was above all true of the private service sector where, outside the banks and one or two of the large retailers, the vast majority of young people entering employment were offered little in the way of structured job training.

Although there has been a dramatic drop in the number of apprenticeships in recent years, there have been radical changes in the arrangements in the form of the modern apprenticeships announced by the Conservative government in 1993. This initiative seeks to revive and improve apprenticeship training in traditional sectors and extend it to new sectors of the economy. The initiative offers a relatively high quality work-based education and training route (Maguire, 1999). Modern apprenticeships share some features with those of the traditional kind but they also have some distinct new features (Gospel and Fuller, 1998). They are similar in the following ways:

1 The rights and obligations of the employer and employee are formalized in a contract or agreement.

2 Periods of off-the-job training alternate with productive work.
3 The costs of training are to some degree shared between the employer and apprentice – the employer agrees to furnish skills training while the apprentice works for a lower wage rate than a qualified worker until the training period is completed.

There are also some differences:

1 Modern apprenticeships divide the costs between three parties because the state offers a subsidy for the off-the-job training component.
2 There is some external monitoring and accountability carried out by Training and Enterprise Councils.
3 The modern apprenticeships cover a wider range of occupations.
4 The curriculum of a modern apprenticeship is written down in an industry framework document designed to ensure consistency and adequate attainment.
5 Attainment is not based on a time-serving but the acquisition of competence-based National Vocational Qualifications level 3.
6 The scheme was initiated by government though with employer involvement in design and delivery.

In the words of a recent report:

> The programme takes the best of the old apprenticeship tradition and builds on it – in particular by providing public subsidies to help employers meet the costs of training, by setting minimum standards, and by linking the apprenticeships to national qualifications. Participating employers report that these apprenticeships now represent an important part of their skills strategy and are raising the quality and quantity of their training efforts. They seem too to be helping them recruit better quality people.
>
> (IRS, 1999b: 16)

Various evaluations of the scheme have reported positive results and responses (for example, Ernst and Young, 1995; Saunders, 1997). A more balanced assessment is made by Gospel and Fuller (1998). These latter commentators acknowledge the strengths of the modern apprenticeship scheme (higher standards than hitherto; a mixed balance of work and training; employed status), they also point out the weaknesses: uncertainty about the attained level of skill between and even within sectors; concerns about the emphasis on competence and whether this neglects real theoretical understanding; concerns about high standards will be maintained by the various stakeholders; concerns about sufficient numbers – especially on the demand side. On balance, the initiative is welcomed but there are worries about whether the institutional support (for example from industry bodies) is adequate in the UK and about whether beyond a finite number of enlightened firms who think about training in strategic terms, employers are sufficiently prepared to see the initiative really take off and become secure.

Altogether, 250,000 young people have been involved in the scheme, which was formally launched in 1995, with nearly 130,000 participating in early 1999. Evidently, the number remains small as does the number of employers involved. Significantly, however, the arrangements have not simply taken root in manufacturing, where there is a longstanding apprenticeship tradition. Sectors such as finance and catering are also involved.

Also important to note is that a combination of changes in educational provision and employers' demand for young workers has contributed to a decline in the proportion of 16 year olds entering the work force from 62 per cent in 1975 to only 9 per cent in 1992. The number remaining in full-time education beyond the age of 16 has increased substantially: by 1994–95, 72 per cent of 16-year-olds and 59 per cent of 17-year-olds were in full-time education (IPD, 1997c: 50).

National Vocational Qualifications

Like modern apprenticeships, National Vocational Qualifications (NVQs), together with their Scottish equivalents, date back to the Conservative governments of the mid-1980s. They were intended to help deal with some of the major weaknesses of the UK's VET infrastructure by introducing a wide range of employer-led and workplace-based training qualifications with national accreditation and some government funding. One of the main aims was to promote the training and development of all groups and not just the young. Altogether, there are five levels of NVQ, ranging from the least complex jobs (level 1) to those requiring great responsibility and autonomy as in the case of many management positions (level 5).

Initially, the arrangements met with considerable criticism, not in the least because of the language and bureaucracy involved. Many of these problems have been addressed in a series of modifications. Most significantly, successive governments, Conservative and Labour, have stuck with the core principles, which is relatively rare in the history of UK training and development initiatives. The result is that the arrangements have been given time to bed in.

A recent report (IRS, 1999a: 8), for example, observes that the two millionth NVQ has just been awarded – less than three years after the one millionth – and that at any one time some 800,000 people are working towards a qualification. Awareness of NVQs among employers is high and nearly one in four currently offer employees the opportunity to gain the qualification.

We are aware of many instances where the possibility of obtaining NVQs, often accompanied with the pursuit of Investors in People (discussed below), has been an important catalyst for training and development. At Warners Holidays leisure complex on Hayling Island, for example, around half of the 140 employees have either gained a qualification or are working towards one. In the words of the head chef:

> We used to go through the motions of training people . . . Now the company is making serious efforts to improve things. It has made me more determined to stay here.
>
> (Quoted in Merrick, 1998)

In the same vein, one of the room attendants, who has gained a level 1 NVQ in housekeeping, made the following point:

> Before it was a dead-end job. People simply came in, worked and went home . . . Now NVQs are keeping me here. They've given us all something to work for.
>
> (ibid.)

In another case, Clamason Industries, a medium-sized family-owned business producing high precision metal pressings in the

West Midlands, a training and development initiative involving NVQs is seen as a critical factor in a successful turnaround (Chadda, 1999). NVQ opportunities are available to everyone and nearly half of the 180-strong workforce have or are taking advantage. Especially significant in the turnaround is seen to be the leadership training of supervisors and top managers. In the case of the supervisors, who have had their jobs dramatically changed by de-layering and the introduction of teamworking, the training has enabled NVQ level 4 to be achieved at the same time as the shift in their role to be absorbed.

Lifelong learning

Storey and Sisson (1993: 162–3) suggested that there had been significant innovations in the provision of wider training and development opportunities through open and distance learning activities which are not immediately job-related. Organizations launching major initiatives included BT, Ford, Jaguar, Rover, Kodak, Lucas and Midland Bank.

One of the pioneering open learning schemes was Ford's Employee Development and Assistance Programme (EDAP) launched in 1989. This allowed employees to qualify for grants of up to £200 per annum for personal development activities (Hougham et al., 1991). In the words of the brochure introducing the scheme to Ford employees, 'EDAP is a joint union–management initiative aimed at developing Ford's most precious asset – people. Not just to improve their career prospects – though it can certainly help – but to make the most of them as individuals.' EDAP continues to offer every Ford employee a wide range of courses and other opportunities for personal and career enhancement, ranging from Open University degree funding to assistance with health-related programmes. Grants are decided, notably, by a joint union–management committee at each Ford location. EDAP-backed courses are voluntary and take place outside working hours. It was anticipated that relatively few individuals would take up the opportunity. In the event, the numbers exploded and more than half of the approximately 40,000 employees had taken part within a short time (for further details see Hougham et al., 1991).

The theme of continuous training and development has become more important as the pace of change has quickened and it has become increasingly accepted that the prospects of further and ongoing restructuring will be the norm rather than the exception. Throughout OECD and EU countries, training and development have assumed a new significance. They are seen as important not only in enabling employees to do their present and future jobs within the organization, but also in enabling them to be more employable, i.e. to adapt to employment opportunities elsewhere, should their services no longer be required (CEC, 1998).

In the UK, this thinking is reflected in the publication of a major policy Green Paper early in 1998, *The Learning Age*. Proposals include a developing programme for lifelong learning, a University for Industry and an entitlement to learning credits to help individuals with their vocational development. During the fiscal year 1989/99, the government was committed to opening 'one million individual learning accounts targeted at different parts of the labour market and different needs' (interview with the Secretary of State reported in MacLachan, 1998: 42).

Investors in People

Investors in People (IiP) is a national training standard. It was introduced in the wake of the Training in Britain survey of 1989, which had raised yet again major concerns about the nature and the extent of the training taken place in the UK. Reflecting these findings, the standard is administered by Investors in People, UK and funded, via the Training and Enterprise Councils, by the Department for Education and Employment. It consists of 23 indicators used to assess an organization's training performance grouped together under four principles which are shown in Figure 6.3.

Adams provides us with a useful summary of its modus operandi:

An initial diagnosis can be requested from a TEC-nominated adviser: this provides an action plan. To work towards Investors, the chief executive issues a written 'commitment' to implement the plan. A portfolio of evidence is collected by

---

Principle 1: Commitment
An Investor in People makes a commitment from the top to develop all employees to achieve its business objectives.

Principle 2: Planning
An Investor in People regularly reviews the needs and plans the training and development of all employees.

Principle 3: Action
An Investor in People takes action to train and develop individuals on recruitment and throughout their employment.

Principle 4: Evaluation
An Investor in People evaluates the investment in training to assess achievement and to improve future effectiveness.

Figure 6.3 The Investors in People principles

the organization when it is ready for assessment; assessors visit the organization, assess the evidence and interview a cross-section of employees. If the assessor is satisfied, the employer's case is discussed by a local Investor's panel and it is either 'recognised' as having achieved the standard or further improvements are requested. Recognition lasts for three years. Employers receive a plaque and permission to use the Investors logo on corporate literature.

(IRS, 1996b: 12)

IiP bears all the hallmarks of the times. The system is voluntary, but there is a strong expectation that 'good' management will sign up. There is a reliance on the process of benchmarking of 'best practice' to establish standards and the pressure to introduce a simple disciplinary framework, subject to scrutiny, to help ensure that the organization does not deviate too much from the path of righteousness. Public accreditation, in the form of a kite mark, is available, which can be used to present the organization in a good light to present and prospective employees.

Clearly the success of the initiative very much depended on the take-up. The ambitious target was set of achieving IiP accreditation by 70 per cent or more of organizations with 200 or more employees and 35 per cent of those with 50 or more by the year

2000. In total, this meant some 13,000 organizations with 50 or more employees. Initially, take-up was very slow: by the middle of 1996, scarcely 10 per cent of organizations had achieved the target. By the end of 1998, however, some 11,301 had reached it (Arkin, 1999) – still some way short of the original target, but a considerable achievement in the light of the slow start. Moreover, there is evidence to suggest that some organizations, although not signing up for the formal process, have nonetheless adopted the good practice laid down in IiP.

Research suggests that it has been very difficult for organizations to establish a clear-cut relationship between achieving the IiP standard and improvements in the bottom line, although many feel that it has made a significant difference (see, for example, IRS, 1996b). More definite are the views about the links with intermediate objectives such as improving customer service, employee understanding of the organization's objectives and employee motivation more generally. One recent poll of 600 organizations found that employees in IiP organizations were much more likely to feel valued and see better promotion prospects compared with those working in non-IiP organizations (reported in Pandya, 1999). Perhaps most fundamentally, however, IiP has not only made managers more aware of the importance of training, but also encouraged them to develop a more systematic approach. Ruth Spelman, the chief executive, is reported as saying that, contrary to expectations, IiP is 'not about spending more on budgets for training. Rather it is a mechanism for assessing whether or not an organization's training fits its business needs' (Pandya, 1999).

Our own view is that organizations which are seeking to improve their performance in managing employment relations have to have a very good reason for not signing up for IiP. In the context of the UK's voluntarist training system, it offers precisely the kind of disciplinary framework that is needed to push back the pressures of short-termism.

Continuing problems?

Despite these developments, it would be remiss of us not to point out that some of the old, fundamental barriers to training and development remain even today. Sooner or later these will have to be addressed if organizations are to use learning as a key ingredient in improving competitiveness.

Work organization, employment relations and competitive strategies

In a hard-hitting critique of the potential of the learning organization, Keep and Rainbird (2000: 183) quote the remarks of Pevoto (1997: 212–13), reviewing another 'quick fix cook book' on the learning organization:

> I keep asking myself why was this book written? What the world doesn't need is one more 'quick fix' book, or one more 'cook book' for how to make the organization and its people work better. We have hundreds of those littering the shelves of authors, professors and libraries. I was reminded of the story of the farmer and the agricultural agent wherein the agricultural agent suggested the farmer attended a seminar on new farming methods, and the farmer replied, 'Why, I'm not farming now as well as I know how to'. The same could be said of organizations. Most are not managed or led now as well as people know how to.

Keep and Rainbird go on to point out that, on the evidence supplied by the Skills Survey (Green *et al.*, 1997), underemployment and underutilization of existing qualifications held by employees may also be a reality for a substantial proportion of workers. The survey suggested that 32 per cent of degree holders believed themselves to be in jobs that did not require this qualification, 30.6 per cent of holders of sub-degree qualifications felt they were overqualified for their current jobs, and 22.4 per cent of workers with qualifications were in jobs where no qualification whatsoever was required.

As research by Dench *et al.* (1998) has illustrated, despite the textbook models of worker empowerment and the demands by some employers for workers with better skills in communication, problem-solving and creativity, in reality in many organizations 'the generally low level of autonomy allowed to employees especially in non-managerial roles and in less skilled jobs was a theme emerging from many of our in-depth interviews' (p. 58). Far from wanting self-monitoring, problem-solving innovators, Dench *et al.* conclude that 'in reality most employers simply want people to get on with their job, and not to challenge things' (p. 61). In these organizations it continues to be the case that managers undertake the planning, thinking, design and decision-making elements of work, while the non-managerial workforce get on with following tightly defined procedures and taking orders from above. The scope for real organizational learning (and for the learning to be utilized productively) at all levels in the workforce is thus severely limited.

Given the choice between trying to get employees to work harder and longer or to get them to do more by working in smarter ways, say Keep and Rainbird, the evidence suggests that many (perhaps most) UK organizations appear to prefer the tried-and-tested route of increasing working hours (as also indicated in the previous chapter). Evidently, as well as the many other problems that they bring, long working hours make it more difficult for staff to find the time and energy to learn (the more so in organizations where the current norm is for more and more learning to be undertaken in the employee's own time rather than during working hours).

The point, as Keep and Mayhew (1998a: 42) remind us, is that the problem is not so much inadequate education and vocational training, but the 'inevitable consequence of being in a low skills, low spec environment'. The notion that a set of universalistic trends and competitive pressures are impelling organizations towards competition based on organizational learning, they suggest, is seriously flawed. Alternative avenues to competitive advantage remain viable in the UK, and price-based competition continues to thrive – above all in the service sector. Far from opting for the high skills route to competitive success, many organizations remain wedded to standardized, low specification goods and services where the main factor of competitive advantage is consistent delivery of relatively simple goods and services to a low price (see also Foundation for Manufacturing Industry/DTI/IBM, 1996; Ackroyd and Procter, 1998). This is in turn reflected in Tayloristic forms of work organization that minimize the opportunities for creativity and discretion. In short, training and development are a problem of demand not of supply. Many organizations have to change their product market strategies before the UK can become a high pay, high skill and high productivity economy.

The role of management

A fundamental problem often articulated by managers is that they cannot afford to commit significant resources to training because of the constant pressure from corporate or divisional level to show healthy financial results. As pointed out by Storey and Sisson (1993: 168–70), the evidence available at the beginning of the 1990s suggested that it was not so obvious that UK companies were as out of line with their international competitors in terms of training expenditure as once was thought. Our own research into how managers were made in Japan and the UK showed that Japanese companies which are known to provide exemplary training to their employees often recorded very low levels of overt expenditure on the training function (Storey *et al.*, 1997a).

Reflecting the situation described above and in Chapter 1, the reality is that in many organizations in the UK training and development are treated as a peripheral and low-level non-strategic activity not fully integrated into everyday practice. Managers and supervisors have not as yet as a matter of routine been inculcated with the Japanese practice of regarding staff development as one of their priority agenda items.

Rarely is it the case in UK companies that the extent to which a manager develops his or her own immediate staff is regarded as the critical measure of how well that manager is doing the job. Yet in our research comparing British and Japanese managers we found that the Japanese tended to place subordinate development as one of the highest priorities when defining the nature of the managerial role (Storey *et al.*, 1997a). In contrast, UK managers would much more readily point to the need to be seen to be shouldering 'responsibility' and meeting financial and production targets as the essence of their job.

An outcome of this basic difference in the understanding of what it means to be a manager is to be found also in performance appraisal criteria and evaluation systems in the UK. At best there is token and subsidiary reference to staff development in the evaluative systems used; often this facet of managerial work is simply omitted altogether. Under such circumstances it is of little wonder that training and development are in practice given low priority and regarded as peripheral.

Supervisors and staff themselves rarely act as a constituency to complain about this. On the contrary, they are far more likely to be complicit in the process. Reading the signs about 'what counts', ordinary members of staff routinely declare themselves 'too busy' to be trained. Their supervisors and departmental line managers resist attempts to take any of their staff away from normal duties. Here one witnesses the real, measured priorities asserting themselves at all levels throughout the organization.

Ironically, when, begrudgingly, training does take place, because it has been pared and timed to cause minimal disruption, the resulting experience is often unsatisfactory. Trainees at first-line management level, for example, will rightly observe that the training has come too late, or that it insufficiently targets their specific needs. These problems are not purely technical failings of the kind the prescriptive texts warn about. On the contrary, they are logical outcomes of the endemic training problems in the UK of the kind outlined in this section. The poor training record is an integral feature of the HR/IR context described in this book. Most of the voluminous prescriptive training literature is abjectly neglectful of this reality. It is little wonder therefore that its impact has been so marginal. In Keep and Rainbird's (2000: 191) words,

A fundamental point concerns conceptions of the managerial task. For as long as managers in the UK see themselves primarily as doers, fire-fighters or as 'Action Man'/'Woman' rather than as reflective practitioners the scope for wide-reaching and permanent organizational change will remain limited. If learning at a fundamental and deep level is not at the heart of what it means to be a successful manager, it seems highly unlikely that organizational learning will easily take root within the organizations which these individuals manage and lead.

Relevant here is the way managers are themselves 'made'. Our own Anglo-Japanese comparison (Storey *et al.*, 1997a) suggested

165

that British managers were more likely to encounter a deep-seated preconception that people either 'have what it takes' or they do not. In consequence, a certain sink-or-swim philosophy was allowed to prevail. A corollary was the emphasis placed on being exposed to responsible positions at an early age for a select few. The assumed power of this practice finds support in current conventional wisdom in Western management development literature (for example, Margerison and Kakabadse, 1985). What it neglects, however, is the often happenchance nature of the process. Those given such early challenges often just happened, as our respondents admitted, to be 'in the right place at the right time'. The corollary of this lack of planning is that large numbers of an equally talented cohort become disillusioned and key talents are lost to the company as those left out leave to look for opportunities elsewhere.

In contrast, the Japanese organizations in the study were far more likely to give weight to the importance of continuous development for the whole cohort of entrants over a prolonged period of years. Continuous adjustments might be made but the system remained essentially intact and known to all. The notable feature in the UK, by contrast, was the propensity to vacillate. New programmes and initiatives were launched and old ones swept away almost in their entirety. There were two damaging consequences: managers at all levels saw little point in committing themselves too heavily to a prevailing system because it was thought likely to be temporary; second, there was little inclination to invest time in learning about the current pattern of provision and so British managers (especially those out in the divisions away from corporate HQ) were often remarkably unclear about what training packages and related development devices were available. Sometimes the centrally provided core courses were of the highest world standards but their promulgation often left a lot to be desired.

Fortunately most clouds seem to have some silver lining. One factor is the de-layering of management levels discussed in Chapter 3. The 'action' manager who has been the dominant role model in British management is beginning to disappear – organizations simply cannot afford to employ managers to do or to control what other people are supposed to be doing. A second is the training and development which managers are receiving themselves. This increasingly emphasizes the limitations of the traditional role and the need for managers to become 'enablers', 'facilitators' and 'developers' rather than doers. The missing link in many organizations is the structure of rewards to make this kind of thinking stick.

Conclusions

Although to talk in terms of a renaissance is perhaps going too far, not everything is gloom and doom in training and development. Especially significant is that, at long last, the UK appears to be getting some of the training and development infrastructure that it has so sadly lacked. The modern apprenticeships, NVQs, IiP programme (with the prospect of provisions for lifelong learning to come) are beginning to look like a credible system. Given further teeth by government, more about which in Chapter 10, it could help to deal with the 'market failures' identified at the beginning of the chapter. There are also a number of significant initiatives being attempted at organizational level, *especially* in the area of management development. Crucially, these initiatives suggest that managers do have some measure of 'strategic choice'. Moreover, much that can be done does not involve significant expenditure. Rather it requires rethinking the role of management. Managers have to be encouraged by their own appraisal and reward systems to treat training and development as priority items. Also important is the need for a wider appreciation of the fact that organizations have to change their product market strategies before the UK can become a high pay, high skill and high productivity economy.

Suggested further reading

For more details of the management of learning, see Mabey *et al.* (1998a, chs 5 and 10–12). For management development, see Storey *et al.* (1997a,b) . For a critical review of training developments, see Keep and Rainbird (2000).

7

IMPROVING COMPETENCES AND CAPABILITIES II:
Recruitment and selection

It might be thought that the subject matter of this chapter, traditionally seen as the stock-in-trade of personnel managers, was out of place in a book primarily concerned with raising and examining issues needing to be high on the agenda of managers concerned with the strategic direction of their organizations. However, ensuring that the right people are in the right place at the right time is a critical factor in gaining and maintaining competitive advantage. Moreover, as IRS (1997a: 11) *Employee Development Bulletin* reminds us, 'recruitment and selection are not cheap exercises' (see also ACAS 1997e,f).

The Institute of Personnel and Development (IPD) produces regular information on the costs of recruitment and selection. The latest available estimates are shown in Table 7.1. If anything, however, these figures, substantial though they may seem, underestimate the costs involved. A more extensive list has been produced by the Institute of Employment Studies (IES) including temporary replacement costs (for further details, see Bevan *et al.*, 1997). In a 350-bed hospital employing 700 nurses, for example, IES found that 7.1 per cent of the annual paybill was spent purely on replacing the roughly one-fifth of nurses who left every year. It estimates

Table 7.1 The costs of turnover

Occupational group	Median cost per person £	No. of respondents
Management/administration	5008	398
Professional	4861	341
Associated professional/technical	3671	411
Clerical/secretarial	1746	400
Craft/skilled	1652	228
Sales	3640	237
Operatives and assembly	1456	199
Routine unskilled	735	250

Respondents selected the appropriate cost bands from a range provided in respect of leaving administration, replacement (recruitment, interviewing, placement fees); transition (training, unproductive learning time, induction); and indirect (loss in customer service).
Source: IPD (1997c).

that the average costs involved were £4900 per head (Seccombe and Smith, 1997). Nor is this an extreme case. The publicly funded Skill Needs in Britain Survey (IRS, 1997a) calculated that a labour turnover of 20 per cent was around the national average among organizations with more than 25 employees in 1996–97.

Another graphic example given in the same *Employee Development Bulletin* article relates to public houses (IRS, 1997a). The British Institute of Innkeeping is reported as estimating that labour turnover costs the industry £160 million a year, necessitating the recruitment of 600 employees a week as direct replacements for leavers. The Institute's director is quoted as saying that 'We have to sell 220 million pints of beer – or 3500 pints per pub – just to pay for the people who *don't* want to work for us.'

The context for these and similar statements was set by the growing evidence of skill shortages throughout 1998 as unemployment fell to its lowest level in 17 years and below the level recorded during the last skills crisis in the late 1980s. The Bank of England and the new Monetary Policy Committee especially became worried that the labour market was overheating, with adverse implications for the rate of inflation which they now had the responsibility for keeping in check. Numerous examples were quoted of particular shortages, even in sectors such as engineering which were suffering reductions in orders as the result of the high value of the pound.

In the event, there was some easing of the pressure as the world economy began to slow down throughout 1998. Yet worries about skills shortages, and the associated high turnover rates, were a timely reminder of the importance not only of reducing labour turnover but also of getting recruitment and selection right first time.

Against this background, this chapter is structured in two main sections. The first discusses in a novel way a number of the issues involved in recruitment which rarely, if ever, receive the attention they deserve in traditional textbooks. The second critically reviews developments in selection and the ways in which management performance in this key activity can be improved.

Recruitment

An organization has just two sources of labour supply – the internal and the external labour market. Recruitment internally has typically involved word-of-mouth recommendation or the copying of some of the methods used in recruiting externally, for example, noticeboard advertisements. More recently, appraisals, career development reviews and assessment centres are providing much of the information on which decisions are made. Recruitment in the external labour market involves a variety of methods: advertising, employment agencies and job centres, registers, selection consultants, introductions by existing staff, people who have left the organization, people who applied on previous occasions and casual callers and respondents.

As Chapter 2 has emphasized, ensuring that the right people are in place at the right time and minimizing the need for recruitment requires planning. In the case of groups of employees, this means applying some of the techniques of human resource planning (HRP). In the case of individual employees, the equivalent is known as succession planning.

In practice, there is a substantial body of evidence to suggest that, typically, UK organizations have relied on traditional sources of recruitment without questioning whether or not they continue to be appropriate. In some cases there may be very little option. This is especially the case, for example, where a job requires a statutory recognized qualification. In the majority of cases, however, there is greater choice than has commonly been accepted.

One of the best illustrations of these points comes from the reaction of British management to the implications of the so-called demographic timebomb in the late 1980s. Most large employers such as the banks, the civil service and telecommunications had traditionally relied upon recruitment from school-leavers. But this source of supply was forecast to diminish rapidly. The total number of under 25-year-olds in the labour force was projected to decline by 1 million between 1990 and the year 2000. In fact, these figures on the shrinking size of the age group understated the degree of change. Because of the greater numbers of young people going into higher and further education, the proportion available for employment would be even smaller.

In the event, while some organizations such as the major retailers and the NHS showed considerable imagination, less than one-third of the 2000 organizations surveyed in 1989 seriously considered looking at alternative sources of recruitment such as women returners or workers over 50. Even a smaller proportion, less than 20 per cent, were prepared to consider the unemployed (NEDO/Training Agency, 1989). Fewer still considered radical changes in the existing working arrangements or provisions for retraining to help deal with the problem. This was above all true of manufacturing companies. For the great majority, the preferred solution seemed to be to seek to compete rather than adapt. That is to say, to pay their way out of trouble, i.e. try to compete more effectively for the dwindling pool of young people. Not surprisingly there were considerable fears of a wages spiral.

Other research confirmed that the approach of most organizations had been tactical rather than strategic.

Firms' responses to shortage . . . tend to be sequential, introduced only slowly as the full seriousness of the shortage problem become apparent to firms. They tend to be hierarchical, with more difficult/expensive responses deployed only when easier/cheaper ones have proved inadequate .

(Atkinson, 1989: 22)

As Figure 7.1 shows, the initial reaction was to 'take it on the chin', responding passively in the hope that something would turn up. In a second stage, when the first stage did not appear to be working, organizations began to compete more effectively for the same group of labour. Only the third and fourth stages involved strategic responses such as seeking alternative supplies of labour such as older workers and restructuring existing working arrangements. Very few managements, anticipating the results of the NEDO study, had progressed to these stages, however; and even then they had only done so by working through the other stages rather than thinking through the most appropriate solution for their own circumstances.

Stemming the flow

It is the obvious thing to say, but cutting down on turnover is the most effective way of dealing with the problem of recruitment. In an IRS survey, so-called natural wastage was the most commonly

	Tactical	
On the chin		*Compete*
Do nothing		Intensify recruitment efforts
Allow hiring standards to decline		Schools liaison
Work overtime		Increase pay
Demand side		**Supply side**
Create		*Substitute*
Training		Recruit and retain older workers
Improved development		Reduce wastage
	Strategic	

Figure 7.1 Four types of response to labour shortages
Source: Atkinson (1989: 23)

cited reason (56 per cent) for skills shortages (IRS, 1998b). Around one-third (34 per cent) of respondents also mentioned poaching by other employers, adding to the sum total of the flow from the organization.

It may be that the organization needs to adapt recruitment and retention policies in one or more of the ways suggested in an ACAS guide *Recruitment Policies for the 1990s* (ACAS, 1997a). As well as seeking to attract and retain the growing number of over-25s in the labour force, especially women, and compete more effectively for young people, organizations are recommended to consider:

1 Improving training
2 Improving job design
3 Ensuring pay rates are competitive
4 Developing equal opportunities policies
5 Introducing flexible working patterns such as part-time work and job-sharing
6 Introducing arrangements for child care
7 Introducing career breaks
8 Improving links with local schools and colleges
9 Reviewing entry requirements and qualifications.

Improving induction, so often neglected in many organizations, can make a significant difference. This has been the experience of Virgin Our Price, for example. Following the merger of Virgin Megastores and Our Price in 1994, management found itself confronted by staff turnover figures which suggested that around one-quarter of non-management employees were leaving within the first six months of employment. A revamped induction programme, offering structured training for the first three months linked to a two-year learning programme and a 10 per cent pay increase at the end of the first year is reported to have resulted in a dramatic fall in turnover among new recruits from around 20 per cent to 2.5 per cent (for further details, see IRS, 1998j; for further details of how to handle induction, see ACAS, 1997f; IRS, 1998k).

Sadly, too few organizations take these kinds of initiative largely because of the implications of the wider context discussed in Chapter 1. In the words of Roncoroni (1998), the managing director of the L&R consulting group,

The trap that most businesses fall into is that they worry only about managing costs, not about creating value. Typically, they use crude measures such as headcount, and put in short-sighted restrictions.

Roncoroni quotes a hotel reservations company employing around 200 agents with a staff turnover of more than one-third every six months. Grade 1 agents brought in on average £700,000 per annum more than a new starter. Yet under the system of per-formance grades, it took two years to reach grade 1 and only about 13 per cent of new recruits ever made it. He observes,

> Just suppose the company could increase the number of people reaching grade 1 to 40 per cent, and cut the number of people in grade 4 to 10 per cent. That could potentially add anywhere from £10 million to £17 million a year in additional revenue – the equivalent of adding up to seven weeks of sell-ing at no extra cost.
>
> That's on top of the reduced recruitment and training costs, and the fact that team leaders could devote a lot more time to developing people instead of recruiting and running induc-tion programmes.

Being clear about needs

The perceived need to trigger the recruitment process may result from a variety of developments: retirement, resignation, dis-missal, plus changes in technology, procedures or markets. In these circumstances, there is a tendency to set the process in motion as soon as possible. It is sensible, however, to see such developments as an opportunity to review whether or not a new appointment is really necessary. This is not the same, it needs to be emphasized, as a freeze on replacement. Such a gesture at first sight appears very decisive. In our experience, however, recruit-ment freezes are often an excuse for saving money with little thought being given to the longer term. Other things being equal, it makes sense to start from a zero base.

A critical double-check is to draw up a definition of the job or specification of the person required. This is going to be necessary in any event if potential candidates are to have the information

- Job title and other identifying features
- Key tasks
- Purpose and objectives
- Relationships with others inside and outside the organization
- Performance standards to be met in undertaking tasks and achieving objectives
- Limits of authority over expenditure, working methods, sales, information, equipment and personnel matters
- Particular problems, difficulties, distasteful aspects and constraints
- Pay
- Hours and working conditions

Figure 7.2 The information required for job descriptions
Source: Watson (1994: 187)

with which to make a decision about applying. Critically important, however, is that it can help to minimize the excessive informality that pervades the process in many organizations. It can also mean that an initial decision to replace, for example, can be reversed in the knowledge that the position can be dealt with in another way.

Beginning with the job description, all of the information listed in Figure 7.2 will be required at some stage in the recruitment process, even if is not necessary for the advertising. The last point in Figure 7.2 may be more difficult: it will be useful not only to potential candidates but also in the process of review which is one of the continuing themes of the book. The other side of the coin, the person specification, has become more controversial as expectations in terms of equal opportunities have begun to bite. Originally, the two bases on which most prescriptive formulations were based, Rodger's (1970) Seven Point Plan and Fraser's (1971) Five-fold Framework, contained terms such as 'acceptability' and 'circumstances', both of which would be frowned on today because of their scope for infringing equal opportunities.

Recruitment should also be seen as an opportunity for more radical change. For example, Fowler (1999: 40), who was responsible for preparing the DfEE-sponsored publication, *Recruitment: Mind the Gap*, has suggested that organizations should ask the following two questions:

1 Would a change in the way that its products or services are delivered reduce the need to recruit people?
2 Could products or services be redesigned so that the requirement for scarce skills is reduced or eliminated?

Fowler makes the point that has been confirmed in research (see, for example, Hunter and MacInnes, 1991; Arrowsmith and Sisson, 1999) that working methods sometimes remain unchanged for years simply because 'this is the way things have always been done'. Changing the content of jobs and/or simplifying the product or service may avoid the need for recruitment altogether. At the very least, to emphasize one of the underlying messages of this book, asking the questions will make people think about the way they do things and how their methods might be improved.

Fowler also suggests that recruitment raises the opportunity to exploit the market. There could be tasks that could be contracted out to external providers to ease the recruitment problem. It may also be possible to buy-in standard components or off-the-shelf software packages to replace some activities.

Other possibilities which emerge from the IRS survey mentioned earlier include the employment of temporary workers, either in-house or from agencies (IRS, 1998b). It may be that the activity in question could be better done if it was 'externalized' in the form of being subcontracted. At the very least, some form of 'market testing' provides yet another opportunity to double-check whether or not the organization should realistically be seeking to do something in-house. Such market testing should not target only 'ancillary' workers either. Indeed, it makes most sense, above all for SMEs, to see if other, higher-status posts could be treated in the same way. This may include, as Chapter 9 shows in more detail, many of the activities traditionally associated with the specialist personnel function.

Making better use of the internal labour market

Another source to which organizations are encouraged to look is the internal labour market. Typically, an aspect of the unquestioning behaviour in many UK organizations is to think in terms of a very segmented or 'balkanized' internal labour in which, despite the rhetoric of flexibility, there is little or no movement between jobs and the people who perform them. Other things being equal, however, it might be expected that the internal labour market ought to be the main source of recruitment. Crucial knowledge and experience can be enhanced to the benefit of the organization. If the recent interest in 'knowledge management' means anything, it surely should mean retaining the reservoirs of tacit knowledge that individuals build up.

Significantly, more than 90 per cent of respondents to the IRS survey said that they were changing the ways that they were using existing employees to deal with skills shortages. Top of the list of specific activities came training in general (68 per cent) followed by 'training up' (58 per cent). Other changes reported included the use of teamwork (36 per cent) and greater flexibility (34 per cent).

A major problem here, which is often camouflaged by understandable worries about the implications of a recruitment-from-within strategy for equal opportunities, is the vested interest of key groups in the organization. Historically, it often used to be the craftworkers who were pilloried for standing in the way of the progression of their supposedly unqualified colleagues. Today, it is much more likely to be 'professional' employees who are the culprits.

An example involves the administration of university business schools. In recent years, as the previous chapter has pointed out, there has been a dramatic increase in the number of managers on MBA programmes as the result of the introduction of evening, modular and distance learning modes of delivery, together with executive courses more generally. On the face of it, the resulting increase in the need for a range of support staff represents a very considerable opportunity for development for some of the more able clerical and secretarial employees. In some universities, however, there has been an insistence of restricting entry to 'administrative' posts to candidates with a degree or a professional qualification of some kind. The net result is that a number of 'administrators' are doing jobs they are not really equipped for, while those who could do them very well are not only denied the opportunity but, to add insult to injury, often have to 'carry' their higher paid colleagues in the process.

Rethinking external sources

Too few UK organizations have been prepared to question traditional sources of supply. Understandably there is a natural reluctance to dilute standards, although this can sometimes be the cover for vested interests, as the example given above suggests. This does not necessarily mean, however, that things have to stay the same for ever.

One way in which an organization can respond is to take on apprentices or trainees. Indeed, it has long been the dream of policy-makers that UK organizations should do this more in order to increase the overall supply of skills. The problem, as the previous chapter has suggested, is that the odds have been stacked against doing this in the UK.

On the face of it, the IRS survey quoted earlier suggests that this may be changing (IRS, 1998b). More than two-thirds reported that they were taking on apprentices and trainees to deal with skills shortages. Along with training generally, this was the activity most often reported.

One specific example is that of Logica. In partnership with the University of East London Business School, it has developed a new recruitment and training model which it hopes will provide a long-term solution to the skills shortage it is facing. Sixteen non-technical people have undergone an intensive training programme to learn computing skills at the university. Of these, 14 successfully completed the course and have been recruited into technical jobs within the managed services division with recruits receiving further training and being integrated into the company graduate training scheme. The success of this pilot scheme has persuaded Logica to repeat the exercise in the following year (for further details, see IRS, 1998b).

Ageism in particular continues to be a major problem, however. This is despite the success of the large multiple retail chains in employing older people to deal with the threatened 'demographic timebomb' in the late 1980s and early 1990s. It was a subject of some comment, for example, that not only was it possible for stores such as B&Q and Tesco to fill the gap with older workers, but also that those employees actually did the job much better. Their social skills were often superior to those of youngsters and their interest in DIY activities especially was a substantial selling point. Moreover, contrary to expectation, they also found that many of these returning retirees were willing and able to use new technologies, their training in this respect taking no longer than for younger workers. The really amazing thing was that no one had thought about this before the crisis; it took an external threat to force organizations to review the way they did things.

Others learnt, equally amazingly with the virtue of hindsight, that working time arrangements could, in some circumstances, be a critical consideration in recruitment and retention. The building societies and banks, for example, launched more generous maternity leave and child care schemes in order to attract and hold onto female employees. These and other organizations introduced fleximime working and leave arrangements to recruit and retain more female employees.

During this same period, one of us was involved in an MBA project commissioned by a local assembler of household heating equipment which will help to illustrate the significance of the point. Turnover among the predominantly women assemblers had risen dramatically with the influx of one or two major new employers into the area offering enhanced levels of pay. In the event, the answer to the problem was found among those employees who stayed with the organization, despite the apparently greater attractions of the incoming competitors. More-or-less unbeknown to senior managers, the company had acquired a reputation for having a relatively relaxed regime in so far as time keeping was concerned. In its own way, it was an early example of a 'family friendly' employer: the production manager and his supervisors informally allowed women to take time off in the event of their children being ill, for example. Rather than compete head-to-head for those younger workers primarily interested in the highest level of pay, the organization was encouraged to think in terms of a variety of different part-time shifts with recruitment aimed specifically at women-returners with schoolchildren. In the event, the switch in emphasis proved extremely successful as it did in a number of organizations.

On the face of it, there does not appear to have been as much change in these areas as the others quoted. Less than one in five in the 1998 IRS survey said they were targeting different age groups

(17 per cent) or using 'family friendly' policies (19 per cent) to help solve their problems (IRS, 1998b). As the authors suggest, this may be because they are already doing this, although the figures for other activities suggest otherwise.

Selection

Selection involves making decisions about the appropriateness of individuals for specific jobs. One particular reason why selection has taken on a new prominence in the past decade or so is the example of the Japanese companies setting up operations in Britain. The seriousness with which these newcomers have been seen to treat these issues (and the amount of resources they have devoted to them) has proved to be especially influential. The most publicized of these cases have been Nissan and Toyota. Both have been seen to operate highly systematic and carefully structured recruitment processes for all levels of employee (see Figure 7.3).

Choosing appropriate methods

A wide range of selection methods is available. Tables 7.2 and 7.3, for example, which are derived from a survey of practice by *Employee Development Bulletin* (IRS, 1997a), show that these typically include application forms, biographical data, interviews, psychometric and aptitude tests, interviews and assessment centres. Evidently, as both tables show, there is a wide range of different use largely dependent on occupation or sector. The interview is used almost without exception, reflecting its relative cheapness and need for people to be seen to be acceptable. Application forms are the next most widely used method, although these are less extensively used for managers than other groups. CVs come third, being used by a majority of organizations in the case of managers, professional/technical workers and graduates. Of the three forms of test listed, those of personality primarily affect managers, followed again by graduates and professional/technical workers. By contrast, tests of ability/aptitude and literacy are more in evidence in the case of clerical/secretarial workers than the other groups. Any kind of testing for manual workers, it seems,

Despite the rhetoric of 'people as our most important asset', the not untypical prac- tice in the UK has been to treat employee resourcing in a very ad hoc and peremp- tory fashion. In a highly unregulated legal environment 'hire and fire' has been common practice. Until recently, line workers in car plants, for example, were often 'requisitioned' by production managers merely a matter of days before they were deemed to be required. The request to the personnel department might be to 'find 20 workers by next Monday'. Ex-milkmen or painters and decorators registered at the labour exchange could find themselves on the line within a day or two. In the event of a cutback in production these people would equally speedily find them- selves laid off.

The seriousness with which Japanese companies in Britain have been seen to treat this issue (and the amount of resources they have devoted to it) has proved to be especially influential in causing managers to reflect. First there was Nissan, which was seen to operate a carefully structured recruitment exercise for all levels of employee. In its first round of recruitment for supervisors, for example, Nissan invited no fewer than 200 applicants to be interviewed for just 22 jobs. The initial shortlisting to reach the 200 figure was itself undertaken by senior managers. A week-long period of selection exercises followed and 75 were invited back for a further battery of tests. This second phase of selection included attitudinal and per- sonality profiling as well as competence testing. Reports and assessments were fed to senior managers who themselves conducted the final interview. The process of resourcing the production staff was similarly meticulous and also involved mul- tiple tests and interviews.

Similarly, Toyota used what have been described as 'decidedly un-British recruit- ment practices' (*The Guardian*, 17 December 1992) to start up its new plant at Burnaston near Derby. Employees spent six months in an expensive recruitment and selection process, undergoing assessment for a total of 16 hours. Toyota used a five-page application form followed by a series of mental and physical tests, and an interactive video test to judge how candidates would respond to different types of situation, a 75 minute targeted interview and then 6 hours on a simulated pro- duction line. The Director of Human Resources at Burnaston said, 'We didn't want the traditional 20 minute interview and the "you go to the same football match as me so you must be OK" line. We want people who can work as a team and who have ideas for improvements and can demonstrate an ability to learn.'

Figure 7.3 Nissan and Toyoto – decidedly un-British recruitment practices?

is used by a minority of organizations only, which is surprising in view of the importance of ability/aptitude. Biographical data, it seems, is rarely used, despite the publicity it has received.

In recent years, managements have increasingly been encour- aged to adopt a multi-method approach to selection instead of relying on just the interview. The reason, put simply, is that no

Table 7.2 Selection methods

	% of organizations using method	
	Some occupations	*All occupations*
Ability/aptitude tests	76	15
Application forms	94	72
Assessment centres	45	0
Biographical data	5	1
CVs	76	37
Interviews	99	99
Literacy/numeracy tests	50	8
Personality questionnaires	61	8
Telephone screening	24	1

Source: *Employee Development Bulletin* (1997a: 11)

Table 7.3 Selection methods by occupation

	% of organizations using method				
	Manual/ craft	*Clerical/ secretarial*	*Professional/ technical*	*Graduate*	*Manager*
Ability/aptitude tests	36	52	47	43	48
Application forms	90	85	78	86	75
Assessment centres	5	5	21	31	29
Biographical data	1	1	3	3	4
CVs	38	54	68	64	73
Interviews	99	99	99	100	100
Literacy/numeracy tests	20	35	18	19	19
Personality questionnaires	10	14	35	38	57
Telephone screening	3	9	7	4	6
N	123	155	148	120	152

Source: *Employee Development Bulletin* (1997a: 11)

selection method is very reliable, i.e. consistent in the results it gives, or valid, i.e. able to predict the future behaviour or performance of candidates. Perversely, the most popular method, the interview, especially in its unstructured form, has one of the lowest levels of predictive accuracy (Anderson and Shackleton, 1993). It is far too easy to make mistakes if the interview is the only method used.

The *Employee Development Bulletin* survey suggests that the message may be getting through. The smallest number of methods (the application form and/or CV and interview) affects only manual workers. Clerical/secretarial workers are usually subjected to three methods (the interview, application form and/or CV and a test of ability/aptitude or literacy) as are graduates and professional/technical workers. In the former case, assessment centres are typically used in conjunction with the application form and/or CV and interview, whereas in the case of professional/technical workers some form of testing makes up the trio. Finally, managers can find themselves involved in as many as four or five methods including multiple interviews and some form of testing.

Overall, the survey evidence suggests that organizations have been striving for a 'greater professionalism' in selection, reflecting the growing recognition of its importance touched on in the introduction to this chapter and concerns about meeting the requirements of legislation in the area of equal opportunities. The latter consideration is an especially important consideration in the public services, encouraging managers to lead the way in revising and updating their arrangements (IRS, 1997a: 17).

In terms of the specific developments in each of the main areas, *Employee Development Bulletin* (IRS, 1997a,c) draws attention to the following:

1 There has been a move towards more structured and situation interviewing together with an increase in multiple interviewing (for further details see next section).
2 Application forms are being redesigned to ease completion and interpretation (especially important where they are used as an integral part of the screening process) as well as to meet the requirements of equal opportunities legislation.

3 The main development in testing has been an increase in their coverage reflecting the search for techniques which are rather more systematic than the traditional interview – more organizations are using them and for a wider range of groups. For example, in 1991, in a similar survey, just under half of organizations used ability/aptitude tests, whereas the figure in 1997 had grown to three-quarters; of those using any form of test, almost half reported an increase in applications as opposed to just under 7 per cent saying that usage had declined.

The use of tests, above all those concerned with personality, continues to be a subject of heated debate (see, for example, Sternberg, 1998). Fletcher reminds us that 'numerous surveys and studies have illustrated the negative way in which psychometric measures are seen by a large slice of the applicant population' (1998: 38). He also usefully draws attention to a number of lessons arising from research on attitudes to such testing about the conditions that can be used to make testing a more positive and acceptable experience:

1 Candidates need to understand the place of tests in the selection process, including how the data will be used, how much weight they will be given, whether there is a simple pass/fail criterion, whether the tests are common ones.
2 Candidates need to see the relevance of the test to the requirements of the job, which is not always obvious.
3 Candidates need to be convinced of the accuracy of the test, which means presenting them with evidence that the measures used predict performance and are free of bias.
4 Candidates need to be reassured of the competence of those using the tests, which means they have had proper training and have the requisite British Psychological Society competence qualifications.
5 Candidates need to know that feedback will be available to them at some stage.

'Using psychometric tests', concludes Fletcher, 'can be a help or a hindrance; it all depends on how you go about it.'

Improving interview performance

For many organizations, above all SMEs, it is the interview that is likely to remain the predominant and, regrettably, the only method. Understanding the weaknesses of the interview, and the steps that can be taken to minimize them, is therefore vital. Indeed, improving interview performance is probably the most cost-effective investment that an organization seeking to improve its management of employment relations can make.

The longstanding research evidence (see, for example, Wanous, 1980), confirms that the interview is the most abused as well as the most widely used method. Watson puts it rather nicely: 'Employment interviewing is like driving: most people rate themselves highly; the consequences of mistakes can be serious; and when something goes wrong there is a tendency to blame the other party' (1994: 211). By its very nature, the interview involves a subjective process. Less well known is that the evidence shows very clearly that there are a number of instantly recognizable behaviours that it brings out in us. In Watson's words again:

> interviewers are systematically prone to adopting certain stereotypes; they deem people from a particular background to be of a certain 'type'; they emphasise similarities with themselves; they tend to give undue emphasis to first impressions – the 'primacy' effect; they are influenced by accents; and they relate candidates to one another rather than agreed criteria – the 'contrast' effect. They also tend to give overwhelming importance to negative features – selection, in other words, is essentially a process of rejection.
>
> (1994: 212)

Our own experience of employment interviews is that it is very difficult to get people, above all senior managers, to recognize these problems. It nonetheless helps to remind people of the 'mistakes' they are likely to make in an interview unless they think very hard about them.

There are also a couple of increasingly recognized crucial steps that organizations can take to minimize the dangers. One is to have more than one person do the interview. This may seem costly, but it is likely to be well worth it. It is not simply that there are two opinions. Having two or more people involved is much more likely to mean that there is some rudimentary discussion beforehand of the things that are going to be looked for.

In very few cases, the survey evidence suggests, do organizations 'risk everything by relying on just one interview attended by one interviewer'. Indeed, there were only around 40 cases in a total sample of 678 in the *Employee Development Bulletin* survey (IRS, 1997a: 12), more than half of which involved manual occupations. In the case of secretarial/clerical occupations, the norm was one interview with two or more interviewers. Practice in the case of the other groups usually involved two or more interviews each with at least two interviewers. The arrangements for managers, as in the case of the number of selection methods used, tended to be the most complicated. Overall, there was no noticeable increase in the number of interviews that each candidate had to undergo; having more than one interviewer was, however, much more likely.

The second step that organizations are urged to take is to introduce some structure to the interview. Structured interviews, it has been shown (Anderson and Shackleton, 1993), can double the predictive accuracy of unstructured ones. Typically, structured interviews involve asking the same or similar questions to each of the candidates, reflecting the job and person specifications, so that there is a stronger basis for making a comparison. Structured interviews also usually involve several elements. Most will involve 'biographical' questions in which the candidate is asked about aspects of previous experience. 'Situational' or 'problem-solving' questions are also recommended: these give an opportunity to present the candidate with an hypothetical situation as relevant as possible to the job as a way of seeing how they handle it. There may also be occasions when a 'stress' element is felt to be called for. In this case the interviewer puts the interviewee under some pressure, perhaps criticizing an aspect of their previous career or performance, to see how they respond. The key point is that this has to be carefully considered and not done in the heat of the moment.

Here the *Employee Development Bulletin* survey (IRS, 1997a) suggests there is considerable room for improvement. Although, overall, the use of structured and situation interviews was widespread – around three-quarters said they used them for some occupations – less than half did so for all occupations. Indeed, the number using structured interviews for all occupations was only around 40 per cent and for situation interviews even less at just under 30 per cent.

Conclusions

The British tradition in the spheres of recruitment and selection can be characterized by a lack of planning and analysis and a reluctance to experiment. In the 1980s, the concurrence of publicity about the demographic dip and the influence of Japanese implants, led to the placing of resourcing issues much higher on the agenda than had normally been the case. While the recession which followed undid much of this work, the basic lessons are still broadly in evidence and can be fairly easily identified. It means rather less informality and not trying to do the job 'on the cheap'. Human resource planning and succession planning can make a considerable difference to improving recruitment and selection. Managerial time and money are involved, but are relatively small compared with the costs of getting things wrong, as the increasingly persuasive evidence from surveys of labour turnover costs clearly demonstrates. It also means taking a broader view of external supply as well as making more use of the internal labour market. The latter may require confronting some of the vested interests very often at the root of its 'balkanization'. The weaknesses of the interview have to be recognized and steps taken to remedy them such as having more structure and, wherever possible, supplementing them with other methods such as routine tests of ability. As we have seen throughout previous chapters, the need for such attention does not simply reflect changes in demographics: changes in technology and in organizational form can also drastically recast the demand and supply of labour. Critically, too, HRP and succession planning make good business sense. Recruitment and selection, to go back to the beginning of the chapter, certainly do not come cheap; the worse they are done, the more expensive they are.

Suggested further reading

The annual IPD report on the costs of recruitment and selection is worth studying to reinforce the importance of the issues dealt with in this chapter. For more detailed treatment of both recruitment and selection, see Iles, 1999. The various ACAS guides cited are an excellent source of practical advice.

8

MANAGING WITH TRADE UNIONS

This chapter deals with a number of strategic issues which management has to face in dealing with trade unions. One is the decision about the nature and extent of the recognition of trade unions. A second (assuming recognition involves negotiation and not just individual representation) is the structure of collective bargaining. Key decisions here are the units and the levels of collective bargaining. Is management going to deal severally or collectively with trade unions? Is management going to deal with trade unions indirectly through the intermediary of an employers' organization or assume direct responsibility? Is the management in a multi-establishment organization going to deal with trade unions at the organization level or at the level of individual establishments? A third area is the choice of methods for resolving conflict. Here particular attention is given to two of the features which figured prominently in the so-called new style agreements pioneered by the electricians' union and some of the Japanese companies investing in the UK in the 1980s, namely 'strike-free' provisions and pendulum arbitration. The fourth and final area is the nature of the collective bargaining relationship and the key development of partnership agreements.

Recognizing trade unions

Recognition, it must be emphasized, is not an open-and-shut issue: management has to decide the nature and the extent of recognition. Typically, trade unions are recognized for the purpose of negotiating pay and conditions. Many variants of much narrower and much broader recognition are available, however. For example, a company may recognize a trade union simply for the purposes of representing the individual grievances of employees such as is the case with the retail staff of Sainsbury. At the other extreme, trade unions may be involved in business and investment planning; the joint consultation process at ICI is a case in point.

At first sight, the decision whether or not to recognize trade unions might appear to be a foregone conclusion. Surely, it might be thought, management are unlikely to recognize trade unions unless they have to. Trade unions are concerned with representing the collective interests of employees, whereas management may want to stress the individual. Trade unions represent an external influence, an alternative focus of loyalty, which might be thought to disrupt the unitary approach of the company. Trade unions are interested in rules and regulations which impinge on management decision-making and desire for flexibility. Trade unions sometimes use sanctions and take strike action in pursuit of their objectives. Moreover, even if trade unions were once necessary to offset the excessive power of employers, surely this is no longer the case? Managements, it is argued, have learnt the error of their ways and recognize the vital contribution that their employees make.

In the UK, it is important to stress, managements do not have to recognize trade unions. By the time this book is published, the enactment of the Employment Relations Bill published in January 1999 means that there will be legal support for trade union recognition in workplaces with more than 20 employees. In the event of an employer refusing to negotiate, and the union being able to convince the Central Arbitration Committee (CAC) that it has 'majority' support, there will be a procedure requiring management to recognize the union for the purposes of negotiating over pay, hours and holidays and to inform and consult with it over training. A union with a 'reasonable' level of support (i.e. at least 10 per cent) will also be able to pursue recognition via the CAC, depending ultimately on a ballot in which the union will have to secure majority support from employees in the bargaining unit and at least 40 per cent of those eligible to vote. In the event of a failure to agree, it is likely that the CAC will be given the power to make an award which becomes part of the individual employee's contract of employment. Similar processes are available to de-recognize the union.

Whether or not these procedures make a great deal of difference remains to be seen. As Chapter 1 has pointed out, according to the first findings of the 1998 Workplace Employee Relations Survey (WERS), union recognition had fallen from 66 per cent of work-places in 1984 to 53 per cent in 1990; between 1990 and 1998 it fell a further eight points to 45 per cent (Cully *et al.*, 1998: 28). Meanwhile, the proportion of workplaces with no union members increased from 27 per cent in 1984 to 36 per cent in 1990 to 47 per cent in 1998. 'This signals, clearly, a transformation in the landscape of British employment relations, particularly when contrasted with the rela-tive stability and continuity that has characterised the system for much of the post-war period' (Cully *et al.*, 1998: 28).

It will take further and more detailed analysis of the 1998 WERS findings to get an accurate picture of the balance between the effects of restructuring, on the one hand, and the withdrawal of recognition by management, on the other. Evidently, there have been few positive implications for trade unions and collective bar gaining, given the political as well as economic climate of the 1980s and 1990s, the shift from manufacturing to services, the reduction in the size of workplaces, the changes in the occu-pational structure and the feminization of the workforce. Table 8.1, for example, suggests that there are strong associations between the size of workplaces and the extent of recognition.

Also important, however, as Table 8.1 confirms, are manage-ment attitudes. Indeed, Cully *et al.* suggest that the association between recognition and management attitudes are even stronger than that between size and recognition:

Nearly two-thirds of employees are union members in the 29 per cent of workplaces where management are in favour of union membership. In workplaces where managers are reportedly neutral, union density is relatively low, and in the

Table 8.1 Union presence by workforce size and management attitude

Workplace size	Union density: % of employees who are members	Any union members: % of workplaces	Union recognition: % of workplaces
25–49	23	46	39
50–99	27	52	41
100–199	32	66	57
200–499	38	77	67
500 or more	48	86	78
Management views on union membership:			
in favour	62	98	94
neutral	23	40	29
not in favour	7	16	9
All workplaces	36	53	45

Base: all workplaces with 25 or more employees.
Figures are weighted and based on responses from 1889 managers.
Source: Cully *et al.* (1998: 15).

17 per cent of workplaces where management are not in favour, union membership is very low indeed. Whether union membership begets union recognition, or supportive employer policies provide an environment in which union membership can flourish is difficult to establish, but these figures suggest anti-union sentiments on the part of employers provide a considerable hurdle to overcome if unions are to win members and recognition.

(Cully *et al.*, 1998: 15)

Significant from this point of view is that younger workplaces (i.e. those at their present address for less than ten years) are less likely than older ones to recognize trade unions – 28 per cent in the former category recognize unions, compared with 53 per cent in the latter. Also, of workplaces five or more years old, although 14 per cent recorded a fall in the number of unions (which may, in part, be explained by union mergers), only 3 per cent had completely derecognized (Cully *et al.*, 1998: 16).

In any event, the reality is that in many UK companies, whatever the senior managers may feel about trade unions, they are in no position to withdraw recognition. It is not simply that they might face opposition from trade unions. They do not have an alternative set of employment relations policies that they can realistically hope to put in place of those agreed with trade unions. Few have the managers with the relevant interpersonal skills to manage individually. Hardly any could afford the superior levels of pay and conditions which would almost certainly be necessary to persuade their employees to give up trade union membership.

Not only negative reasons are important, however. Trade unions also fulfil a number of important managerial functions which help to explain why a number of the foreign-owned companies coming into the UK have been willing to recognize them. One is the agency function which is especially important where there are large numbers of employees engaged in relatively homogeneous activities: management escapes the time-consuming and costly process of dealing with employees individually and also avoids inconsistencies which can be a major problem. A second is that trade unions voice the grievances and complaints of employees (Freeman and Medoff, 1984). In the words of Henry Mond, who had a significant influence on ICI's early policy towards trade unions, 'the trade unions are extremely useful to us in bringing to our notice matters that we should not otherwise be aware of' (quoted in Reader, 1973: 66). A third, and in many respects the most important, function that trade unions perform is in helping to manage discontent by legitimating procedures and management prerogative.

This last point can be illustrated by drawing on US as well as UK experience. As Kochan et al. (1986) show, throughout the 1970s a number of major US companies, including the car manufacturers Ford and General Motors, experimented with some aspects of HRM much as many UK managements have done in the 1980s. They found, however, that their pursuit of 'individualism' at the expense of their relationship with trade unions was counterproductive; there was a great deal of mistrust on the shopfloor about management's motives and many of the individual initiatives did not have the hoped-for benefits. It was only when management began to involve the trade unions in the programmes of change that they wished to introduce that they began to achieve the breakthrough that they were looking for.

In the UK, the point can be illustrated by reference to the major clearing banks. In the 1980s and early 1990s, although not going so far as to withdraw recognition, management in several cases tended to take an aggressive position in their dealings with their trade unions, taking advantage of restructuring to force through individual performance-related pay. In the second half of the 1990s, following a number of disputes, growing evidence of poor employee morale and rising complaints from customers, there were major reappraisals often leading to new HR/IR appointments. For example, on the occasion of the recent three-year pay and partnership deal, Norman Haslam, the new group employee relations director recruited by Barclays from British Aerospace, is quoted as saying:

> Barclays has had quite an adversarial relationship with the unions and there was a tendency to ignore them in the hope that they would go away . . .
>
> But the dispute changed that. It was clearly time to work with the unions to establish an approach based on partnership. Negotiations over the pay system provided an opportunity to do this . . .
>
> Partnership does not mean an end to redundancies, but it does mean that they will be handled better.
>
> (Walsh, 1999: 13)

In the words of Jim Lowe, assistant secretary of the Bank, Insurance and Finance Union (BIFU):

> Clearly, the bank sat down at the end of the dispute and realised it must be doing something wrong. It has shot from being the worst in the banking industry to being one of the best.

One thing seems evident. Management needs to make a clear choice. If they are not going to recognize trade unions for the purposes of negotiating pay and conditions, they need to have a system of highly developed personnel and HR policies and practices in place. If management is going to recognize trade unions, it needs to remember that the relationship has to be managed. In the case of a 'greenfield' operation, for example, this means selecting a trade union to represent its employees. This can be done either unilaterally, possibly following the competitive consideration of a number of alternative union presentations (what has become known as the 'beauty contest') or in conjunction with the regional TUC. In the case of 'brownfield' sites, it means having clear views about the structure of collective bargaining or the relationship they want to have with trade unions. There is a great deal in the adage that managements get the trade unions they deserve.

The structure of collective bargaining

As well as the nature and extent of the recognition, management has also to come to a view about the most appropriate structure of collective bargaining. This is above all true of the large, multi-establishment organizations where union recognition continues to be the norm. Key issues are the units and the levels of collective bargaining.

The unit

In the 1980s, a great deal of attention focused on the 'single-union' arrangements associated with some of the Japanese companies such as Nissan and Toshiba (see, for example, Bassett, 1986; Wickens, 1987; Trevor, 1988). In practice, however, where a number of unions are already recognized, a single union agreement is not normally a practicable proposition. The key issue is whether management is going to deal with the various trade unions it may recognize on a one-to-one basis or collectively around a so-called single table (IRS, 1989b; Marginson and Sisson, 1990). In practice, this latter means bringing manual and non-manual trade union representatives together, since many companies moved to single-table bargaining for their manual and non-manual employees in the 1970s.

At the time of the third Workplace Industrial Relations Survey in 1990, there was overall an average of two bargaining units for each workplace with recognized trade unions (Millward *et al.*, 1992: 86). There were 43 per cent of establishments which had just one bargaining unit, which was, in fact, the predominant mode overall in both private manufacturing and services. The public sector was an exception: here, multiple bargaining units were more common.

At first sight the logic of single-table arrangements appear to be irrefutable. Operating in this way saves managerial time and reduces the possibility of inconsistencies, anomalies and leap-frogging by one bargaining group over another. In addition, the single-table approach fits well with the trend towards harmonization and single-status workplaces. In general, it can be said to help establish and support a progressive organizational climate appropriate to a strategy which is respectful of joint regulation.

There are, however, some practical considerations to be taken into account. As has been pointed out in Chapter 5, in many organizations there continue to be substantial differences in the terms and conditions of employment between manual and non-manual employees. Many managements are afraid that putting the two groups together will mean levelling up more quickly than they can afford. In these circumstances, some managements may feel that they can gain some tactical advantage from playing off one group against another, although this hardly sits well with a desire to harmonize. Trade unions may also be opposed to the idea fearing that they will lose their individual identities.

Even when these considerations are not uppermost, there is a need to recognize that it will be necessary to have tiered arrangements. Otherwise there is a danger that groups will not feel their interests are being properly dealt with or the 'single table' becomes extremely overloaded with issues which do not affect the majority of employees.

The other important issue in terms of bargaining 'units' relates to which groups of employees will actually be covered by collective agreements. Although as we noted earlier, the extent of overall derecognition of trade unions has been small, there has, nonetheless, been a significant trend towards taking certain groups out of the collective arrangements.

Evidently, many employers have taken the view that they do want to take certain groups out of collectively agreed arrangements for pay and other terms and conditions. Prime targets for this have been successive levels of managerial employees. Other groups such as sales and IT staffs have been picked off as union membership density has dwindled and as the opportunity has arisen.

The level

There have been major changes in the levels of collective bargaining in recent years. There is no dispute about the general trends (see, for example, Brown *et al.*, 1995: 134–9; Sisson and Marginson, 1995: 97–100), which are:

1 A shift from multi-employer (national) to single-employer bargaining.
2 A shift from multi-establishment (company) to single-establishment bargaining especially in the large enterprises.

Multi-employer or single-employer bargaining?

In the case of the shift from multi-employer to single employer bargaining, there was pressure from Conservative governments in the 1980s. But this was not the most important consideration. As Sisson has argued, the decline in multi-employer bargaining in the UK is long-running (Sisson, 1987). Multi-employer agreements in the UK, unlike those in other EU countries, are not enforceable in law and the emphasis is on procedures rather than substantive terms. This means that multi-employer agreements have never had the authority of those in other countries.

In the case of the shift from multi-establishment to single establishment bargaining, the most important consideration has been the growth in the number of large, multidivisional organizations. This has meant the adoption of profit and cost centre management which puts pressure on 'bottom-line' responsibility for labour costs. Responsibility for pay determination, it is argued, should be given to the management with bottom-line responsibility for profit and costs. If there is a mismatch between levels and responsibilities, local management can shirk its responsibilities. Pay and conditions, it is also argued, need to be closely related to (a) the profitability of individual businesses, (b) differences in performance and skills, and (c) differences in local labour market conditions – the organization may be overpaying in some instances and underpaying in others. In some companies, for

197

example General Electric and Pilkington, this can even mean that the individual business unit on a multibusiness site can become the level of bargaining. The consequence that will have to be lived with, however, is that people at the same location, possibly even doing very similar jobs, may be on different terms and conditions.

One point, however, must be made absolutely clear. Despite these trends, there is no consensus about what is the 'right level' of collective bargaining. This is above all true of the choice between multi-employer and single-employer bargaining on which there has been an extremely vigorous debate. Certainly in industries such as clothing, construction and printing, managements as well as trade unions are committed to maintaining the system of multi-employer bargaining.

The case against multi-employer bargaining is broadly as follows:

1 *It is inflationary* – pay and conditions of employment need to be closely related not only to the profitability of individual companies and to differences in performance and skills but also to local labour market conditions.
2 *It is inflexible* – much-needed changes, for example in payment systems, working practices or training, are difficult to bring about and the industry tends to move at the pace of the slowest.
3 *It is an abdication of responsibility* – if employees really are the most important asset, it is difficult to justify relinquishing the control of pay and conditions to an external body.
4 *It gives trade unions too much power* – they can bring their relatively limited resources to bear on a single set of negotiations.

Conversely, the case *for* multi-employer bargaining goes like this:

1 *It is neither inflationary nor inflexible* – in most cases it sets minimum terms and conditions and allows considerable scope for local adaptation.
2 *It is relatively efficient* – management in many companies, particularly small companies, does not have the time, let alone the expertise, to negotiate the total package of pay and conditions.
3 *It sets standards* – these standards help to ensure that companies are not undercut by others in the same industry.

4 *It usually provides a national disputes procedure* – such a procedure is a useful safety valve.
5 *It maximizes the bargaining power of management* – trade unions are less able to 'pick off' individual companies or engage in leap-frogging.

Supporters of national (multi-employer) agreements can point to the dispute in engineering in 1989–90 to show what can happen in the absence of national agreements (for further details see IRS, 1989a).

Much depends on the specific circumstances of the industry or the individual organization (as is argued in more detail below). Even more important, however, are the prevailing beliefs of senior managers about what is most appropriate. There is a widely held view, for example, that the decentralization of pay determination is an important instrument or lever in promoting the management of change. In practice, it is not at all clear that this is the case (Arrowsmith and Sisson, 1999).

It is important not to get swept up by the 'flavour of the month'. Decentralized negotiations may be highly appropriate in some situations but equally highly inappropriate in others. This is why it is essential to study the circumstances before coming to a decision.

In making a choice between multi-employer and single-employer bargaining, three main sets of considerations need to be taken into account. The first relates to product market factors. Firms which operate in a highly competitive market where a large number of firms each has a small market share are likely to favour multi-employer bargaining. Labour market circumstances are a second set of factors to be considered. The more labour intensive the industry the more likely it is that firms will want to stabilize wage costs by resorting to multi-employer bargaining. Third, this form of bargaining also tends to be favoured when the technology used by different firms is similar (ACAS, 1983). It is not difficult to understand therefore why multi-employer (national) agreements are popular in industries such as clothing, construction and printing. Each of them is composed of a large number of small and highly competitive firms, which employ very similar types of worker and which face large national trade unions.

Company-level or establishment-level bargaining?
Another choice facing managers in the unionized firm is whether to opt for company-level or workplace-level bargaining. Factors which need to be taken into account here include size of establishments, geographical dispersion of workplaces, diversity of product range and the degree of interdependence between sites. The larger the size of the separate establishments the more likely it is that management will favour decentralization. The more dispersed they are – especially if operating in markedly different labour markets – again the greater the likelihood that decentralized bargaining will be favoured. If the range of products is diverse and especially if the process of production is highly interdependent, then this will favour centralized bargaining (CIR, 1974; ACAS, 1983; IRS, 1989c). It is not difficult to understand, therefore, why the car manufacturers, the clearing banks and the retailers prefer multi-establishment to single-establishment bargaining. In the case of the car manufacturers, interdependency is the critical factor; in the case of the banks and the retailers it is the size of establishment and similarity of services (and hence skills) which are important.

Nonetheless, many managers now find themselves in a period of flux and some of these fundamentals are in danger of being forgotten in the headlong dash for decentralized bargaining. The current desire to relate terms and conditions to the fortunes of separate business units may push the above considerations to the sidelines. The extent to which this will present a serious problem to UK managers will depend upon the level at which real decisions are going to be made.

Levels of management decision-making
The research evidence is very clear (Marginson *et al.*, 1988, 1993; Kinnie, 1985a,b). Although the level of bargaining has attracted most of the attention, it is not the only or, from the point of view of management, the most important issue to be considered. Far more important is the level of management decision-making. One might expect that with the tendency towards devolved financial responsibility to business units (see Chapter 3) that company-level managers would be involved less in workplace industrial relations. However, the survey evidence shows that the reverse has been the case: in 1990 there was a greater propensity for senior corporate

managers to be involved in establishment industrial relations matters than previously (Millward et al, 1992: 209). To put it bluntly, much of the decentralization that has taken place is an illusion. Things may 'happen' at local level, but they are not decided there. Many of the key issues of employment relations policy are likely to be determined at higher levels in the organization. Shifts towards harmonization or the introduction of quality circles or TQM are good examples. The same is true of specific conditions of employment: most companies will have what might be described as a taboo list – a list of the issues that managers must not make concessions on at local level. The working week is a good example: this is decided at higher levels of the organization in most companies. Some companies even have seven-day 'approval' notices which require managers taking an initiative to circulate colleagues in other units for their views before going ahead.

As for pay determination, a range of possibilities can be found even in the most apparently decentralized of companies. Management may dictate the increase or require local managers to justify their proposals in a mock negotiation, or they may leave local managers in no doubt of what they expect, or they may tackle the issue in the annual budgeting process – local managers, for example, may be given complete freedom to pay what increases they think fit providing there is no increase in labour costs.

At first sight, it may appear to be contradictory to decentralize responsibility and yet to retain a significant degree of central control. It is perfectly sensible, however. Senior managers are trying to get the best and to avoid the worst of both worlds. One important consideration is what might be described as the limited horizons problem. It is all very well making local managers 'operationally' responsible; they cannot be expected to have the time or the expertise, however, to do the long-term 'strategic' HR thinking that is going to be required. It is not very efficient to do so either – the organization is not getting the benefits of the synergies of the large organization. Simply bringing local managers together to discuss and debate the issues can be enormously beneficial in saving time and in arriving at solutions to common problems.

There is also the 'coercive comparison' problem. The theory of decentralization is fine: local managers are given responsibility to determine local issues in the light of local circumstances. The reality is very different. Individual units in the same organization are not 'islands unto themselves' especially if their employees are members of the same trade unions or professional organizations. It does not make sense to give local managers total autonomy – the price of one unit's freedom to do what it wants can be disastrous for other units. Concessions made in one unit can have extremely costly repercussions in others and the organization is left wide open to 'pattern bargaining' or 'leap-frogging' claims by trade unions.

Pattern bargaining, it must be emphasized, is not simply a hypothetical possibility. A successful example took place in the engineering industry in 1989–90. The breakdown of national negotiations over a reduction in the working week led to a classic case of the 'rolling strike'. The Confederation of Shipbuilding and Engineering Unions levied its members throughout the industry to set up a sizeable strike fund; it then targeted individual employers in a series of waves; it conducted strike ballots in individual companies to conform to the relevant legislation – using the proceeds of the levy to pay substantial strike pay to the members voting to take industrial action in support of the claim.

The result was considerable success in achieving a reduction of the working week throughout large parts of the engineering industry and a considerable fillip for trade union morale. The irony is that it was the use of these very tactics (known also as whipsawing in the USA) which led the engineering employers to introduce a national procedure agreement in the first place in the 1980s. Indeed, most advocates of decentralized bargaining often conveniently forget that it was management who introduced centralized bargaining in many situations in order to stop unions engaging in pattern bargaining.

A useful exercise for managers to undertake when contemplating decentralized bargaining is to list which terms and conditions will be handled in which way. Which will be subject to *instruction* from the centre (for example the basic length of the working week, or health and safety rules). Which will be the subject of advice or *guidelines* from the centre (perhaps a specific type of job evaluation will be recommended). On other issues the units may have more autonomy although they may be expected to consult or even be *required to consult* before acting on changes, say, to the grading system. Or, at minimum, it may simply be that individual units are expected to provide the corporate centre with *information*.

The problem is that, in practice, very few organizations go through this type of exercise before they decentralize. This is yet a further example of the lack of strategic thinking in employment relations. Usually, arrangements are simply built up incrementally. In our experience, even where systematic analyses are conducted, they are rarely as formal as the exercise outlined above suggests they could be.

Resolving conflicts

How to resolve the conflicts that may arise between management and trade unions has been an especially prominent concern in collective bargaining in the UK. This is because there are two major differences between the UK and other countries in the content and status of collective agreements. First, in the UK the relationship between management and trade unions has been built on procedural rules whereas in other countries it has been built on a code of substantive rules in force for a specified period. Second, in the UK priority has been given to voluntary rather than compulsory collective bargaining; that is, the procedural rules are made by the parties themselves rather than imposed by government, and along with any substantive rules are deemed to be gentlemen's agreements, binding in honour rather than legally enforceable contracts.

The result is that in the UK the procedure agreements have to take the full strain of the relationship. They have had to deal with disputes over the making as well as the interpretation of agreements. This can also involve a variety of levels – in the case of the industries with multi-employer agreements, for example, this can mean the 'industry', the 'company' and the 'workplace'. Unlike in most other countries, where collective agreements are legally enforceable, there is also no 'closed season' for collective bargaining; negotiation in the UK is highly informal and more-or-less continuous. Typically, then, procedure agreements in the UK have involved a hierarchy of levels usually ending in a form of conciliation involving a third party.

Strike-free?

In the 1980s much was made of the clauses in 'new style' agreements prohibiting the taking of industrial action under any circumstances. In practice, however, the issue is largely symbolic. This is because the general rule in the UK is that collective agreements normally lack contractual status unless the parties decide otherwise. If the management and trade union do not sign a legally enforceable agreement, there is no redress against the union in the event of its members taking industrial action in breach of the agreement. Only if the union has not followed the provisions of the legislation in relation to balloting, picketing and secondary action is it open to the management to seek legal redress. Management can seek redress against individual employees but, as the Royal Commission on Trades Unions recognized more than two decades ago (Donovan Commission, 1968), this does not really amount to much. Individual members are unlikely to have the level of assets to make prosecution worthwhile and, in any event, are unlikely to return to work with enthusiasm if they are being sued by their management. The sanction of dismissal, which management is free to use under the law, is viable only if management is going to close down the unit or has an alternative workforce at its disposal.

In the circumstances, it might be wondered why management has not moved in the direction of making collective agreements legally enforceable, especially as this is the norm in other countries. Trade union opposition is a consideration, but not the only one. British management has shown no great enthusiasm. Much as many managements would have liked procedural agreements to be legally enforceable, they have been much less enthusiastic about giving substantive agreements the same status. If collective agreements were legally enforceable, it would be more difficult for management to change the substantive terms to suit changing circumstances.

Arbitration?

Along with the 'strike-free' provisions, a particular form of arbitration figured prominently in many of the 'new style' agreements of the 1980s. It is known as pendulum or straight choice arbitration. Standard arbitration involves a third party making a judgement about the outcome of a dispute; in coming to this judgement, the arbitrator is free to suggest the outcome that he or she feels is most appropriate. Under pendulum arbitration, the arbitrator has to make a 'straight choice' between the positions of one or other of the parties.

This form of arbitration was developed in the USA in the public services where strikes are outlawed. The main theoretician of pendulum arbitration is Carl Stevens. In a celebrated article entitled 'Is compulsory arbitration compatible with bargaining?' (Stevens, 1966), he argues that the threat of pendulum arbitration might stimulate compromise where there was no right to strike. In particular, pendulum arbitration might help to resolve some of the weaknesses of conventional arbitration: the 'chilling effect' – the reluctance to engage in realistic bargaining in the knowledge that there is another step; and the 'narcotic effect' – the tendency for compulsory arbitration to become habit-forming.

As with other features of the 'new style' agreements, it should not be assumed that management will regard any form of arbitration as a good thing. Indeed, there are strong grounds for thinking the opposite. Resort to arbitration in effect means giving responsibility for making key management decisions to a third party. The point was put very succinctly in the Treasury's evidence to the Megaw Committee set up to look at pay determination in the public services: 'the only sure way for employers to avoid the risk of awards they cannot afford is refuse to go to arbitration. It follows that arbitration should not take place without their consent, but only on mutual agreement' (quoted in Bassett, 1986: 110).

As for pendulum arbitration, it is worth taking into account the comments of some of those involved in pendulum arbitration in the 1980s. In its 1984 annual report, ACAS was clear that the arrangements depended on a high degree of trust and might not be appropriate to every situation. Lewis believed that 'the requirement to find entirely in favour of one side's final position made the arbitration process more "adversarial" and less "inquisitorial"' (Lewis, 1988: 10). Kessler (1987) and Lewis (1988) both questioned whether or not it is appropriate to exclude provisions for conciliation and mediation. Arbitration, in other words, should only be the last resort. The 1990 Workplace Industrial Relations Survey (WIRS) revealed that 68 per cent of managers with pay and conditions procedures in their establishments reported that they had provision for some kind of third-party intervention to resolve disputes (this represented a decline from 79 per cent in 1984: Millward *et al.*, 1992: 208). The incidence of 'straight choice' arbitration, however, was low – it accounted for only 7 per cent of those establishments which had made arrangements for third-party arbitration.

The partnership question

The principles of 'partnership' have already been outlined in Chapter 2. Three main sources for the ideas can be identified. One is the USA where the 'new industrial relations model appeared in the 1980s in the work of Kochan and his colleagues at the Massachusetts Institute of Technology (Kochan *et al.*, 1986). A second source is continental Europe. The notion of social partnership in the sense of national-level relations had long been a feature of a number of EU countries. In the wake of the completion of the single European market with economic and monetary union (EMU), the European Commission has sought to promote social dialogue not only as a way of responding to demands for developing social policy, but also to deal with the expected restructuring and to bring about much-needed modernization of work organization as a means to competitive success (see, for example, CEC, 1997, 1998).

The third source is the UK itself, where trade union debates over 'new realism' in the mid-1980s led to the proposal that they should develop a joint approach with employers 'to create the conditions for economic success and social cohesion in the 1990s' (Edmonds and Tuffin, 1990). Out of this came a joint statement of intent, *Towards Industrial Partnership* (IPA, 1992) signed by leading management and trade union representatives in membership of the Involvement and Participation Association, which in turn was the catalyst for the negotiation of so-called partnership agreements by companies such as Blue Circle and Welsh Water (Hyder).

Two fundamental issues are involved. The first is the role of trade unions. Historically, trade unions have tended to be seen, and to have seen themselves, as the permanent opposition, challenging management's authority, as well as seeking to improve the position of their members by establishing a floor of both procedural and substantive rights. Under the pressure of intensifying international competition and declining membership in many countries, however, there have been moves to redefine relations with management in terms of what have been called 'productivity coalitions' designed to promote organizational performance and hence the future employment of their members.

The second is the importance of collective employee 'voice'. Other things being equal, managers may eschew any form of indirect representation whatsoever. It is not just a question of the individual employee needing representation to help balance the inequality of power with the employer. As previous chapters have pointed out, the views of employees are vital to the success of changes in work organization. In the absence of a representative voice, there is a danger that these views either are not expressed, for fear of antagonizing managers, or are simply ignored. The insecurity that much of the de-layering and downsizing of recent years has produced, it is also argued, is proving to be counter-productive. There is little or none of the trust that managers are encouraged to seek as the basis for a new 'psychological contract': trust depends on the legitimacy of decisions, and joint regulation is one of the most tangible ways of expressing such legitimacy. In effect, advocates of the new thinking argue, a coalition for change is required involving all the major stakeholders.

'Partnership' agreements in the UK differ considerably in their details, reflecting the involvement of companies as diverse as Rover (IRS, 1992), Blue Circle (IRS, 1997d), Tesco (Allen, 1998), BGT (British Gas call centres) (IRS, 1998h), Hyder (formerly Welsh Water) (IRS, 1998c) and Legal and General (IRS, 1998a). Some idea of their contents and timescale that can be involved appears in Figure 8.1, which summarizes the first four phases of an unfolding eight-year relationship at Hyder. Like other water companies, Welsh Water had for many years before privatization in 1989 been the subject of detailed central agreements covering the different groups of employees: manual, non-manual and craft.

To understand the potential significance of this type of development, the term 'collective bargaining' which has so far been used

Partnership 1 – 1990
This introduced the following key features:

- Replacement of the traditional annual pay negotiations by an objective formula (embracing the November RPI percentage; links with the local labour market undertaken by an independent organization (Cardiff Business School); and a profit-related component).
- A new single-table representative council supported by joint 'issue' groups.
- New working time arrangements involving greater flexibility, a form of annual hours arrangements and a reduction in the working week for manual and craft employees.
- The harmonization of the working conditions, policies and procedures of all employees.
- The introduction of monthly pay through credit transfer for all employees.
- A commitment to introduce a new pay structure.
- A range of measures to improve productivity through greater flexibility.
- A no-compulsory redundancy policy.

Partnership 2 – 1993
This introduced the following key features:

- Introduction of a jointly prepared unified pay structure for all employees.
- Performance appraisal and new understandings on performance management.
- Provisions for handling reductions in the workforce including opportunity for employees to leave at mutually acceptable dates; recognition of the need to consult and involve employees on how jobs would be managed in the future.
- Further refinements to the pay formula.
- A renewal of the employment security provisions.

Partnership 3 – 1995
A distinguishing feature of this phase was its preparation. To ensure future developments matched needs, senior personnel managers and full-time officers carried out a series of 'road shows', meeting small groups of employees covering over 75 per cent of the workforce. The agenda embraced a review of developments and the concerns of employees, the identification of issues. The continued uncertainty about the nature of partnership resulted in a restatement of the basic principles:

> What you give – sharing responsibility for continued improvements in performance. Dwr Cymru can be assured that everyone shares the responsibility in meeting our business objectives and improving the highest levels of customer service. What you get – the benefits of Partnership are that out people have continuing employment and pay security with good conditions of employment.

The employment security provisions were put on a ongoing basis to help alleviate fears about their regular review. The position of temporary staff was also addressed through new review procedure.

208

The 1998 agreement ('Working Together')
This extends the basic principles of previous agreements to the newly acquired electricity supply and distribution business (SWALEC), seen as vital to preparing for some challenging business issues needing to be faced over the next five years, e.g. open competition in electricity in 1998, regulatory reviews in electricity and water in 1999/2000, ongoing competition in the open gas market and completion of the Green Seas policy in water and the associated costs of achieving European Blue Flag water quality standards. In the case of a major event, for example significant regulatory intervention, change of government policy, serious loss of market, all parties are committed to work closely together to reduce the impact on key elements of the agreement, which could include the right of either side to give appropriate notice of termination.

Figure 8.1 The phases of the Hyder partnership agreement
Source: Thomas and Wallis (1998: 162–5); *Employment Trends* (1998)

to describe relations between management and trade unions has to be unpicked. Collective bargaining, it will be recalled from Chapter 4, embraces two processes. One is joint regulation. Here the implication is that the outcome of the process is an explicit agreement between the two parties. If the union withholds its agreement, management does not proceed. Or if it does, it recognizes that it may face industrial action. The other is joint consultation. Here the implication is that the management will seek the views of the union and take them into account in making its decision. It may go ahead with a decision, however, even if the union expresses its opposition.

In most other EU member states, the two processes are separate. The most obvious example of such a dual system is to be found in Germany where it is enshrined in the legal framework. Joint regulation is largely the responsibility of employers' organizations and trade unions and takes place outside the workplace at the level of the industry or the *Land*. Inside the workplace, the responsibility for representing the interests of employees rests with the statutory works councils, which have limited rights of joint regulation but extensive powers of joint consultation as well as information, which means a much wider range of issues is discussed between management and employee representatives.

As Marchington (1994) describes, joint consultation in the UK has had something of a chequered history. Provisions for joint consultation were a key recommendation of the Whitley Committee at the end of the First World War and in some sectors, notably in some of the public sector, the arrangements survive to this day. Joint consultation, in the form of production committees, was also popular at the end of the Second World War. In the 1960s and 1970s, however, it came in for a great deal of criticism. The feeling seemed to be that if an issue was important enough, it should be the subject of joint regulation. Although the decline seems to have been arrested in the 1980s, the first findings of the 1998 WERS confirm that only a minority of workplaces have a joint consultation committee.

There has as yet been no systematic evaluation of the impact of 'partnership' agreements. Certainly many of the participants are enthusiastic. For example, claimed benefits at Hyder include the establishment of a 24 hour call centre to suit customer needs; improved quality; significant reductions in costs; customers' standards as measured by the director-general in the 'good to very good' category; continuous change accepted; and a willingness to work with contractors, agency and temporary staff, which had been the source of major problems in the 1980s. For their part, employees have benefited from greater employment and pay security; harmonization of conditions and greater equality; training and development opportunities and greater control of immediate working lives.

There is also wider evidence to suggest that partnership works. In the UK the IPA has produced both case study and survey evidence establishing positive links between the principles of partnership, the practice of partnership and organizational performance (IPA, 1997, 1998). Even more widespread support comes from the report of the major ten-country study of the role of direct participation in organizational change sponsored by the European Foundation for the Improvement of Living and Working Conditions (1997). Not only did the effects of direct participation increase with the degree of employee representative involvement in its introduction, but also the more extensively employee representatives were involved, the more successful direct participation was deemed to be in the view of managers.

Even so, doubts have been expressed by management on both operational and ideological grounds. On operational grounds, there are worries about the time and effort involved and how these trade off against the likelihood of benefits (see, for example,

Marchington, 1998; see also IPA, 1997). The sheer scale of the changes required is another consideration. The changes required in the role and style of managers are especially fundamental, as Thomas and Wallis (1998: 166–9), who helped to draw up the Hyder agreements, admit in their appraisal of the implications of having partnership arrangements (see Figure 8.2). The feasibility of trying to build long-term relationships in the midst of so much uncertainty is yet another consideration. Worries have also been expressed about the quality of local trade union representatives on whom partnership places considerable burdens.

On ideological grounds, there remains a strong resistance to collectivism in general and to trade unions in particular on the part of many managers in the UK. Unions are promoting partnership, some cynics would say, for tactical reasons – managers should not be doing anything that stops unions from withering on the vine. The important link, others would argue, is between the organization and the individual employee. Involving a trade

---

For management
- A willingness to commit the act of faith that the benefits would outweigh the costs
- A need for a change in management style – from being 'doers' to facilitators
- A need for greater openness
- A need for a change in approach to the trade unions – problem solving
- Employment security has removed poor performers through the redundancy route leading to extra strain on the performance management system
- Greater activity has led to expectations of greater reward

For trade unions
- The nature of partnership restricts the number of opportunities for the trade union officers to demonstrate publicly their value to their members
- Opposition for opposition's sake had to be replaced by a recognition that the long-term interests of the members were best served by helping the organization to be more successful
- Acceptance of the need for joint communication
- Trade union officials and senior representatives had to some extent to let go the reins of their power
- Full-time officials in particular faced charges that they were in 'management's pocket'

Figure 8.2 Some of the key implications of partnership agreements
Source: Based on Thomas and Wallis (1998: 166–9)

union is tantamount to bringing a third party into what is a close family relationship. Yet another group, though they may not admit it, find the whole business of consultation, be it with individuals or their representatives, extremely uncomfortable – some believe that seeking the views of employees undermines their managerial authority.

For trade unions, involvement in the kinds of coalition for change being envisaged poses both opportunities and threats (see, for example, Claydon, 1998; Monks, 1998). Trade unions have to face up to the implications of the different trajectories of work organization regardless of any strategic position they adopt. More positively, it can be argued, there is much to be gained from trade unions, at national and workplace level, presenting themselves as the champions of the 'quality' forms of work organization and the training and developments opportunities that go with them.

Many within trade unions see partnership agreements as a major threat, however. In particular, they are worried that they will compromise the traditional role of unions which is to defend their members' interest. Employee representatives will become part of management. One trade union official involved in the negotiations at Hyder expressed the basic dilemma like this:

> Partnership does mean a different, sometimes a more challenging role for the trade unions. It is easy to confront to say NO. It is far more difficult to create a new role working with employees and the company to develop a better future not only for ourselves but more importantly for our customers.
> (IPA, 1997: 16)

There is also a worry that partnership agreements will compromise the basic trade union role of establishing minimum standards and make it more difficult to manage the tensions between members of different organizations and interest groups, for example, skilled and unskilled, full-time and part-time, with significant implications for the ability to maintain collective strength.

For the moment, partnership agreements remain very much a minority movement, affecting up to fifty organizations, with their wider adoption seeming to depend on the political context. There is as yet no indication that the Labour government of Tony Blair, for all its commitment to partnership, will bite the bullet

and legislate for the universal right to employee voice. Management and unions will be left to make their own decisions,
although things could change. Should it win a second term in
office, the Labour government, as Chapter 1 intimated, could
well decide to bring forward further legislation.

In the circumstances, it might seem appropriate to wait and see.
In our view, however, the strategic choice for management is
becoming increasingly stark. They either seize the opportunity
presented by the coming of partnership agreements to put their
relationship with trade unions onto a new and, hopefully, more
positive footing or they withdraw recognition altogether.
Management cannot hope to manage the relationship with trade
unions exactly to their liking. Conceivably there may be situations
where the union is in serious decline and so it does not make sense
to force the issue, although even in such situations, it needs to be
remembered, there will still be a need for some form of collective
employee voice. There is nonetheless a great deal in the adage
'managers get the unions they deserve'. Absolving themselves of
any responsibility for managing the relationship is likely to produce the worst of all possible worlds. Blaming the union for
everything that goes wrong may give managers an important
psychological scapegoat, but the 'trench warfare' traditionally
associated with such a relationship is hardly a basis for the
improved management of employment relations being advocated
throughout this book.

Much more positively, there is in our view a strong argument
for management and trade unions using partnership agreements
to extend the coverage of consultation to a wider range of issues
and at higher levels in the organization along the lines discussed
here and in Chapter 2. There is an understandable reluctance on
the part of management to make many of the issues touched on
throughout the book, such as changes in work organization, training, or future business plans, the subject of joint regulation. If
everything has to be the subject of agreement, the process of
decision-making will be slowed down. Yet there is a strong case
for management to discuss these issues with trade union representatives: not only do these representatives have a contribution to make, but their involvement will add to the legitimacy of
what management is seeking to do.

Conclusions

The focus of this chapter has been upon a number of strategic issues which managers have to face when dealing with trade unions. Four areas were selected as being especially critical: decisions about the nature and extent of union recognition; the structural arrangements to be made for conducting collective relations; choices about methods for resolving conflicts; and, finally, a decision about the basis of management/union relations in the light of developments in partnership agreements.

These four sets of decisions were grounded in an account of the changing contours of management/union relations. In particular, trends in the areas of recognition and derecognition, shifts in bargaining levels and changes in the form and nature of union/management interactions were explained. The overriding message was that, despite the fluidity of the institutional IR mechanisms (and there are suggestions in the recent WERS data that the pace of change may be accelerating), there are nonetheless enduring issues requiring attention. The fundamental issue is whether UK management and trade unions are going to be able to put their relationship on a more positive footing. The way that this might be done – by developing joint consultation over a much wider range of issues and at a higher level in the organization through partnership agreements – is clear enough. The imponderable, as with so many of the other aspects of managing employment relations covered in the book, is whether management in particular is willing and able to invest the time and resources to do so.

Suggested further reading

The two volumes reporting the findings of the 1998 Workplace Employee Relations Survey (Cully *et al.*, 1999: Millward *et al.*, 2000) contain much useful up-to-date information on trade union workplace organization. Details of partnership agreements will be found in the various IRS reports cited in the chapter. For a range of different views on partnership, see Claydon (1998), Coupar and Stevens (1998) and Monks (1998). See also Tailby and Winchester (2000).

9

MANAGING THE HR/IR FUNCTION

Previous chapters have been concerned largely with the policy and practices of employment relations. Our focus now turns to an issue rarely treated in textbooks, namely the management of the function. Where this issue is considered, it is typically done so in terms of a specialist function, i.e. employment relations is something that is done by a specialist group of people. This is not necessarily the case, however. Indeed, only a minority – around 17 per cent according to the 1990 Workplace Industrial Relations Survey (Millward *et al.* 1992: 27–38) – of workplaces with 25 or more employees have specialist HR/IR managers. Furthermore, key issues are the balance of responsibility between line and staff and the way that any specialist activity is to be delivered.

Our approach here is to see things through the eyes of a chief executive or general manager deciding the role and organization of the HR/IR function. The first section considers the contribution he or she might expect the function to make and provides an opportunity to reinforce the message that it involves both strategic and operational dimensions. The second explores how this contribution might be achieved, drawing attention to the key decisions that have to be made about the balance of responsibility between line managers and any specialist HR/IR managers employed, the way specialist service might be delivered, and the specific role and status of any specialist employed. The third section considers how the contribution of the specialist function might be monitored to ensure that it is both effective and efficient.

The nature of the HR/IR contribution

A review of the writings on the specialist HR/IR function in the UK suggests that its practitioners have never been able to escape a preoccupation with the 'management of ambiguity' (see, for example, Legge, 1978; Hall and Torrington, 1998). Much of the ambiguity is implicit in the nature of employment relations activities. Both operational and strategic dimensions are involved and are implicit in Storey's (1992: 35) contrast between personnel/industrial relations and HRM depicted in Figure 1.1 in Chapter 1. Patently, there is a wide range of operational activities to be done. People, including the top management team, have to be recruited. Training has to be organized. Someone has to make sure people get paid, that the organization fulfils its legal requirements, for example in the area of dismissal and redundancy or health and safety, and that (where they are recognized) relationships are maintained with trade unions.

Not only is there a very wide range of activities, however, but also a considerable number of detailed operations exist in each case. Many of these can be devolved to line managers, as is discussed below. Yet there is also considerable expertise involved which is why organizations employ the personnel specialist.

Managing employment relations is not just a matter of operations, as previous chapters have tried to show. It also involves a significant strategic dimension. At the very least, as Chapter 2 in particular has argued, this means a set of disciplines which have to be the responsibility of the senior management team. These include regular stocktaking, simple scenario planning and regular monitoring and control. A clear allocation of responsibilities and a basic personnel database make up the portfolio, together with a need to express business plans in employment relations terms. Underpinning these are the need for an awareness of one's own assumptions and prejudices and a sense of direction.

If this strategic dimension is missing, trouble can be expected.

Each of the preceding chapters has given examples of what can go wrong: inconsistencies of approach, which can be a major source of conflict; a failure to react to sudden changes in labour supply; a misfit between the approach to pay and to work organization; costly mistakes in selection; the failure to recognize the significance of working time arrangements. All of these can be attributed, directly or indirectly, to a lack of a strategic dimension.

Second, and more positively, a strategic dimension is essential to securing the benefits of the competitive advantage that effective employment relations management can bring. Securing the fit between the business strategy and employment relations policies and the adoption of policies and practices which are complementary as well as appropriate are not things that are likely to happen by accident.

The range of activities is reflected in the position of HR/IR specialists in managerial hierarchies. These specialists, far from being the single, homogeneous occupation which their professional organization, the IPD, often seems to assume, are involved in a variety of different roles and activities. One typology sees the range extending from 'clerks', who make up the majority and who are involved in basic operational matters; to 'contract managers', who are responsible for pay and, where appropriate, negotiations with trade unions; to a small number of 'architects' at the pinnacle who are involved in policy-making as a member of the senior management team or with a seat on the board of directors (Tyson and Fell, 1986: 21–7).

In practice, of course, much depends on the size of the organization and level at which specialists are employed. Clerks are likely to be found at each of the main levels and in the SME. Contract managers and architects, by contrast, are likely to be the preserve of the larger workplaces and the divisional and headquarters levels of multi-establishment organizations.

The overworked owner-manager of an SME is likely to say that this may be fine so far as the large plc or public service organization is concerned. For a small business, however, managing employment relations surely cannot be so important, given everything else that has to be done.

In key respects, however, managing employment relations in the SME is at least as important as in the large plc if not more so.

As so many SME representatives themselves are fond of saying, managing employment relations in this context is inextricably bound up with interpersonal relationships. Yet this makes things more complicated, not less. It is much more difficult, in times of problems, to hide behind the rules and regulations of the larger organization. Very often there is no second chance to make mistakes as there usually is with the plc. An inability to recruit or to hold onto an effective top management team, for example, can be fatal for the business.

Realizing the HR/IR contribution

As Chapters 1 and 3 have suggested, behind the widespread internal restructuring of organizations have been three major developments. One is the break-up of centralized functional bureaucracies into quasi-independent businesses and units. The second is the flattening or de-layering of management hierarchies, i.e. the reduction in the number of tiers of managers. The third is the development of internal markets in which goods and services are traded between business and units as well as between headquarters and divisions. In this case the questions increasingly being asked relate to how to handle the activities involved. Each of these developments has had an effect on views about realizing the HR/IR contribution.

A key role for line managers

Most commentators agree that, in recent years, there has been a general trend towards the greater involvement of line managers in personnel work (Hall and Torrington, 1998). A recent Industrial Society (1998c) survey of 706 organizations, for example, found that around two-thirds claimed to be devolving greater responsibility to line managers. Areas where devolution are most likely to take place are job interviews, performance appraisal, health and safety monitoring, promotion selection, discipline and dismissals, induction, recruitment specifications, annual records and employee communications and counselling (IRS, 1998g). Training and development tend to be only partly delegated, while pay determination seems to be the area where there is the greatest reluctance to devolve.

The rationale for line managers assuming greater responsibility for managing employment relations is difficult to quarrel with. The costs of apparently non-productive support is obviously one consideration. More fundamentally, it can be argued, managing people is an element of every manager's job and cannot be transferred to staff specialists. Significantly, too, greater divisionalization brings greater accountability in every sphere of management. Last, but by no means least, greater devolution enables employment relations decisions to be tailored to suit local circumstances and to be taken more quickly. Furthermore, other things being equal, line managers who make their own decisions are likely to have greater commitment to those decisions.

At the same time, devolution allows specialist HR/IR managers to concentrate on more strategic concerns. This is important for two reasons. First, there is an inevitable danger that the strategic dimension is neglected if the specialist is too involved in operational matters. Second, the more the specialist becomes involved in operational matters, the greater the likelihood that line managers will abdicate responsibility, blaming the specialist for any mistakes that follow. The result is that the specialist is sucked into a vicious circle, which is summarized in Figure 9.1.

In practice, as the list of pros and cons of devolution summarized in Figure 9.2 suggests, experience has been mixed. Most organizations which have devolved greater responsibility report that there is a downside as well as an upside. Personnel specialists, it seems, are not necessarily willing to abandon their operational role, especially as devolution increases the difficulties of measuring their contribution and may increase tensions with line managers (Bach, 1999). Line managers, while supporting devolution in principle, may be unwilling to undertake enhanced people management responsibilities, especially if they are uncertain about whether they will get the necessary training and support (Hall and Torrington, 1998: 49). A major underlying problem has been that it has proved difficult to devolve a clearly defined workload to line managers, the dividing line between executive action and administrative support being especially difficult to delineate.

Complicating matters further is a major difference of opinion

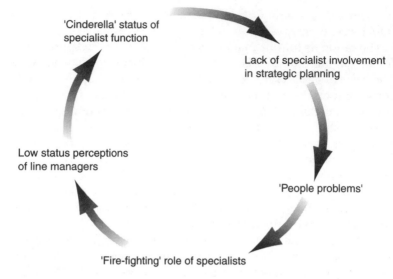

Figure 9.1 The HR function's vicious circle

Pros	Cons
• Local management accountability	• Lack of time to perform HR/IR duties adequately
• Line management responsibility for people issues	• Increase in line manager's workload
• Potential costs savings	• Additional costs of training line managers
• Increase in speed of decision-making	• Increase in grievances/tribunal cases
• Policies/practices to suit local conditions	• Lack of consistency in decision-making
• Strategic role for central HR/IR	• Potential for HR/IR to be marginalized
• Short lines of communication	• Less consistent communications
• Increased awareness of people management issues throughout the organization	• People management not considered to be line manager's job

Figure 9.2 The pros and cons of HR/IR delegation
Source: IRS (1998g: 27)

among HR/IR managers about the direction in which the specialist function should go. Given the increasing importance, discussed in Chapter 1, of the links between business strategy and the management of the HR/IR function, many believe that HR/IR specialists need to put some distance between themselves and the operational detail. Indeed, one acknowledged American HR expert Thomas Stewart, a senior editor of *Fortune* magazine and author of *Intellectual Capital: the New Wealth of Nations* (1998) is quoted in an article appropriately titled 'Strategic role requires HR to take "heretical" action' (John, 1998) as suggesting that 'a view is emerging that the strategic and bureaucratic paper-pusher roles can no longer co-exist – the only way to go is to tear the HR function apart, outsource and downsize it, and call it something else.'

Although there have been no comments as extreme as this in the UK so far, many senior practitioners would appear to be edging towards this position. The senior HR managers of BP Chemicals, whose case is discussed below in connection with the use of benchmarking, are one example. Their colleagues at the Navy, Army and Air Force Institutes (NAAFI) are another. A major restructuring of the specialist function has involved reductions in numbers, the devolution of operational responsibility to line managers and a considerable amount of outsourcing, which even extends to writing employee references. In the words of Mike Nicolson, the HR director,

> Previously, our personnel function was seen as providing administrative support and welfare-type services to the organization. It wasn't strategically focused. Our role now is to ask questions such as 'where is the business going?' and 'how can HR contribute to its success?' and then to provide answers.
> (Quoted in IRS, 1999c)

The other view, which can be associated with senior HR figures in both the UK (see, for example, Torrington, 1998) and the USA (for example, Ulrich, 1997) is that HR specialists are unlikely to be able to make the kind of strategic contribution the first group craves unless they are able to demonstrate considerable expertise in operational matters. Thus Ulrich (1997) identifies a 'multiple-role model' for HR/IR specialists embracing the following:

1 Partner in strategy execution
2 Administrative expert
3 Employee champion
4 Change agent.

Table 9.1 Definition of HR roles

Role	Outcome	Metaphor	Activity
Management of strategic human resources	Executing strategy	Strategic partner	Aligning HR and business strategy; 'organizational diagnosis'
Management of firm infrastructure	Building an efficient infrastructure	Administrative expert	Re-engineering organization processes; shared services
Management of employee contribution	Increasing employee commitment and capability	Employee champion	Listening and responding to employees
Management of transformation of change	Creating a renewed organization	Change agent	Managing transformational change: ensuring capacity for action

Source: Ulrich (1997: 25)

Table 9.1 outlines the roles, outcomes and activities associated with these metaphors and listed below are the key competences he suggests that HR professionals need in order to reflect this broader portfolio:

1 Understanding of the business
2 Knowledge of HR practices
3 Ability to manage culture
4 Ability to manage change
5 Personal credibility.

(Ulrich, 1997: 253–4)

This is a debate which is going to run and run. Our own view is that both camps are somewhat guilty of exaggerating the role of HR/IR specialists in deciding future directions. Our experience is that chief executives and their senior line manager colleagues usually determine the role and influence of the specialists. They do so either explicitly, by deciding what the role should be, or by default, leaving a vacuum which the specialist has to fill as best they can.

Our own research also chimes with the evidence of recent US surveys (see IRS, 1998f). This suggests that, while HR/IR specialists may view success in terms of being treated as a business partner, for senior managers the credibility of the HR function derives from its ability to deliver employment relations services.

It is certainly difficult to believe that, given the overall state of the function described in Chapter 1, UK HR/IR specialists will be able to jettison operational activity for some time to come. Indeed, there is unlikely to be any strategic dimension unless the infrastructure of policies and practices is put in place.

Two final comments are worth making. The first is that senior managers should be wary about taking devolution too far. At risk from excessive devolution is the ability to integrate policies and practice in a coherent fashion. The point can be best illustrated by reference to management development. In our comparison of Japanese and British career and development systems (Storey *et al.*, 1997a), a key element in the success of the Japanese system was the integration of different aspects of the employment relationship. Our conclusion was that an especially challenging task for British organizations would be to find ways in which corporate and individual goals could be linked – especially the development of systems through which different personnel policies, such as career management and management development could be more closely integrated. This implies, as Guest and Mackenzie (1996) have also suggested, that the fashion in the UK for devolving responsibility for career management away from the centre of the organization may have to be reversed if there is to be any real progress, since the only way to monitor and update a career management system systematically is for this to be resourced and done centrally. From their research, Guest and Mackenzie found that it was often difficult to obtain a clear picture of what was happening in organizations because a policy of devolution meant that accountability had been left to local management, some of whom had used this to introduce their own preferred arrangements.

The second point is to do with training. Devolution requires line management training in people skills and it is clear from the first findings of the 1998 WERS that this is not happening; supervisors, it will be recalled from Chapter 1, are being trained in employee relations skills in only around one-quarter of the larger work-places.

A practical example of what can and should be done comes from Coca-Cola Schweppes (for further details see IRS, 1998g). Between them, the HR department and the central training unit put on an extensive mandatory skills training programme for line managers to help them to assume their employment relations responsibilities. Each team leader has a training skills matrix, which lists the core skills for the post, and is expected to complete the full programme over a two-year period. Nine elements are included:

1 Recruitment and selection
2 Team briefing
3 Managing absence
4 Managing discipline and employment law
5 Coaching
6 Problem-solving
7 Being an effective manager
8 Training the trainer
9 Zero-accident behaviour.

In our view, it is especially important that negotiating skills are added to this list.

Delivering specialist services

So far, our treatment has assumed that there will be a specialist in-house activity. Traditionally, its size and composition will have been governed by three factors: diversification, divisionalization and strategic style (Sisson and Marginson, 1995: 104–6). Diversification concerns whether companies are involved in related activities, and the associated degree of integration between different activities, or in unrelated activities or whether they are spatially diversified but undertake the same kind of activity in many different locations. As Chapter 3 pointed out, divisionalization relates to internal structure, which can be primarily territorial (i.e. segmented according to regions or districts) or business-based (i.e.

segmented into product or service divisions). Strategic style concerns the level at which strategic business decisions are taken (business unit, division, national subsidiary or corporate headquarters), the role of corporate headquarters in business development (planning, reviewing, monitoring) and the degree to which it stresses numbers-driven rather than issue-driven planning.

Differences along these three axes generate differences in the extent to which companies are centralized or decentralized in their overall management approach, with consequent implications for their employment relations policies. For example, where there is a high degree of integration in production or service provision, as in the cases of automobile manufacturers (Ford, General Motors/Vauxhall, Peugeot–Talbot and Rover), management will tend towards a centralized approach. A centralized approach is also likely where the organization is carrying out the same activity in different locations, because of gains to be made in standardized operating procedures and common purchasing. Here the main clearing banks (Barclays, Lloyds, NatWest and HSBC) and multiple retailers (such as Sainsbury and Tesco) would be examples. A decentralized approach is more likely where different kinds of business activity, which are not closely related, are being undertaken in different locations. The extreme case would be that of the diversified conglomerate or industrial holding companies

Variations in the size of corporate personnel function, for example, are only partially accounted for by the employment size of companies. The largest corporate personnel functions tend to be found amongst single-business enterprises and amongst strategic planners, whereas conglomerates and financial controllers tend to have small numbers of specialist staff or no corporate function at all. Similarly it is no coincidence that it is the single-business enterprises, such as the automobile manufacturers, clearing banks and multiple retailers, which have multi-establishment bargaining or pay determination, whereas it is the conglomerates which are more likely to have decentralized arrangements.

Increasingly in recent years, there has been a change in the relationship reflecting the process of marketization discussed in Chapter 3. HR/IR specialists, in the words of the IRS *Management Review* (1998g: 3), have become ' "economic" actors selling and marketing their wares in the same way as other service providers'. The separation of the roles of purchaser and provider, the *Review* goes on, has proved especially attractive in public services because it facilitates a move towards 'a more business-like structure, in line with past and present government policy'.

A complicated pattern or 'mixed' economy has emerged. Indeed, no fewer than four main options for delivering personnel activities can be identified as well as the traditional department:

1 *External consultancy* in which the organization and its units go outside to completely independent business for help and advice on IR and HR matters.
2 The *in-house agency*, in which the personnel department or some of its activities, for example, graduate recruitment, is seen as a cost centre and its activities are cross-charged to other departments or divisions.
3 The *internal consultancy* in which the personnel department sells its services to the parent organization or its units – the implication being that managers in the parent organization will enjoy some freedom in deciding to go elsewhere if they are not happy with the service that is being provided.
4 The *business within a business* in which some of the activities of the function are formed into a quasi-independent organization which may trade not only with the parent organization and its units, but also externally.

These options can be explored in more detail by consulting Adams (1991).

In theory, the total portfolio of employment relations activities can be outsourced. In practice, however, as Fowler (1997: 43) points out, there are three main arguments against total outsourcing:

1 A significant proportion of personnel work is so central to the culture and strategic objectives of the organization that it can be undertaken effectively only by the organization itself.
2 Some situations are unpredictable and require immediate action.
3 There is no significant market for the provision of a total personnel function – rather it is characterized by many providers of specialist services, such as executive search, job evaluation, training courses and so on.

In most cases, it is particular activities which have been out-sourced. Some have traditionally been so. These include recruitment (in the form of executive search), training and job evaluation. Pensions and payroll administration have also been long-standing candidates in some organizations. More recently, the IRS *Management Review* (1998g: 35) suggests, the net has widened to 'range from employee communications to helping and preparing for Investors in People Accreditation'. The NAAFI, as reported above, has even outsourced compiling employee references and arranging pensioners' social functions.

The main reasons for outsourcing are also fairly consistent. Typically they are to secure access to specialist services and expertise (61 per cent), reduce costs (46 per cent) and enable HR specialists to take on a more strategic role (38 per cent) (IRS, 1998g).

The other forms of delivery listed above typically involve some kind of service contract in which there is charging for activities performed. The types of possibility open to general managers are indicated by practice. For example, the London Borough of Hackney has substantially reduced the size of its HR/IR function and split it into two at the same time as it has devolved responsibility for day-to-day activities to line managers. A so-called core unit is responsible for the following areas:

1 Strategy development
2 The council's regulatory framework
3 Providing advice to executive board members and council members
4 Corporate servicing
5 Corporate commissioning
6 Overall resource planning.

For its part, the trading unit, as the name suggests, sells services to the core units and service directorates. In the words of the IRS *Management Review*:

> Managers can purchase the unit's consultancy services on a unit-by-unit basis or opt for a 'gold card' approach, whereby they enjoy an all-inclusive service and have benefit of unlimited support via an advice line. There is no minimum limit on the level of consultation purchased and a customer can buy as

little as one job evaluation. The cost of a single job evaluation is £55. If the HR consultancy is required to respond to a job evaluation request within five working days, the cost increases to £75.

(1998g: 45)

As Figure 9.3 suggests, there are pros and cons in the case of each of the main alternatives to the traditional department. Most are common to any outsourcing activity. Especially important here is the expertise to manage a market as opposed to an employment relationship. Key considerations, as Storey (1998c) emphasizes, are the importance of clarifying the objectives of each outsourcing decision and the need to specify high standards in areas such as quality, reliability and delivery. Perhaps the key question, however, should be the significance an organization attaches to the HR/IR function. If it is a core competence, there is a strong argument for keeping it in-house as companies such as NatWest Bank have done.

A seat at the top table?

Another debate concerns the representation of the HR/IR function in the senior management team, which in the case of the large plc, raises the issue of main board representation. The background is set by the research evidence suggesting that it is relatively rare. In the case of multi-establishment organizations, the two Warwick Company-level Industrial Relations Surveys (Marginson *et al.*, 1988, 1993) amongst a representative sample of 176 multisite companies employing 1000 or more in the UK where the respondent was an executive responsible for personnel and industrial relations at corporate level are the major source. Although the two samples are not directly comparable, they nonetheless would seem to confirm that not only was specialist board representation restricted to a minority of companies (30 per cent), but also there was no change between 1985 and 1992 – a matter of some surprise given the upsurge of interest in HRM and recognition of the need for a strategic dimension to managing employment relations.

In the case of independent establishments in the trading sector, the 1990 WIRS survey (Millward *et al.*, 1992: 50–1) found virtually

228

Pros	Cons
Internal consultancy	
• Concentrate on HR/IR strategy	• Must sell/market services
• Central HR/IR function becomes part of strategic core	• Cost-based transactions
• Self-financing	• More open to external competition in terms of costs and quality of services
• Better able to show HR/IR's contribution	• Better able to identify HR/IR's shortcomings
• Customer/supplier relationship	• Potential for conflict with purchasers
• Sell services externally	
External HR/IR consultants	
• Access specialist skills/expertise	• Conflicting advice
• HR/IR can stick to core activities/ strategic role	• Poor value/expensive advice
• Independent/objective opinion	• Lack of knowledge in specific areas
• Controversial decisions more acceptable from outsiders	• Lack of understanding of organizational culture
• Cross-transfer of skills	• Proposals 'off-the-shelf'/not tailored to business needs
Outsourcing HR/IR	
• Economies of scale	• Poor quality service
• Removes time-comsuming complex activities	• Poor management control
• No requirement to keep up to date with technological change	• Additional cost/time to manage contract
• Removes activities providing little added value	• Loss of skills/knowledge
• Accesses to specialist skills/expertise	• Possible costs of bringing service back in-house
• Reduced labour costs	• Greater dependence on supplier

Figure 9.3 Pros and cons of alternative means of HR/IR delivery
Source: IRS (1998g: 35)

no change in the proportion with someone with specific responsibility for personnel and industrial relations work on the senior management committee. Overall, only half reported such representation, with the proportion increasing with size; such representation was also more likely in manufacturing than in services.

In any case, the significance of board representation has been questioned. Some commentators have suggested, on the basis of more focused survey evidence, that 'formal positioning on the board, or lack of it, did not seem to make much difference to the extent of personnel's influence' (Torrington, 1998: 32). Personnel specialists often found ways around it by informal networking. Rather, what counted was more informal sources of 'corridor power'. (Interestingly, however, most non-board members aspired to this status and were fighting for it or expressing discontent about not having it.)

Our own view, which has been spelt out in detail elsewhere (see, for example, Sisson, 1994b), continues to be that, other things being equal, having a seat at the top table is important. It is not just a question of the intuitive argument that if personnel specialists are not even present, the input they can make is inevitably limited to dealing with the personnel implications of implementing strategic decisions.

The Warwick Company-level Industrial Relations Survey results confirm that companies with a main board personnel director were, according to both the personnel and financial respondents to the survey, more likely to take personnel matters into account in strategic business decisions. They were also more likely to accord personnel a role in the monitoring and control of business units. Board-level representation was also correlated with a number of other significant features: personnel policy committees, bringing together different management functions at corporate level were reported in over 40 per cent of companies; regular meetings (more than once a year) were held between corporate personnel managers and those in business units in just over half of cases. This latter rose to three-quarters in companies with a main board director for personnel. Company-wide policies were strongly associated with the existence of a corporate personnel policy committee: the implication is that such committees are primarily concerned to develop guiding principles rather than specific policies (Purcell, 1995: 78–9). The survey undertaken by IRS (1998g) in preparing its review of the evolving HR function offers further support.

Auditing the specialist function

Pressure to establish the effectiveness and efficiency of the HR/IR function has gone hand-in-hand with the debate over methods of delivery. On the basis of its survey of more than forty major organizations and from other sources, the IRS (1998g: 48–50) identifies three main types of indicator that can be used:

1 Quantitative or hard measures, i.e. numerical measures of inputs, outputs and outcomes (a full list will be found in Figure 9.4).
2 Qualitative or soft measures such as the attitudes or percentages of managers and employees gained through surveys and focus groups.
3 Process analysis – covering detailed scrutiny of the clarity or efficiency of particular HR/IR processes and activities, again using focus groups and surveys, plus arrangements such as IiP accreditation.

Market testing is another device that can be used. Indeed, this is explicit in a number of the purchaser/provider splits that have been introduced. If the purchaser is unhappy with the service, they can buy services from elsewhere. Here the guide produced by IPD in conjunction with the Chartered Institute for Public Finance for use in cases of compulsory competitive tendering is helpful. It suggests that overall quality of the potential contractors and in-house function could be assessed on the basis of the factors and weightings listed in Table 9.2. For further details see Fowler (1997).

Some organizations use benchmarking to audit the specialist HR/IR function. This is true, for example, of the civil service agencies (Cabinet Office, 1998). In the words of the Department of Trade and Industry, the process of benchmarking is defined as recognizing 'the importance of understanding how the best of the competition is performing and of a commitment to implement changes to match or exceed them' (DTI, 1997b). The obvious points of comparison are close competitors, but some organisations recommend going beyond to identify best practice wherever it may be found. Thus, Xerox, where benchmarking is credited with being one of the main factors behind the revival in

231

HARD

Recruitment and selection

- Number of long-term vacancies
- Average time to fill vacancies
- Proportion filled through promotion, demotion or lateral movements of personnel
- Average time spent in a job or function per employee

Training and development

- Number of trainee days/number of employees
- Total training budget/total employment expenditure

Compensation and benefits

- Total compensation cost/total revenues
- Basic salary/total renumeration
- Number of salary grades/employees

Employee relations

- Number of resignations/total headcount per year
- Average length of service per employee
- Rate of absenteeism
- Average length of absence per employee
- Number of supervisors and managers per employee

Overall HR management

- Total revenue per employee
- Total headcount this year compared with last year
- Proportion of part-time employees to total number of staff
- Employment cost/total expenditure
- Number of HR professionals per employee
- Age distribution of employees

SOFT

Internal customer satisfaction

- Employee satisfaction surveys
- Employee focus groups
- Line management survey of HR's performance
- Senior management views of HR's performance

Figure 9.4 Hard and soft measures of HR effectiveness
Source: IRS (1998g)

Table 9.2 Factors and weightings that can be used to assess the quality of service providers

Quality factors	Maximum score
Know-how and experience	20
Access to specialist data and advice	15
Acceptability and relevance of proposed methods	15
Compatibility of style with that of purchaser	20
Price	30

Source: Fowler (1997)

the 1980s, has evaluated organizations as diverse as railways, insurance and electricity generation.

Originally, benchmarking was used in such areas as new product development involving cross-functional teams and there was a tendency to exaggerate 'asset management' at the expense of 'people management' (Holberton, 1991: 24). More and more, however, benchmarking has become a valuable tool in managing employment relations. An important catalyst was the coming to the UK of Japanese companies such as Nissan, whose performance levels have helped to destroy some of the myths about the attitudes of UK workers and to put the emphasis on the policies and practices of management.

The detailed case of BP Chemicals is reported in *Employment Trends* (IRS, 1997b) and involves a similar approach to the one suggested in Figure 9.5. Four HR managers were joined by two manufacturing colleagues and given the task of finding a way 'to achieve best-in-class standards of human resource management, promoting the objective to become a world class chemicals company'. The methods used to identify appropriate benchmarks included brainstorming, analysis of the HR department and interviews with non-specialists; the final indicators chosen were very similar to the list in Figure 9.3. A number of 'activity drivers' were also produced to take into account non-quantitative elements and, in particular, the business strategies that would have an impact in terms of generating work for the HR function. These included organizational changes, turnover, unionization, technology, age profile, growth rate and staff development.

Step 1 Decide composition of audit team, which should include senior line management representation if the exercise is to have any credibility.

Step 2 Identify the personnel department's main customers. The personnel department may be seen to have a number of customers. In the case of the headquarters personnel department, it is likely to be the senior management team in a critical function-type organization such as a large retail chain store or a bank. In a decentralized multidivisional organization, on the other hand, it will more likely be the general managers of the strategic business or service units.

Step 3 Review personnel department's mission, i.e. reason for the personnel department's existence, its principal activities and its most important values.

Step 4 Review personnel department's role in formulating the organization's strategy.

Step 5 Review role of personnel department in developing key HR and IR policies and practices – human resource planning, recruitment, selection and retention, training and development, reward management, and employee relations – and the extent to which HR and IR policies and practices are 'owned' by line managers as well as the personnel department.

Step 6 Review delivery of personnel policies and practices. Are there HR and IR activities currently being undertaken by personnel managers which could be done as well or better by line managers? Are there technically better ways of delivering HR and IR service currently being undertaken by personnel managers, e.g. computerized databases which could be accessed by line managers? Are there HR and IR activities currently being undertaken by personnel managers which could be done better or more efficiently by external agencies? Are there better ways of organizing the HR and IR activities for which the personnel department is going to be responsible, e.g. the in-house agency, the internal consultancy, the business within a business? Are the structure of the personnel department and the skills and experience of its staff appropriate to the service for which it is going to be directly responsible?

Step 7 Make external comparisons to estabish 'best' practice. They do not have to be close competitors, however. Indeed, as the example of Xerox quoted in the text suggests, there are benefits in extending the analysis beyond an organization's immediate competitors; such competitors may not be a positive role model so far as the management of HR and IR is concerned.

Step 8 Review analysis and policy implications with 'customers'.

Step 9 Implement agreed improvements.

Figure 9.5 Auditing the HR/IR function

The next step was to interview a diagonal slice of the organization to elicit the views of 'internal' customers on HR's performance. It emerged that people did not understand what HR did, that it had a low profile in the organization, and that even the making of mistakes of detail, such as miscalculating pay, had an adverse effect on opinion.

The third step took the form of visits to nine other organizations (three in BP and six elsewhere). Typically, these were half- or full-day visits and, as in the case of BP employees, involved interviews at a number of levels. As well as appreciating that the qualitative issues were more important than the quantitative, the benchmarking team concluded that 'best practice' included:

1 A formal client focus for HR.
2 The devolution of people management, to include some traditional HR responsibilities, to line management to the greatest extent possible.
3 A smaller, more strategically focused, central HR function which can take responsibility for clarifying and communicating business objectives to the workforce and instigating change in response to manufacturing imperatives.
4 Teamworking and flexibility within HR to cope with peaks and troughs.
5 A strong commitment to training and the transformation of the basis of reward systems from performance to competence.
6 The simplification of HR processes so that they are transparent, easy to administer and relevant to business needs.

On the basis of this, BP not only made major changes to the organization of the specialist HR/IR function – each member, for example, was expected to provide a 'one-stop shop' for its unit as well as taking 'lead' responsibility for a designated area such as employment law or reward systems – but also instituted a regular review process of HR specialists. An overall contract covering the entire HR department set out the services the department would supply to the rest of the organization and for which collective responsibility was to be assumed. In addition, an individual contract for each HR adviser was introduced against which client managers could appraise performance at the end of the year.

Some organizations conduct regular benchmarking. In the

Industrial Relations Research Unit's pay and working time project, for example, there is a benchmarking 'club' in one sector of
the engineering industry run by the trade organization with financial support from the DTI. The club, which embraced a dozen of
so of the major UK employers, made regular comparison between
member firms and, wherever possible, with major international
competitors. There had also been visits to Japanese companies in
the sector.

As Humble (1988: 33) pointed out more than a decade ago, it
does not require an 'espionage' system to collect the data to carry
out the basic forms of benchmarking: job adverts and recruitment
brochures, as well as annual reports and articles in such publications as *People Management*, *Personnel Today*, Incomes Data Services and Industrial Relations Services publications carry a great
deal of useful material. The great majority of large UK companies
are multinational in scope and so can look inside as well as outside for useful benchmarks.

Conclusions

Managing employment relations, this chapter has argued,
involves both strategic and operational dimensions. Attainment
of a quality workforce capable of delivering competitive advantage in world markets does not happen by accident. It means
devising and practising a mutually reinforcing set of employment
practices which ensure that HR planning is actually done, that
appropriate selection methods are used, that the performance
management elements of goal-setting, communication, appraisal
and reward are tackled in a way which fits the business needs, that
a positive relationship is developed with trade unions, and so on.
The challenge could not be more fundamental.

There is no question about where the responsibility lies for
ensuring that the organization has an effective and efficient
HR/IR function to help achieve the desired objective: it is with the
chief executive and the senior management team, whether it be
a large multinational corporation or a small business. In terms
of best practice, the predominant view is very clear. Operational
responsibility for employment relations should rest with line

managers, with advice and support being provided by specialists from inside or outside the organization depending on its size. The same is true of the strategic dimension, the only difference being the level of management and expertise involved. Market principles should be applied to the delivery of the HR/IR function, as they are in other areas of management, to ensure the highest levels of performance. In each case, however, the critical decisions revolve around the balance – between line and staff, between internal and external delivery – for which there is no magic formula. Managing employment relations is a continuous and ongoing process and is never a question of automatic policies or practices. Critically, it is these decisions which will be the major factor in shaping the contribution of any specialist HR/IR managers the organization employs.

Suggested further reading

Strongly recommended are Ulrich (1997), Hall and Torrington (1998) and IRS (1998g). Torrington (1998) is very good on the challenge facing the HR/IR function. The two volumes reporting the findings of the 1998 Workplace Employee Relations Survey (Cully *et al.*, 1999; Millward *et al.*, 2000) also contain much useful information on the presence of HR/IR specialists in UK workplaces.

10

THE KEY ISSUES

We began in Chapter 1 by suggesting that just about every book on the subject and many a company chairman's statement make the same point: it is people that make the difference. The workforce is the most vital asset. Technology and capital can be acquired on varying terms by a wide range of players around the world: the real, sustainable competitive edge has to come ultimately, therefore, from the way that capable and motivated teams put these resources to work. We also pointed out that, in too many organizations, these statements were regarded as cynical hype because managers were either unable or unwilling to take the necessary steps to deliver these visionary insights.

In the intervening chapters we have endeavoured to track and explain potential and actual developments in the activation of this message. We have emphasized that there is a considerable gap between the rhetoric and reality of managing employment relations. The much-vaunted development-oriented, flexible, well motivated, efficiently operating, highly skilled and well paid economy is hardly in evidence. We have argued this not just because of many fundamental contradictions in approach, but also because of a number of deep-seated structural conditions and, in particular, the tendency towards short-termism in management's approach which is encouraged by

238

key features of the UK's business system and the lack of countervailing pressures in the form of an appropriate regulatory framework.

We have also recognized that managers and students of management looking to analysts for guidelines concerning the way to proceed in employment management will not be satisfied or well served merely by a critique of the management of employment relations. A growing number of managers are only too aware of the problems that stem from the wider structures in which they have to work. In successive chapters we have endeavoured to suggest how those managers who are anxious to improve their approach might proceed. We have focused on the most promising forms of intervention – developing a strategic approach, organizing for high performance, promoting involvement and participation, training and development, and so on. Additionally, we have drawn attention to some of the basic problems that will need to be confronted and how, drawing on the growing evidence from empirical research, some of these might be addressed. A continuing theme has been how managers might audit progress in developing a more strategic approach to managing employment relations.

We have also sought to build into our analysis significant elements of a forward look. We have stressed that restructuring is likely to be an enduring feature, reflecting the implications of economic and monetary union (EMU) as well as wider globalization pressures. We have also suggested that UK management is not going to be left entirely to its own devices in employment relations matters as it was in the 1980s and 1990s. The Labour government, however 'business-friendly' it is seeking to be, is going to be playing a much more significant role.

One scenario is that it is in the field of employment relations especially that a second-term Labour government, anxious to promote the 'knowledge economy', will give practical expression to its much-vaunted 'third way'. At face value, this will involve the rejection of both the legally regulated approach associated with the traditional European social model and the free market approach associated with UK Conservative governments of the 1980s and 1990s. Along with its EU partners, there is likely to be resort to a wide range of measures to support the four pillars of what might be described as the 'new' European social model: improving employability, developing entrepreneurship, encouraging adaptability in businesses and their employees, and strengthening the policies for equal opportunities. As well as a framework of individual employment rights, this is likely to involve fiscal measures to promote lifelong learning accounts and put real teeth into Investors in People; the publication and promotion of 'best practice' guides and codes in key areas; support for the kind of social auditing or benchmarking discussed below; pressure on large organizations, in the private as well as the public sector, not only to adopt 'best practice' themselves but also to take steps to make sure it is disseminated among the SMEs making up their supply chains – the enormous potential of the leadership role of multinational companies is clearly demonstrated in the European Round Table of Industrialists' (ERT) report on the ways in which practical partnerships between large and small companies can help to stimulate job creation (ERT, 1997) – and the use of public service contracts to the same end. The use of regulatory frameworks in other areas to enforce employment standards, such as financial services, where the link between training and quality is so critical, is also a distinct possibility. There could even be moves to shift the balance in corporate governance arrangements, which are so inimical to investment in human capital. All these measures are likely to be underpinned by a chorus of support for cooperation and partnership at every level – national, regional, local authority and organization – creating a very different kind of regulatory environment for managing employment relations to the one we have been used to (for the contrasts between the 'traditional' and the 'new' social models, see Figures 10.1 and 10.2).

Important though this changing context will be, our main focus in this final chapter, as it has been throughout the book, is on the key issues facing those responsible for managing HR/IR in organizations. Three issues are singled out for special attention. Each is important in its own right. Together, however, they give us an opportunity to pull many of the strands of our analysis together and remind the reader of the main points.

	Key features	*Outcomes*
The 'European' model	strong trade unions collective bargaining legal regulation (*employee rights*)	$\left\{\begin{array}{l}\text{security}\\\text{relatively high pay}\\\text{inflexibility}\\\text{lack of competitiveness}\\\text{unemployment}\end{array}\right.$
The 'US' model	weak trade unions little collective bargaining management regulation (*management prerogative*)	$\left\{\begin{array}{l}\text{insecurity}\\\text{relatively low pay}\\\text{flexibility}\\\text{competitiveness}\\\text{employment}\end{array}\right.$

Figure 10.1 Models of HRM/IR: the current stereotypes

Main ingredients	*Outcomes*
flexibility security education and training direct participation ('empowerment') indirect participation ('partnership')	$\left\{\begin{array}{l}\text{quality people/}\\\text{quality goods and services/}\\\text{competitiveness}\\\text{'good' jobs}\end{array}\right.$

Figure 10.2 The 'new' European social model

Balancing flexibility and security

The aim of reconciling 'security for workers with the flexibility which firms need' (CEC, 1997) can easily be criticized as being idealistic and unrealistic. Even with the best will in the world, it can be argued, management cannot guarantee security, such is the volatility and unpredictability of demand. In its response to the European Commission's Green Paper, the Swedish employers' confederation (SAF) put it quite bluntly: 'It cannot be accepted' (EIRO-online, 1999). Instead, SAF argues, the main question should be whether the enterprises have enough scope for developing a flexible and effective work organization. The

241

problem in Europe was that legislation and rules of the game put far too much emphasis on security and static employment relations.

Yet there are powerful reasons for thinking that balancing flexibility and security will be one of the key issues. First of all, there is the business case. The basic problem has been spelt out in Chapter 1. Most recent attention has been on external flexibility, i.e. the ability of the organization to vary its commitments through reductions in the number of employees or changes in their status (for example from permanent to temporary) or through subcontracting. The real advances, it is argued, are much more likely to come from internal flexibility leading to improved organizational capacity. In the words of the European Commission's Green Paper *Partnership for a New Organization of Work*,

> It is about the scope for improving employment and competitiveness through a better organization of work at the workplace, based on high skill, high trust and high quality. It is about the will and ability of management and workers to take initiatives, to improve the quality of goods and services, to make innovations and to develop the production process and consumer relations.
>
> (CEC, 1997: 5)

The problem, as IRRU's study of TQM for the Department of Trade and Industry suggests (Collinson *et al.*, 1998), is that it is difficult to maintain the credibility of, let alone the commitment to, attempts to promote improvements in the quality of the goods or services if the only way in which management seems capable of managing the turbulence in its environment is through redundancy. There has to be some optimism.

Secondly, there are the political considerations. It is not just that it is very difficult for politicians to quarrel with the argument that information and consultation about restructuring are a fundamental social right. Arguably, one of the main reasons for the shift in position of most governments on social policy issues, whatever their overall political persuasion, reflects concerns about the economic and social costs of restructuring. The reality is that it is governments, not business, which have to cope with many of the implications of unbridled market capitalism. Unemployment is not just bad politics. The costs, in terms of unemployment, social welfare and the like are considerable, as are the burdens of social deprivation and exclusion that can result. Similarly, governments are increasingly concerned about the responsibilities for the costs of training and retraining for employability, especially given the investment they recognize they have to incur to improve the education system. Critically, these and other cost implications of restructuring threaten public finances and the desire to reduce personal tax levels. Getting business to share the burden is a major objective.

In terms of practical implications, a great deal of attention has focused on some measure of employment security. For example, a key feature of a number of recent partnership agreements has been an explicit trade-off between far-ranging internal flexibility and a measure of employment security. Organizations which have introduced 'flexicurity' arrangements come from manufacturing and services and include the Rover Group, which set the trend with its New Deal agreement, Blue Circle, Co-op Bank, the Halifax, Hyder (Welsh Water), Lloyds/TSB and United Distillers.

On the face of it, there is considerable scope for such arrangements. The first findings of the 1998 WERS, it will be recalled from Chapter 1, suggest that only 14 per cent of workplaces with more than 25 employees have any provision for guaranteed job security or no compulsory redundancy policy.

It is not just employment security that is important, however. Two other areas feature prominently on policy-makers' agendas. One is the promotion of employability via training. In the words of the report of the European Commission's Higher-level Group on restructuring:

> Companies have an obligation and a direct interest in helping to maintain the employability of their workforce ... Companies should introduce training programmes, which prepare workers for:
>
> - different approaches to their work as the result of technological, organizational or economic change;
> - changing jobs and acquiring new skills within the same company; adapting to the needs of the labour market, should they be forced to leave the company.

The effort involved entails training which goes beyond the immediate needs of the job in question and prepares the worker for future requirements.

(CEC, 1998: 16)

The other area is information and consultation. Quoting from the same report:

Good forward planning and dialogue allow more effective management of industrial change. With their help we can make the right choices for the future and turn change to our advantage . . .

The systematic development of social dialogue within companies, nationally and at European level is fundamental to managing change and preventing negative social consequences and deterioration of the social fabric (national levels). Social dialogue ensures a balance is maintained between corporate flexibility and workers' safety.

(CEC, 1998: 5)

Interestingly, the Higher-level Group report also goes on to suggest that 'the best means of spreading good social practice in business to encourage companies to report publicly on their practices and policies in a structured manner is a managing change report, i.e. an annual report on employment and working conditions' (CEC, 1998: 13). All companies with more than 1000 employees, it suggests, should produce a management of change report (MCR) in consultation with employees and their representatives. The suggested framework appears in Figure 10.3. They go on,

The group recommends that the MCR be considered as a criterion for the award of all government contracts and grant aid at European, national and regional levels. Adjudicators should look closely at the policies and practices of companies with particular reference to work organization and rhythm of work, communication and involvement; training and retraining for self-development through life-long learning; health and safety at work; and the contribution and involvement of employees in environmental management.

(CEC, 1998: 13)

A. Policies

1 Dealing with structural change	• policies and procedures
2 Communication and involvement/ social dialogue	• at different levels
	• including collective and individual arrangements
3 Education and training	• overall policies and commitments
4 Employee health and safety	• at different levels in the organisation
5 Equal opportunities	• including race, sex, disability

B. Practices

1 Communication and involvement	Identifying specific systems, practices
2 Training, retraining and education	and arrangements which are in place
3 Health and safety	under each of the policy areas, giving
4 Structural change	more detail on those seen as most
	critical, effective and/or innovative. For
	example, identifying what is being done
	to adapt work organisation and rhythm
	of work to the opportunities offered by
	the new information technologies.

C. Performance

1 Performance systems	• Monitoring of performance under each policy, data on education systems, review or audit mechanisms.
2 Performance in the year	• range of measurements
	• indication of initiatives implemented

Figure 10.3 Proposed framework for a managing change report
Source: CEC (1998)

Managing individually and collectively

A distinctive feature of our treatment has been the attempt to break away from the conventional segmentation, which results in books on personnel management and separate books on industrial relations. Our aim has been to reflect the trends in practice whereby initiatives engage with, and have implications for, both sets of activity. We now need to return centrally to this issue of the interplay between individualism and collectivism and emphasize that it is not a question of *either or* as it was so often presented by protagonists of collective bargaining in the 1960s and 1970s and of HRM in the 1980s and 1990s. Both, as Coupar and Stevens (1998) have argued, will be critical.

Of course, managing individually is important. The notion of communicating with employees only through a trade union, for example, is obviously not appropriate, if it ever was. The relationship with the individual is important in other areas as well – selection and recruitment, training and development, involvement and participation, and the rest. The requirements for adaptability, speed of response, and for direct effective communications also mean that there cannot be a return to the type of detailed proceduralism of the 1960s and 1970s discussed in Chapter 1.

Even so, there is a need to manage collectively as well as individually. As Chapter 4 has argued, the case for collective employee voice does not rest on social justice alone, fundamental though this is. It is the business case which is important. Employees and their representatives have a significant contribution to make to improving performance. Their knowledge and experience of the details of operations on the ground, the problems and the pitfalls and how they might be dealt with, are superior to those of management. These details, after all, are their job. The notion that individuals will be open with managers about what they think is naive in the extreme. Most people feel too powerless. There is always a worry that suggestions for change will be interpreted as criticism, which will be held against the individual who makes them. Significantly, as Chapter 4 showed, it was these kinds of concerns, revealed in anonymous employee attitude surveys, which encouraged the food retailer Sainsbury to introduce a system of works councils for the purposes of information and consultation throughout its stores in 1996, as the direct relationship between supervisors and employers, most of whom were part-time women, was simply not producing the contribution to continuous improvement that senior managers were looking for.

Collective voice or dialogue, to use the Higher-level Group's terms, is also critical to maintaining the balance between flexibility and security. Opposition to collective employee dialogue must always give rise to the suspicion that management has got something to hide or is concerned about the implications for its prerogative. If senior managers really believe in information and consultation, they should be exploiting, in the best sense of the term, all the means at their disposal. Indeed, a further strong argument for dialogue is that it offers an extremely valuable discipline; management needs to think through and be able to justify its decisions to its employees. Again, it makes no sense, other than in terms of the power relationship, not to take advantage of this important opportunity.

Sometimes the argument is put forward that, while collective employee voice may be appropriate for large, homogeneous groups of manual workers, clerical employees and retail assistants, along with professional employees, do not need it. Obviously, there may be employees who do not wish to have collective representation. If so, that is their prerogative. Other things being equal, however, the case for collective employee voice is as strong for professional groups as it is for others. Relevant here are the findings of IRRU research into the relative failure of the introduction of a computerized information system in a major pharmaceutical company (see Lloyd and Newell, 1998). A key factor in the failure was the lack of any real dialogue between management and employees (in this case sales representatives). In the absence of any representative structures, the views of employees were either not expressed, for fear of antagonizing senior managers, or simply ignored.

In the case of most large multi-establishment organizations, collective bargaining with trade unions will remain the main vehicle for collective employee voice. In the UK context it appears unlikely that wholesale derecognition of trade unions is feasible for the main body of organizations. This is true not only in the public sector where requirements of comprehensive and universal coverage and of standardized levels of service obtain, but also for the larger private sector organizations which in the main do not have the wherewithal, in terms of either financial resources or the interpersonal skills of individual managers, to emulate the likes of IBM or Marks & Spencer other than in a most superficial way. It is a lesson that the clearing banks thankfully learnt quickly in the early 1990s. Significantly, some of the banks such as Barclays and NatWest, have been to the fore in negotiating partnership agreements with their union representatives encompassing, among other things, the restructuring process and its implications.

There needs also to be a clear acceptance of strategic responsibility at company level for managing employment relations. The first element is a company-level commitment to relationship-building. Restructuring often means that much responsibility is devolved to operating units. At the same time, the lateral responsibility between HR/IR specialists and line managers has become increasingly blurred. One consequence of this fluidity has been massive equivocation about fundamentals. Is there a corporate stance or philosophy on employment relations or is this something to be determined severally by the business units? In the light of the analysis in previous chapters, our suggestion is that the company or organization should be the level at which employment relations strategy should be developed. Managers from individual units need to be involved and they should have primary responsibility for operating decisions. It is too much, however, to expect them to be responsible for developing strategy on their own especially if, at the same time, the division or headquarters is going to impose financial targets that in effect crowd out attention to the medium and long term. It also does not maximize the advantages of belonging to a multi-unit organization in terms of experience and expertise. In many organizations, making explicit what is already the reality – whatever the apparent 'decentralization of bargaining' might imply – would be a bonus in itself: it would save a great deal of time and energy as well as removing much of the ambiguity about how much autonomy the individual unit really has.

Second, having resolved the equivocation about responsibilities, there is a need in many cases to reassess the relationship with trade unions at company level. In many organizations this is a taboo issue – trade unions are to be kept as far away as possible from the levels where the serious decisions are made. The experience of managements that have maintained relationships with trade unions above the individual units, however, suggests that the advantages considerably outweigh any disadvantages. Trade union involvement in the general direction of employment relations developments can smooth many of the wrinkles that might otherwise emerge in the individual units. It also does not necessarily follow that a joint approach at the organization level means that the bargaining has to take place at this level as well. There is a tendency to forget that employees and their representatives value their autonomy as much as managers do.

The third element concerns actual mechanisms. To repeat our view expressed in Chapter 8, management needs to seize the opportunity presented by the coming of partnership agreements to put their relationship with trade unions onto a new and, hopefully, more positive footing. Most importantly, they should seek to use partnership agreements to extend the coverage of consultation over a wider range of issues and at higher levels in the organization along the lines discussed throughout the book. Experience in other EU countries, where works councils are the norm, suggests that the separation of joint regulation (collective bargaining) from joint consultation can facilitate joint management/worker discussions of critical issues including product markets, investment and operational improvements.

Although the principles have a general application, the target group for this particular programme is mainly the large, multi-establishment organizations which are already unionized. Elsewhere, and especially in the SMEs which are so increasingly important, the insistence on the 'single-channel' system of collective employee voice, whereby negotiations, consultation, communication and participation are handled through the medium of trade unions is unlikely to be viable (although the possibility of framework agreements or joint opinions on HR/IR matters involving the TUC and some of the main SME representative organizations would make a great deal of sense). Here the mechanism for information and collective consultation has to be some form of employee-based committee or council.

In especially small organizations, say those with less than 20 employees, a regular meeting between the senior managers and all employees would seem to be appropriate. In larger organizations, some form of a representative system is required. In terms of its arrangements, something like the 'workforce agreement' provisions of the Working Time Regulations offer a basic blueprint. All employees would be eligible to stand as employee representatives as well as vote in elections; voting would also need to be in secret and votes fairly and accurately counted.

In terms of content, the report of the Higher-level Group on restructuring quoted earlier offers a starting point. Key issues, it will be recalled, include major structural changes; training, retraining and education; health and safety; equal opportunities;

and performance. As the authors of the report emphasize however, these are indications only and should not be seen as a straitjacket. A sensible management would see such arrangements as an opportunity to inform and consult with employees on any matters that are likely to affect them and to which they can make a contribution. The fundamental logic, it needs to be remembered, is not an exercise in social justice but a key element in business strategy.

Integration, integration, integration

Our final point embraces the previous two and enables us to emphasize one of the main undercurrents of our treatment throughout the book. It is the need for integration: integration in the sense of employment relations policies and practices being complementary as well as appropriate; and integration in the sense of employment relations policies and practices being compatible with business strategy. Without a doubt, this represents the biggest challenge facing those responsible for managing employment relations.

The unspoken assumption of the bulk of the prescriptive textbooks and punditry is that success comes from following supposed best practice in each of the main areas of employment relations management. Our developing understanding of the practice of employment relations suggests that it is not like this. First of all, it is not individual practices which are associated with success: what make the difference are bundles of mutually supportive and reinforcing practices. Incrementalism may appear to make sense but, in managing employment relations, the danger is that the implementation of individual practices, however appropriate they may appear to be in their own right, is likely to be unsuccessful unless they are supported by complementary arrangements.

Absolutely clear is that slavish following of the latest fad can be totally counterproductive, breeding cynicism from top to bottom of the organization. The most powerful illustration of this comes in the area of pay systems. It is not just that senior UK managers seem obsessed with performance pay – be it the payment by results systems of the 1950s and 1960s or the individual performance pay of the 1980s and 1990s – despite all the evidence that pay is not the prime motivator in performance. Even more fundamentally, there seems to be a conviction that not only is 'managing through the payment system' the most effective means of managing human resources, but it is also sufficient for doing so. Despite the rhetoric attaching to the notions of the psychological contract, UK management seemingly feels much more comfortable with the equivalent of a subcontracting relationship with employees than it does with other forms of contract carrying mutual obligations.

The second lesson is that it is the management of the interdependencies which is the key to success. It is not enough, in other words, simply to identify and implement the components of reportedly effective bundles of practices as much of the technology-driven literature appears to assume. In themselves, these bundles do not have an automatic effect any more than individual practices do. Each component of the bundle has considerable implications for the others and managing the connections is fundamental.

Successful teamworking, for example, requires considerable attention not only to training and development but also to communications, involvement and participation. Payment is critical. The reluctance of most organizations to think in terms of team-based pay is a major drawback. An arrangement which has been developed in partnership is likely to be more effective, even if technically inferior, if it is owned by the people who will be working with it.

Detailed application can make a difference at every point in the loops. Take training and development, for example. The significance of training and development in overall terms is well attested. The focus of training is very important, however. The TQM study referred to earlier (Collinson et al., 1998) found that there was a strong tendency for employees most favourable to quality programmes to be those who said that they had been trained specifically in quality ideas and teamwork. By contrast, other forms of training, and the total amount of training, had little or no effect. Significantly, too, only one-fifth of the overall sample saw quality or teamwork as the main purpose of their training, which suggests that much of this training might have been insufficiently focused.

Another important observation arises from IRRU's 'lean production' study and concerns team leaders and lean production (IPD, 1997a; Purcell and Terry, 1997). Most of the organizations observed attached great importance to the training of team leaders. Yet even the best readily admitted that what they had been doing was not good enough. The problems that team leaders were having coping with the problems of managing people and production, and with the twin roles as leaders and members, were especially fraught. An important consideration was that the more that team leaders were trained for leadership, the greater the gulf created between them and their fellow team members.

Evidently, it is difficult to draw up hard-and-fast rules in this area. Three things have become clear, however, and they are an appropriate point on which to end the book. The first is that policies and practice configured or tailored to the organization's specific circumstances are likely to be much more effective than those plucked off the shelf or bought from a consultant. HR/IR is not a technological area where there is an automatic best practice solution. Arrangements developed to suit the circumstances – and which, ideally, are 'owned' by those who have to work with them because they have been involved in their development – are likely to perform better than those that might appear to be technically more correct.

The second is an adequately resourced personnel function. This does not mean, as Chapter 9 has argued, large personnel departments. It does not necessarily mean, especially in the case of SMEs, a specialist personnel manager. Critically, it does mean ensuring that senior managerial time and resources are made available to ensure that there is proper planning and monitoring of the implementation of arrangements. Unfortunately, the reduction of personnel departments and the devolution and decentralization of personnel functions to line managers has often not taken these requirements into account, contributing to the 'ad hocery' and short-termism encouraged by features of the wider business system in the UK.

The third and most fundamental point to have become clear concerns management itself. The way managers are managed has to change before there can be any serious prospect of improving the performance of HR/IR management more generally. Time and time again it emerges that management may apparently be doing all the right things so far as other employees are concerned. Critically, however, they are not changing the arrangements of their managers. Yet innovations such as TQM and teamwork do not stand a chance of success as long as organizations continue to appraise and reward their managers on the basis of 'hard' operational or financial targets rather than the softer development and interpersonal skills issues which are so essential to the success of these initiatives. Similarly, appeals to middle and first line managers to involve their employees in the process of continuous improvement will fall on deaf ears as long as senior managers continue to take pride in modelling themselves on the absolute dictator; 'telling' middle and first line managers that they have to develop and involve their staff is hardly an appropriate starting point. The acid test for us, when regaled with the detail of major change programmes that organizations are proposing to introduce in employment relations, is to ask whether or not the changes embrace the management of managers. Sadly, there is too often an inability to understand the question, let alone answer it.

Suggested further reading

The European Commission's Green Paper (CEC, 1997) *Partnership for a New Organization of Work*, and the report of the Higher-level Group on restructuring (CEC, 1998) are important, if controversial, statements. For alternative views on the key issues facing the HR/IR function in particular, see Sparrow and Marchington (1998b).

REFERENCES

ACAS (1983) *Collective Bargaining in Britain: Its Extent and Level.* Discussion Paper No. 2. London: ACAS.

ACAS (1997a) *Recruitment Policies for the 1990s.* London: ACAS.

ACAS (1997b) *Personnel Records.* London: ACAS.

ACAS (1997c) *Teamwork: Success through People.* London: ACAS.

ACAS (1997d) *Appraisal-related Pay.* London: ACAS.

ACAS (1997e) *Job Evaluation: an Introduction.* London: ACAS.

ACAS (1997f) *Recruitment and Induction.* London: ACAS.

ACAS (1998a) *Employment Policies.* London: ACAS.

ACAS (1998b) *Employee Communications and Consultation.* London: ACAS.

ACAS (1998c) *Employee Appraisal.* London: ACAS.

ACAS (1998d) *Hours of Work.* London: ACAS.

Ackroyd, S. and Procter, S. (1998) British manufacturing organisation and workplace industrial relations: some attributes of the new flexible firm, *British Journal of Industrial Relations*, 36(2), 163–83.

Adams, K. (1991) Externalisation vs specialisation, *Human Resource Management Journal*, 1(4), 40–54.

Allen, M. (1998) All-inclusive, *People Management*, 11 June (partnership at Tesco).

Anderson and Shackleton (1993) *Successful Selection Interviewing.* Oxford: Blackwell.

Applebaum, E. and Batt, R. (1994) *The New American Workplace. Transforming Work Systems in the United States.* Ithaca, NY: ILR Press.

Arkin, A. (1998) Central processing unit, *People Management*, 25 June, 56–7.

References

Arkin, A. (1999) Investing in the future, *People Management*, 11 February, 40–1.

Armstrong, M. (ed.) (1992a) *Strategies for Human Resource Management: a Total Business Approach*. London: Kogan Page.

Armstrong, M. (1992b) *Human Resource Management: Strategy and Action*. London: Kogan Page.

Armstrong, M. and Baron, A. (1998a) Out of the box, *People Management*, 23 July, 38–41.

Armstrong, M. and Baron, A. (1998b) *Performance Management: the New Realties*. London: Institute of Personnel and Development.

Arrowsmith, J. and Sisson, K. (1999) Pay and working time: towards organization based arrangements?, *British Journal of Industrial Relations*, 37(1), 51–75.

Arrowsmith, J. and Sisson, K. (2000) Managing Working Time, in S. Bach and K. Sisson (eds) *Personnel Management: A Comprehensive Guide to Theory and Practice*. Oxford: Blackwell.

Atkinson, J. (1984) Manpower strategies for flexible organizations, *Personnel Management*, August, 28–31.

Atkinson, J. (1989) Four stages of response to the demographic downturn, *Personnel Management*, August, 20–4.

Atkinson, J. and Meager, N. (1986) Is flexibility just a flash in the pan?, *Personnel Management*, September, 3–6.

Bach, S. (1995) Restructuring the personnel function: the case of NHS Trusts, *Human Resource Management Journal*, 5(2), 99–115.

Bach, S. (1999) Personnel managers: managing to change?, in S. Corby and G. White (eds), *Employment Relations in the Public Services*. London: Routledge.

Bach, S. (2000) From performance appraisal to performance management, in S. Bach and K. Sisson (eds), *Personnel Management: A Comprehensive Guide to Theory and Practice*. Oxford: Blackwell.

Bach, S. and Sisson, K. (eds) (2000) *Personnel Management: A Comprehensive Guide to Theory and Practice*. Oxford: Blackwell.

Baird, L. and Meshoulam, I. (1988) Managing two fits of strategic human resource management, *Academy of Management Review*, 13(1).

Barney, J. (1991) Firm resources and sustained competitive advantage, *Journal of Management*, 17, 99–120.

Bassett, P. (1986) *Strike Free: New Industrial Relations in Britain*. London: Macmillan.

Beatson, M. (1995) *Labour Market Flexibility*. Employment Department Research Series No. 48.

Becker, B. and Gerhart, M. (1996) The impact of human resource management on organizational performance: progress and prospects, *Academy of Management Journal*, 39, 779–801.

255

Becker, B. and Huselid, M. (1998) High performance work systems and firm performance: a synthesis of research and managerial implications, *Research in Personnel and Human Resources*, 16(1), 53–101.

Beer, M., Spector, B., Lawrence, P., Mills, D. and Walton, R. (1985) *Human Resources Management: a General Manager's Perspective*. Glencoe, IL: Free Press.

Berggren, C. (1993) Lean production – the end of history?, *Work, Employment and Society*, 7(2), 163–88.

Bevan, S., Barber, L. and Robinson, D. (1997) *Keeping the Best: a Practical Guide to Retaining Key Employees*. Brighton: Institute of Employment Studies.

Blyton, P. (1994) Working Hours, in K. Sisson (ed.), *Personnel Management: A Comprehensive Guide to Theory and Practice in Britain*. Oxford: Blackwell.

Boxall, P.F. (1992) Strategic human resource management: beginnings of a new orthodoxy?, *Human Resource Management Journal*, 2(3).

Brading, E. and Wright, V. (1990) Performance-related pay, *Personnel Management Factsheets*, No. 30. London: Personnel Publications.

Brewster, C. and Connock, S. (1995) *Industrial Relations: Cost-effective Strategies*. London: Hutchinson.

Broad, G. (1994) The managerial limits to Japanization: a manufacturing case study, *Human Resource Management Journal*, 4(3).

Brown, D. and Armstrong, M. (1997) Terms of enrichment, *People Management*, 11 September, 36–8.

Brown, W.A. (1989) Managing remuneration, in K. Sisson (ed.), *Personnel Management in Britain*. Oxford: Blackwell.

Brown, W.A. and Walsh, J. (1994) Managing pay in Britain, in K. Sisson (ed.), *Personnel Management: A Comprehensive Guide to Theory and Practice in Britain*. Oxford: Blackwell.

Brown, W., Marginson, P. and Walsh, J. (1995) Pay determination and collective bargaining, in P.K. Edwards (ed.), *Industrial Relations: Theory and Practice in Britain*. Oxford: Blackwell.

Buchanan, D. and Preston, D. (1992) Life in the cell: supervision and teamwork in a manufacturing systems engineering environment, *Human Resource Management Journal*, 2(4).

Byrne, J. (1993) The horizontal corporation, *Business Week*, 20 December, 76–81.

Cabinet Office (Development and Equal Opportunities Division) (1998) *Benchmarking Human Resource Activities*. London: Cabinet Office.

Cannell, M., Ashton, D., Powell, M. and Sung, J. (1999) Ahead of the field, *People Management* 22 April, 48–9.

Cappelli, P., Katz, H. and Osterman, P. (1997) *The New Deal at Work*. Boston, MA: Harvard Business School Press.

References

Carly, M. (1998) Board-level employee representation in Europe, *Transfer*, 4(2), 281–96.

Carrington, L. (1991a) Working as a team member, *Personnel Today*, 22 January, 38–39.

Carrington, L. (1991b) Investing in opinion, *Personnel Today*, 19 March, 30–32.

CEC (1989) *Comparative Study on Rules Governing Working Conditions in the Member States*, SEC (89) 1137. Luxemburg: Office for the Official Publications of the European Communities.

CEC (1997) Green Paper, *Partnership for a New Organization of Work*. Bulletin of the European Union. Supplement 4/97. Luxemburg: Office for the Official Publications of the European Communities.

CEC (1998) *Managing Change: Final Report of the Higher-level Group on Economic and Social Implications of Industrial Change*. Luxemburg: Office for the Official Publications of the European Communities.

Chadda, D. (1999) Pressing ahead, *People Management*, 11 February, 50–2.

Chandler, A. (1962) *Strategy and Structure*. Cambridge, MA: MIT Press.

CIR (1974) *Industrial Relations in Multi-plant Undertakings*, Report No. 85. London: HMSO.

Clark, J. (1993) Full flexibility and self-supervision in an automated factory, in J. Clark (ed.), *Human Resource Management and Technical Change*. London: Sage.

Clark, J. (1995) *Managing Innovation and Change*. London: Sage.

Claydon, T. (1998) Problematizing partnership: the prospects for a cooperative bargaining agenda, in P. Sparrow and M. Marchington (eds), *Human Resource Management The New Agenda*. London: Financial Times/Pitman.

Clegg, H.A. (1960) *A New Approach to Industrial Democracy*. Oxford: Blackwell.

Colling, T. (2000) Personnel management in the extended organization, in S. Bach and K. Sisson (eds), *Personnel Management: A Comprehensive Guide to Theory and Practice*. Oxford: Blackwell.

Colling, T. and Ferner, A. (1995) Privatization and marketization, in P.K. Edwards (ed.), *Industrial Relations: Theory and Practice in Britain*. Oxford: Blackwell.

Collins, M. (ed.) (1991) *Human Resource Management Audit*. Birmingham: North Western and West Midlands Regional Health Authorities.

Collinson, M., Edwards, P. and Rees, C. (1998) *Involving Employees in Total Quality Management*. London: DTI.

Connock, S. (1991) *HR Vision*. London: IPM.

Constable, J. and McCormick, R. (1987) *The Making of British Managers*. Corby: British Institute of Management.

Coupar, W. and Stevens, B. (1998) Towards a new model of industrial partnership: beyond the 'HRM versus industrial relations' argument, in P. Sparrow and M. Marchington (eds), *Human Resource Management: the New Agenda*. Financial Times/Pitman: London.

Cressey, P. (1998) European Monetary Union and the impact of UK industrial relations, in T. Kauppinen (ed.), *The Impact of EMU on Industrial Relations in European Union*. Helsinki: Finnish Industrial Relations Association.

Cully, M. and Woodland, S. (1998) Trade Union recognition and membership 1996–1997: an analysis from Certification Officer and LFS data, *Labour Market Trends*, July, 354–64.

Cully, M., O'Reilly, A., Millward, N. *et al.* (1998) *The 1998 Workplace Employee Relations Survey: First Findings*. London: DTI.

Cully, M., Woodland, S., O'Reilly, A. and Dix, G. (1999) *Britain at Work*. London: Routledge.

Dale, B.G., Boaden, R.J. and Lascelles, D.M. (1994) Total quality management: an overview, in B.G. Dale (ed.), *Managing Quality*, 2nd edn. Hemel Hemstead: Prentice Hall.

Davenport, T.H. (1993) *Process Innovation: Reengineering Work through Information Technology*. Boston, MA: Harvard Business School Press.

Deci, E.L. (1975) *Intrinsic Motivation*. New York: Plenum Press.

Dench, S., Perryman, S. and Giles, L. (1998) *Employers' perceptions of key skills*, IES Report 349. Sussex: Institute of Employment Studies.

DoE (1968) *Company Manpower Planning*. London: HMSO.

Donovan Commission (1968) *Royal Commission on Trade Unions and Employers' Associations* (The Donovan Report), Cmnd 3623. London: HMSO.

DTI (1997a) *Competitiveness – Our Partnership with Business: a Benchmark for Success*. London: HMSO.

DTI (1997b) *A Benchmark for Business*. London: DTI.

DTI (1998) *The Competitiveness White Paper*. London: DTI.

DTI/DfEE (1997) *Partnerships with People*. London: DTI.

Edmonds, J. and Tuffin, A. (1990) *A New Agenda*. London: GMB/UCW.

Edwards, P.K. (2000) Discipline: towards trust and self-discipline?, in S. Bach and K. Sisson (eds), *Personnel Management: A Comprehensive Guide to Theory and Practice*. Oxford: Blackwell.

EIRO-online (1999) Comparative supplement on national perceptions of, and the direction indicated by, the European Commission's Green Paper *Partnership for a New Organisation of Work*. Dublin: European Foundation for the Improvement of Living and Working Conditions.

Employment Department (1992) *People, Jobs and Opportunity*. London: HMSO.

Ernst and Young (1995) *Evaluation of the Modern Apprenticeship Prototypes*. London: Ernst and Young.

References

ERT (1997) *A Stimulus to Job Creation: Practical Partnerships between Large and Small Companies*. Brussels: ERT.

European Foundation for the Improvement of Living and Working Conditions (1997) *New Forms of Work Organisation. Can Europe Realise Its Potential? Results of a Survey of Direct Employee Participation in Europe.* Luxemburg: Office for the Official Publications of the European Communities.

Ferri, F. and Smith, K. (1996) *Parenting in the 1990s*. London: Family Policy Studies.

Flanders, A. (1970) Collective bargaining: a theoretical analysis, in A. Flanders, *Management and Unions: the Theory and Reform of Industrial Relations*. London: Faber.

Fletcher, C. (1998) A deciding factor, *People Management*, 26 November, 38–40.

Fombrun, C.J., Tichy, N.M. and Devanna, M.A. (1984) *Strategic Human Resource Management*. New York: Wiley.

Foundation for Manufacturing Industry/DTI/IBM (1996) *Tomorrow's Best Practice: a Vision of the Future for Top Manufacturing Companies in the UK*. London: FMI.

Fowler, A. (1997) How to outsource personnel, *People Management*, 20 February, 40–3.

Fowler, A. (1999) Catch as catch can, *People Management*, 14 January, 40–1.

Fraser, J.M. (1971) *Introduction to Personnel Management*. London: Nelson.

Freeman, R.B. and Medoff, J.L. (1984) *What Do Unions Do?* New York: Basic Books.

Fröhlich, D. and Pekruhl, U. (1996) *Direct Participation and Organisational Change – Fashionable but Misunderstood? An Analysis of Recent Research in Europe, Japan and the USA*. EF/96/38/EN. Luxemburg: Office for the Official Publications of the European Communities.

Gallie, D., White, M., Cheng, Y. and Tomlinson, M. (1998) *Restructuring the Employment Relationship*. Oxford: Oxford University Press.

Geary, J. and Sisson, K. (1994) *Conceptualising Direct Participation in Organisational Change. The EPOC Project*. EF/94/23/EN. Luxemburg: Office for the Official Publications of the European Communities.

Gospel, H. and Fuller, A. (1998) The modern apprenticeship: new wine in old bottles?, *Human Resource Management Journal*, 8(1), 5–22.

Grant, R.M. (1991) The resource-based theory of competitive advantage: implications for strategy formulation, *California Management Review*, 33(3): 114–35.

Grant, R.M. (1995) *Contemporary Strategy Analysis*. Oxford: Blackwell.

Green, F., Ashton, D., Burchell, B., Davies, B. and Felstead, A. (1997) An analysis of changing work skills in Britain. Paper presented to the Low

Wage Employment Conference of the European Low Wage Employment Research Network, CEP, LSE, December.

Guest, D. (1987) Human resource management and industrial relations, *Journal of Management Studies*, 24(5).

Guest, D. (1998) Beyond HRM: commitment and the contract culture, in P. Sparrow and M. Marchington (eds), *Human Resource Management: the New Agenda*. London: Financial Times/Pitman.

Guest, D. and Mackenzie, K. (1996) Don't write off the traditional career, *People Management*, February, 22–25.

Hall, L.A and Torrington, D.P. (1997) *Developments in the Personnel Function*. London: Pitman.

Hall, L. and Torrington, D. (1998) *The Human Resource Function*. London: Financial Times/Pitman.

Hall, M., Lister, R. and Sisson, K. (1998) *The New Law on Working Time. Managing the Implications of the 1998 Working Time Regulations*. London: Eclipse Group Ltd. and Industrial Relations Research Unit.

Hamel, G. and Prahalad, P.K. (1994) *Competing for the Future*. Boston, MA: Harvard University Business Press.

Hammer, M. and Champy, J. (1993) *Reengineering the Corporation*. London: Nicholas Brealey Publishing.

Handy, C. (1984) *The Future of Work*. Oxford: Blackwell.

Handy, C. (1987) *The Making of Managers*. London: National Economic Development Office.

Herriot, P., Hirsch,W. and Reily, P. (1998) *Trust and Transitions: Managing the Employment Relationship*. Chichester: Wiley.

Herzberg, F. (1966) *Work and the Nature of Man*. Cleveland, OH: World Publishing.

Hill, C. and Pickering, J. (1986) Divisionalisation, decentralisation and performance of large United Kingdom companies, *Journal of Management Studies*, 23(1), 26–50.

Hill, S. (1991) Why quality circles failed but TQM might succeed, *British Journal of Industrial Relations*, 29(4), 541–69.

Hill, S. and Wilkinson, A. (1995) In search of TQM, *Employee Relations*, 17(3), 8–22.

Hirsch, W. and Reilly, P. (1998) Cycling proficiency, *People Management*, 9 July, 38–41.

Holberton, S. (1991) How to help yourself to a competitor's best practices, *Financial Times*, 24 June, 24.

Hougham, J., Thomas, J. and Sisson, K. (1991) Ford's EDAP scheme, *Human Resource Management Journal*, 1(3).

Humble, J. (1988) How to improve the personnel service, *Personnel Management*, February, 30–3.

References

Humphries, C. (1997) A training renaissance, *People Management*, 9 October.

Hunter, L.C. and MacInnes, J. (1991) *Employer Use Strategies – Case Studies*, Employment Research Paper No. 87. Sheffield: Employment Department.

Huselid, M. (1995) The impact of human resource management practices on turnover, productivity and corporate financial performance, *Academy of Management Journal*, 38(3) 635–72.

Ichinowski, C., Shaw, K. and Prennushi, G. (1997) The effects of HRM practices on productivity: a study of steel finishing lines, *American Economic Review*, 87(1), 291–313.

Iles, P. (1999) *Managing Staff Selection and Assessment*. Buckingham: Open University Press.

Industrial Society (1998a) *Devolving personnel to the line*, Managing Best Practice No. 45. London: Industrial Society.

Industrial Society (1998b) *Flexible work patterns*, Managing Best Practice No. 46. London: Industrial Society.

Industrial Society (1998c) *Teamworking*, Managing Best Practice No. 47. London: Industrial Society.

Institute of Management (1995) *Survival of the Fittest: a Survey of Managers' Experience of, and Attitudes to, Work in the Post-recession Economy*. London: IM.

Institute of Management (1996) *Are Managers Under Stress?* London: IM.

IPA (1992) *Towards Industrial Partnership: a New Approach to Relationships at Work*. London: IPA.

IPA (1997) *Towards Industrial Partnership: New Ways of Working in British Companies*. London: IPA.

IPA (1998) *The Partnership Company*. London: IPA.

IPD (1996) *IPD Guide on Team Reward*. London: IPD.

IPD (1997a) *The People Management Implications of Leaner Ways of Working*, Issues in People Management. London: IPD.

IPD (1997b) *Impact of People Management Practices on Business Performance*, Issues in People Management. London: IPD.

IPD (1997c) *Working to Learn. A Work-based Route for Young People*, Issues in People Management. London: IPD.

IPD (1997d) *IPD Labour Turnover 1997 Survey Results*. London: IPD.

IRRU (1997) Comments on the European Commission's Green Paper *Partnership for a New Organization of Work*. Coventry: University of Warwick, IRRU.

IRS (1989a) Developments in multi-employer bargaining: 1, *Industrial Relations Review and Report*, 440, May, 6–11.

IRS (1989b) Single union deals, *Industrial Relations Review and Report*, 442, June, 5–11.

IRS (1989c) Decentralised bargaining in practice: 1, *Industrial Relations Review and Report*, 454, December.

IRS (1992) Rover's 'New Deal', *Employment Trends*, 514.

IRS (1993) Annual hours working and harmonisation at Rockware Glass, *Employment Trends*, 543, August.

IRS (1994) Restructuring for growth at Zeneca Agrochemicals, Yalding, *Employment Trends*, 558, April.

IRS (1995) Customer service drive brings new working patterns to BT, *Employment Trends*, 579, March.

IRS (1996a) Flexible workers on call at Tesco, *Employment Trends*, 620, November, 13–16.

IRS (1996b) Making capital out of Investors in People, *Employee Development Bulletin*, 84, December, 11–16.

IRS (1997a) The state of selection: an IRS survey, *Employee Development Bulletin*, 85, January, 8–17.

IRS (1997b) Benchmarking facilitates change and continuous improvement at BP Chemicals, *Employment Trends*, 630, April, 13–16.

IRS (1997c) The state of selection, 2: developments in basic methods, *Employee Development Bulletin*, 89, May, 6–11.

IRS (1997d) Cementing a new partnership at Blue Circle, *Employment Trends*, 638, August, 11–16.

IRS (1997e) Historic single-status deal in local government, *Employment Trends*, 639, September, 5–10.

IRS (1997f) Partnership at work: a survey, *Employment Trends*, 645, December, 3–24.

IRS (1998a) Partnership in practice at Legal and General, *Employment Trends*, 650.

IRS (1998b) Solving the skills crisis: an IRS survey of practice, *Employee Development Bulletin*, 652, 6–20.

IRS (1998c) Flexing the clock part 1: the use of annual hours, *Employment Trends*, 654, April, 4–10.

IRS (1998d) Benchmarking labour turnover: annual update 1998, *Employee Development Bulletin*, 100, April, 10–20.

IRS (1998e) Flexing the clock part 2: the experiences of annual hours, *Employment Trends*, 655, May.

IRS (1998f) Senior executives and HR managers share global goals but disagree about performance, *Employment Trends*, 657, June, 2.

IRS (1998g) The evolving HR function, *IRS Management Review*, No. 10, July.

IRS (1998h) BGT partners new deal, *Pay and Benefits Bulletin*, 453, August, 5–8.

References

IRS (1998i) Hyder maintains long-term partnership, *Employment Trends*, 662, August, 12–16.

IRS (1998j) Improving induction cuts staff turnover at Virgin Our Price, *Employee Development Bulletin*, 104, August, 10–12.

IRS (1998k) Induction, *Employee Development Bulletin*, 104, August, 15–16.

IRS (1998l) Do It All opts for DIY management, *Employment Trends*, 664, September, 6–9.

IRS (1998m) There is value in job evaluation, *Employment Trends*, 665, October, 3–16.

IRS (1998n) Agile production brings success to Grundi Satellite Communications Manufacturing, *Employment Trends*, 667, November, 14–16.

IRS (1999a) NVQs and SVQs mean business, *Employee Development Bulletin*, 109, January, 6–14.

IRS (1999b) Skills for success through modern apprenticeships, *Employment Development Bulletin*, 111, March, 5–16.

IRS (1999c) NAAFI looks to the future, *Employment Trends*, 678, April, 11–16.

John, G. (1998) Strategic role requires HR to take 'heretical' action, *People Management*, 10 December.

Johnson, G. (1987) *Strategic Change and the Management Process*. Oxford: Blackwell.

Kaplan, R.S and Norton, D.P. (1992) The balanced scorecard – measures that drive performance, *Harvard Business Review*, Jan/Feb, 75–85.

Keen, L. (1995) Organisational decentralisation and budgetary devolution in local government: a case of middle management autonomy?, *Human Resource Management Journal*, 5(2), 79–98.

Keep, E. (1989) Corporate training strategies: the vital component?, in J. Storey (ed.), *New Perspectives in Human Resource Management*. London: Routledge.

Keep, E. and Mayhew, K. (1998) Was Ratner right? – product market and competitive strategies and their links with skills and knowledge, *Employment Policy Institute Economic Report*, 12(3).

Keep, E. and Rainbird, H. (2000) Towards the learning organization, in S. Bach and K. Sisson (eds), *Personnel Management: A Comprehensive Guide to Theory and Practice*. Oxford: Blackwell.

Kessler, I. (1994) Performance pay, in K. Sisson (ed.), *Personnel Management: A Comprehensive Guide to Theory and Practice in Britain*. Oxford: Blackwell.

Kessler, I. (2000) Remuneration systems, in S. Bach and K. Sisson (eds), *Personnel Management: A Comprehensive Guide to Theory and Practice*. Oxford: Blackwell.

Kessler, S. (1987) The swings and roundabouts of pendulum arbitration, *Personnel Management*, December, 38–42.

Kinnie, N. (1985a) Local managers' control over industrial relations: myth and reality, *Personnel Review*, 14(4), 2–10.

Kinnie, N. (1985b) Changing management strategies in industrial relations, *Industrial Relations Journal*, 16(4), 17–24.

Koch, J. and McGrath, R.G. (1996) Improving labour productivity – human resource management policies do matter, *Strategic Management Journal*, 17(5), 335–54.

Kochan, T.A. and Barocci, T. (1985) *Human Resource Management and Industrial Relations: Text, Readings and Cases*. Boston, MA: Little Brown.

Kochan, T.A. and Dyer, L. (1992) Managing transformational change: the role of human resource professionals, *Proceedings of the Conference of the International Industrial Relations Association, Sydney*. Geneva: International Industrial Relations Association.

Kochan, T.A., Katz, H.C. and McKersie, R.B. (1986) *The Transformation of American Industrial Relations*. New York: Basic Books.

Labour Market Trends (1997) LFS60. London: Office for National Statistics.

Labour Market Trends (1998a) London: Office for National Statistics, July.

Labour Market Trends (1998b) London: Office for National Statistics, November.

Labour Research Department (1995) Working hours survey, *Bargaining Report*, 154, October. London: LRD.

Labour Research Department (1996) *Flexible Working Time: a Guide for Trade Unionists*. London: LRD.

Lane, C. (1990) Vocational training, employment relations and new production concepts in Germany: some lessons for Britain, *Industrial Relations Journal*, 21(4).

Legge, K. (1978) *Power, Innovation and Problem-solving in Personnel Management*. London: McGraw-Hill.

Legge, K. (2000) Personnel management in the 'lean organisation', in S. Bach and K. Sisson (eds), *Personnel Management: A Comprehensive Guide to Theory and Practice*. Oxford: Blackwell.

Lengnick-Hall, C. and Lengnick-Hall, M. (1988) Strategic human resource management: a review of the literature and a proposed typology, *Academy of Management Review*, 13(3), 454–70.

Lewis, R. (1988) Strike-free procedures: are they what they seem?, *Warwick Papers in Industrial Relations*, No. 20. Coventry: Industrial Relations Research Unit.

Lloyd, C. and Newell, H. (1998) Computerizing the salesforce. The introduction of technological change in a non-union workforce, *New Technology, Work and Employment*, 13(2), 104–15.

Lonsdale, C. and Cox, A. (1998) Falling in with the crowd, *People Management*, 15 October, 52–5.

References

Lupton, T. and Gowler, D. (1969) *Selecting a Wage Payment System*, Research Paper 111. London: Engineering Employers' Federation.

Mabey, C., Salaman, G. and Storey, J. (1998a) *Strategic Human Resource Management*. Oxford: Blackwell.

Mabey, C., Skinner, D. and Clark, T. (eds) (1998b) *Experiencing Human Resource Management*. London: Sage.

Maguire, M. (1999) Modern apprenticeship: just-in-time or far too late?, in P. Ainley and H. Rainbird (eds), *Apprenticeship: Towards a New Paradigm of Learning*. London: Kogan Page.

MacLachan, R. (1998) Paper chase: interview with David Blunkett, *People Management*, 19 March, 42–4.

Mangham, I. and Silver, M.S. (1986) *Management Training: Context and Practice*. London: Economic and Social Research Council.

Marchington, M. (1994) The dynamics of joint consultation, in K. Sisson (ed.), *Personnel Management: A Comprehensive Guide to Theory and Practice in Britain*. Oxford: Blackwell.

Marchington, M. (1998) Partnership in context: towards a European model?, in P. Sparrow and M. Marchington (eds), *Human Resource Management: the New Agenda*. London: Financial Times/Pitman.

Marchington, M. and Wilkinson, A. (2000) Direct participation, in S. Bach, and K. Sisson (eds), *Personnel Management: A Comprehensive Guide to Theory and Practice*. Oxford: Blackwell.

Margerison, C. and Kakabadse, A. (1985) What management development means for CEOs, *Journal of Management Development*, 4(5), 11–19.

Marginson, P. and Sisson, K. (1990) Single table talk, *Personnel Management*, May, 46–9.

Marginson, P., Edwards, P.K., Martin, R., Purcell, J. and Sisson, K. (1988) *Beyond the Workplace: Managing Industrial Relations in Multi-establishment Enterprises*. Oxford: Blackwell.

Marginson, P., Armstrong, P., Edwards, P. and Purcell, J. with Hubbard, N. (1993) *The Control of Industrial Relations in Large Companies*. Warwick Papers in Industrial Relations, 45. Coventry: IRRU University of Warwick.

Marginson, P., Edwards, P.K., Armstrong, P. and Purcell, J. (1995) Strategy, structure and control in the changing corporation: a survey-based investigation, *Human Resource Management Journal*, 5(2), 3–27.

Marsden, D. and French, S. (1998) *What a Performance – Performance-related Pay in the Public Services*. London: Centre for Economic Performance.

Mayo, A. (1991) *Managing Careers: Strategies for Organisations*. London: IPM.

McCarthy, W.E.J. and Ellis, N. (1973) *Management by Agreement: An Alternative to the Industrial Relations Act*. London: Hutchinson.

McKinsey & Co./NEDO (1988) *Performance and Competitive Success: Strengthening Competitiveness in UK Electronics*. London: McKinsey & Co.

Merrick, N. (1998) The leisure angle, *People Management*, 11 June, 36–8.

Miles, R. and Snow, C.C. (1984) Designing strategic human resource systems, *Organizational Dynamics*, Summer, 36–52.

Miles, R.E. and Snow, C.C. (1986) Organizations: new concepts for new forms, *California Management Review*, 28(3), 62–73.

Miller, P. (1989) Strategic HRM: What it is and what it is not, *Personnel Management*, February, 46–51.

Millward, N., Stevens, M., Smart, D. and Hawes, W. (1992) *Workplace Industrial Relations in Transition*. Aldershot: Dartmouth.

Millward, N., Forth, J. and Bryson, A. (2000) *All Change at Work*. London: Routledge.

Mintzberg, H. (1978) Patterns in strategy formation, *Management Science*, xxiv(9), 934–48.

Mintzberg, H. (1985) Of strategies deliberate and emergent, *Strategic Management Journal*, 6(3), 257–72.

Monks, J. (1998) Trade unions, enterprise and the future, in P. Sparrow and M. Marchington (eds), *Human Resource Management: The New Agenda*. London: Financial Times/Pitman.

NACAB (1997) *Flexibility Abused*. London: NACAB.

National Board for Prices and Incomes (1970) *Hours of Work, Overtime and Shift Working*, Report No. 161. London: HMSO.

National Work-life Forum (1998) *Looking for Balance*. London: National Work-life Forum.

Neathey, F. and Hurstfield, J. (1996) *Flexibility in Practice: Women's Employment and Pay in Retail and Finance*. Manchester: Equal Opportunities Commission/IRS.

NEDO/MSC (1987) *Strategic Planning for People*. London: NEDO.

NEDO/Training Agency (1989) *Defusing the Demographic Timebomb*. London: NEDO.

Noble, C. (1997) The management of training in multinational corporations: comparative case studies, *Journal of European Industrial Training*, 21(2–3), 102.

Nonaka, I. and Takeuchi, H. (1995) *The Knowledge-creating Company: How Japanese Companies Create the Dynamics of Innovation*. Oxford: Oxford University Press.

Osterman, P. (1994) How common is workplace transformation and how can we explain who adopts it: results from a national survey?, *Industrial and Labor Relations Review*, 47(2), 173–88.

Overell, S. (1998) Delayering to fire steel profits drive, *People Management*, 25 June, 12.

Pandya, N. (1999) People skills crucial to hi-tech firms, *The Guardian*, 13 February.

References

Pedlar, M., Burgoyne, J. and Boydell, T. (1991) *The Learning Company*. London: McGraw-Hill.

Peters, T.J. (1987) *Thriving on Chaos: Handbook for a Management Revolution*. London: Macmillan.

Peters, T.J. and Waterman, R.H. (1982) *In Pursuit of Excellence: Lessons from America's Best Companies*. New York: Harper & Row.

Pettigrew, A. and Whipp, R. (1991) *Managing Change for Competitive Success*. Oxford: Blackwell.

Pevoto, A.E. (1997) *International Journal of Training and Development*, 1(3), 212–13 (book review).

Pickard, J. and Fowler, A. (1999) Grade expectation, *People Management*, 11 February, 32–8.

Pil, F.K. and MacDuffie, J.P. (1996) The adoption of high-involvement work practices, *Industrial Relations*, 35(3), 423–55.

Porter, M. (1980) *Competitive Strategy: Techniques for Analysing Industries and Competitors*. New York: Free Press.

Porter, M. (1985) *Competitive Advantage: Creating and Sustaining Superior Performance*. New York: Free Press.

Powell, W.W. (1990) Neither market nor hierarchy: network forms of organisation, *Research in Organisational Behaviour*, 12, 295–336.

Price, E. and Price R.J. (1994) The decline and fall of the status divide, in K. Sisson (ed.), *Personnel Management: A Comprehensive Guide to Theory and Practice in Britain*. Oxford: Blackwell.

Purcell, J. (1989) The impact of corporate strategy on human resource management, in J. Storey (ed.), *New Perspectives on Human Resource Management*. Routledge: London.

Purcell, J. (1995) Corporate strategy and its link with human resource management strategy, in J. Storey (ed.), *Human Resource Management: A Critical Text*. London: Routledge.

Purcell, J. and Sisson, K. (1983) Strategies and practice in the management of industrial relations', in G.S. Bain (ed.), *Industrial Relations in Britain*. Oxford: Blackwell.

Purcell, J. and Terry, M. (1997) Return to Slender, *People Management*, 3(21), 46–51.

Quinn, J.B. (1980) *Strategies for Change: Logical Incrementalism*. Homewood, IL: Irwin.

Quinn, J.B. (1992) *Intelligent Enterprise*. New York: Free Press.

Rainbird, H. (1994) Continuing training, in K. Sisson (ed.), *Personnel Management: A Comprehensive Guide to Theory and Practice in Britain*. Oxford: Blackwell.

Reader, W.J. (1973) *The First Quarter Century, 1926–1952. Imperial Chemical Industries: A History. Vol.2.* Oxford: Oxford University Press.

Riley, T. (1992) *Monitoring and Rewarding Employees: Some Aspects of Theory and Practice*. London: ACAS.

Rodger, A. (1970) *The Seven Point Plan*, 3rd edn. London: National Foundation for Education Research.

Roncoroni, S. (1998) The wrong buttons, *People Management*, 9 July, 27.

Sako, M. (1998) The nature and impact of employee voice in the European car components industry, *Human Resource Management Journal*, 8(2), 5–13.

Saunders, L. (1997) *The Impact of Modern Apprenticeships on Young Person's Take-up of Work-based Learning*. London: DfEE.

Scarbrough, H. and Swan, J. (1999) *Case Studies in Knowledge Management*. London: IPD.

Schuler, R.S. and Jackson, S. (1987) Linking competitive strategies with human resource management practices, *Academy of Management Executive*, 1(3), 209–13.

Schuler, R.S., Jackson, S. and Storey, J. (2000) HRM and its links with strategic management, in J. Storey (ed.) *Human Resource Management: A Critical Text*, 2nd edn. London: International Thompson.

Scott, W. and Harrison, H. (1997) Full team ahead, *People Management*, 9 October, 48–50.

Seccombe, I. and Smith, G. (1997) *Taking Part: Registered Nurses and the Labour Market in 1997*. Brighton: Institute of Employment Studies.

Senge, P. (1990) *The Fifth Discipline: the Art and Practice of the Learning Organization*. New York: Doubleday.

Sheard, A. (1992) Learning to improve performance, *Personnel Management*, November, 40–5.

Sisson, K. (1987) *The Management of Collective Bargaining: an International Comparison*. Oxford: Blackwell.

Sisson, K. (ed.) (1994a) *Personnel Management: A Comprehensive Guide to Theory and Practice in Britain*. Oxford: Blackwell.

Sisson, K. (1994b) HRM and the personnel function, in J. Storey (ed.), *Human Resource Management: A Critical Text*. London: Routledge.

Sisson, K. (1994c) Paradigms, practice and prospects, in K. Sisson (ed.), *Personnel Management: A Comprehensive Guide to Theory and Practice in Britain*. Oxford: Blackwell.

Sisson, K. (1995) Human resource management and the personnel function, in J. Storey (ed.), *Human Resource Management: A Critical Text*. London: Routledge.

Sisson, K and Fröhlich, D. (1998) The significance of consultation and delegation in the new forms of work organisation, *Transfer*, 4(2), 195–213.

Sisson, K. and Marginson, P. (1995) Management: systems, structures and strategy, in P.K. Edwards (ed.), *Industrial Relations: Theory and Practice in Britain*. Oxford: Blackwell.

Sisson, K., Arrowsmith, J., Gilman, M. and Hall, M. (1999) *A Preliminary*

References

Review of the Industrial Relations Implications of Economic and Monetary Union. Warwick Papers in Industrial Relations No. 62. Coventry: Industrial Relations Research Unit.

Sparrow, P. and Marchington, M. (1998a) Introduction: Is HRM in crisis?, in P. Sparrow and M. Marchington (eds), *Human Resource Management: the New Agenda*. London: Financial Times/Pitman.

Sparrow, P. and Marchington, M. (1998b) Re-engaging the HRM function: re-building work, trust and voice, in P. Sparrow and M. Marchington (eds), *Human Resource Management: the New Agenda*. London: Financial Times/Pitman.

Steedman, H. and Wagner, K. (1987) A second look at productivity, machinery and skills in Britain and Germany, *National Institute Economic Review*, November.

Sternberg, N. (1998) Survival of the fit test, *People Management*, 11 December, 29–33.

Stevens, C.M. (1966) Is compulsory arbitration compatible with bargaining?, *Industrial Relations*, 5(2).

Storey, J. (ed.) (1989) *New Perspectives on Human Resource Management*. London: Routledge.

Storey, J. (1992) *Developments in the Management of Human Resources*. Oxford: Blackwell.

Storey, J. (1995) Human resource management: still marching on, or marching out?, in *Human Resource Management: A Critical Text*. London: Routledge.

Storey, J. (1997) What a difference a decade makes: management development ten years on, *People Management*, 3(12), 28–34.

Storey, J. (1998a) Do human resources really have a role in strategy?, *Financial Times Mastering Management*, 9, 14–18.

Storey, J. (1998b) *Managing Organizational Structuring and Restructuring*, Unit 4, Managing Human Resources. Buckingham: Open University Press.

Storey, J. (1998c) HR and organizational structures, *Financial Times Mastering Management*, 17: 40–3.

Storey, J. (ed.) (2000) *Human Resource Management*. London: International Thompson.

Storey, J. and Sisson, K. (1993) *Managing Human Resources and Industrial Relations*. Buckingham: Open University Press.

Storey, J., Edwards, P.K. and Sisson, K. (1997a) *Managers in the Making: Careers, Development and Control in Corporate Britain and Japan*. London: Sage.

Storey, J., Thomson, A. and Mabey, C. (1997b) What a difference a decade makes: management development ten years on, *People Management*, 3(12), 28–34.

Storey, J., Wilkinson, A., Morris, T. and Cressey, P. (1999) Banking in the UK, in M. Regini (ed.), *From Tellers to Sellers: Changing Employment Relations in International Perspective*. Boston, MA: MIT Press.

Streeck, W. (1992) *Social Institutions and Economic Performance: Studies of Industrial Relations in Advanced Industrial Countries*. London: Sage.

Tailby, S. and Winchester, D. (2000) Management and trade unions: towards social partnership?, in S. Bach and K. Sisson (eds), *Personnel Management: A Comprehensive Guide to Theory and Practice*. Oxford: Blackwell.

Taylor, R. (1996) Campaign for fewer work hours gains momentum, *Financial Times*, 14 August.

Terry, M. and Newell, H. (1996) Workers' participation in work organization, *Economic and Labour Relations Review*, 7(1), 46–66.

Thomas, T. and Wallis, B. (1998) Dwr Cymru/Welsh Water: a case study in partnership, in P. Sparrow and M. Marchington (eds), *Human Resource Management: The New Agenda*. London: Financial Times/Pitman.

Thomson, A., Storey, J., Mabey, C. *et al.* (1997) *A Portrait of Management Development*. London: Institute of Management.

Torrington, D. (1998) Crisis and opportunity in HRM: the challenge for the personnel function, in P. Sparrow and M. Marchington (eds), *Human Resource Management: The New Agenda*. London: Financial Times/Pitman.

Trevor, M. (1988) *Toshiba's New British Company: Competitiveness through Innovation in Industry*. London: Policy Studies Institute.

TUC (1999) *Partners for Progress, New Unionism in the Workplace*. London: TUC.

Tyson, S. and Fell, A. (1986) *Evaluating the Personnel Function*. London: Hutchinson.

Ulrich, D. (1997) *Human Resource Champions*. Boston, MA: Harvard Business School Press.

Ulrich, D. (1998) A new mandate for human resources, *Harvard Business Review*, Jan/Feb.

Wally, S., Carroll, S.J., Jr and Flood, P.C. (1995) Managing without traditional structures, in P.C. Flood, M.J. Gannon and J. Paauwe (eds), *Managing without Traditional Methods: International Innovations in Human Resource Management*. Wokingham: Addison-Wesley.

Walsh, J. (1999) Barclays unveils landmark pay and partnership deal, *People Management*, 25 February.

Wanous, P. (1980) *Organizational Entry*. Reading, MA: Addison-Wesley.

Watson, T. (1994) Recruitment and selection, in K. Sisson (ed.), *Personnel Management: A Comprehensive Guide to Theory and Practice in Britain*. Oxford: Blackwell.

References

Welch, J. (1998) Lloyds/TSB give staff a job for life, *People Management*, 1 October, 12.

Welch, J. and John, G. (1998) Firms slow to see benefits of recruitment technology, *People Management*, 9 July, 18.

Whitehead, M. (1999) NatWest to put all branch staff on annualised hours, *People Management*, 28 January.

Whittington, R. (1989) *Corporate Strategies in Recession and Recovery: Social Structure and Strategic Choice*. London: Unwin Hyman.

Whittington, R. and Mayer, M. (1994) Beyond or behind the M-form? Organisational structures in contemporary Europe. Paper presented at the Strategic Management Society Conference, Jouy-en-Josas, September.

Wickens, P. (1987) *The Road to Nissan: Flexibility, Quality, Teamwork*. London: Macmillan.

Wickens, P. (1993) Lean production and beyond: the system, its critics and the future, *Human Resource Management Journal*, 3(4), 75–90.

Williamson, O. (1975) *Markets and Hierarchies: Analysis and Anti-trust Implications*. New York: Free Press.

Williamson, O. (1985) *The Economic Institutions of Capitalism*. New York: Free Press.

Womack, J.P. and Jones, D.T. (1994) From lean production to the lean enterprise, *Harvard Business Review*, March/April, 93–103.

Womack, J.P., Jones, D.T. and Roos, D. (1990) *The Machine that Changed the World*. New York: Rawson Associates.

INDEX

272

Index

Index